KNOWLEDGE SYSTEMS

How Intelligent Machines Acquire, Organize, Store, and Apply Knowledge

By Susie Hala

IntelliGloss Press

IntelliGloss AI Education Series

Module 2: Artificial General Intelligence (AGI)

Legal Disclaimer

Educational Purpose Disclaimer

"This publication is part of the IntelliGloss AI Education Series, a structured curriculum support system for AI literacy in grades 6–12."

The information presented in this publication is provided for educational and informational purposes only. This book is intended to support educators, administrators, parents, and learners in understanding the concepts, opportunities, and challenges associated with artificial intelligence in education. It is not intended to serve as legal, technical, policy, cybersecurity, or professional advice.

Readers should consult qualified professionals, institutional guidelines, and local regulations before implementing any educational programs, technologies, or policies described in this book.

Technology and Accuracy Disclaimer

Artificial intelligence is a rapidly evolving field. While every effort has been made to ensure the accuracy and reliability of the information presented at the time of publication, technologies, policies, research findings, and best practices may change over time. The author and publisher make no guarantees that all information will remain current or applicable in future technological environments.

Readers are encouraged to verify tools, platforms, and recommendations independently before using them in educational settings.

Implementation Responsibility

Schools, educators, and institutions are solely responsible for determining how and whether to implement artificial intelligence tools, strategies, or classroom activities discussed in this book. Educational environments vary widely, and policies regarding technology use, student privacy, and curriculum development differ by district, state, and country.

The author and publisher assume no responsibility for outcomes resulting from the implementation of ideas, examples, or frameworks described in this book.

Student Safety and Data Privacy

Artificial intelligence tools may involve the collection or processing of data. Educators and institutions are responsible for ensuring that any technology used complies with applicable student privacy laws, data protection regulations, and school policies, including but not limited to FERPA, COPPA, GDPR, or other relevant regulations depending on jurisdiction.

The author and publisher are not responsible for the privacy practices, security policies, or data handling procedures of third-party platforms or software mentioned in this book.

Third-Party Tools and References
This book may reference third-party technologies, organizations, research studies, or platforms for illustrative and educational purposes. Such references do not constitute endorsements or guarantees regarding the performance, reliability, safety, or suitability of those tools for educational use.

Educators and institutions should conduct their own evaluations and risk assessments before adopting any technology.

No Professional Liability
The author and publisher shall not be held liable for any direct, indirect, incidental, or consequential damages resulting from the use or misuse of the information contained in this book. This includes but is not limited to decisions related to curriculum design, technology adoption, classroom instruction, institutional policies, or educational outcomes.

Educational Interpretation
The concepts and examples provided in this book are intended to support discussion and learning. They should not be interpreted as official standards, mandatory guidelines, or universally applicable policies for artificial intelligence education.

Schools and educators are encouraged to adapt the ideas presented here according to their local policies, cultural context, educational standards, and student needs.

Author's Intent
The goal of this book is to promote responsible AI literacy, thoughtful discussion, and ethical awareness as schools prepare students for a world increasingly shaped by intelligent technologies.

The author encourages readers to approach artificial intelligence education with curiosity, caution, and a commitment to responsible learning.

Title: KNOWLEDGE SYSTEMS: How Intelligent Machines Acquire, Organize, Store, and Apply Knowledge

ISBN: ISBN: 978-1-972925-24-9

Published by
IntelliGloss Press
United States of America

This book is intended for educational and informational purposes. Artificial intelligence technologies and policies evolve rapidly, and the author makes no guarantee regarding the completeness, accuracy, or continued applicability of the information presented. Educators, schools, and institutions are responsible for evaluating and implementing technologies in accordance with their own policies, legal requirements, and educational standards.

Dedication

This book is dedicated to the next generation of learners—
the students who will grow up in a world shaped by intelligent technology,
and who deserve to understand it with clarity, confidence, and purpose.

To the educators who show up every day with dedication and heart,
guiding students through a rapidly changing world—
your role has never been more important.

To the parents and families who support learning at home,
encouraging curiosity, responsibility, and growth—
you are the foundation of every child's success.

And to my granddaughters,
whose curiosity, imagination, and future inspire me to do this work—
this book is for you.

May you not only learn how to use technology,
but understand it, question it, and shape it for the good of others.

About the Author

Susie Hala
Founder of the IntelliGloss AI Education Series

Susie Hala is an author, educator, and curriculum developer dedicated to advancing artificial intelligence literacy in education. Her work focuses on helping schools, educators, and students understand how intelligent technologies are shaping modern society—and why that understanding is essential for the next generation.

Hala is the creator of the IntelliGloss AI Education Series, a comprehensive and growing collection of educational books designed to make complex artificial intelligence concepts accessible, structured, and practical for classroom use. Her work emphasizes clarity, organization, and responsible implementation, enabling schools to introduce AI literacy without requiring advanced technical backgrounds.

In addition to her work in education, Hala brings hands-on experience working with artificial intelligence systems, including early exposure to rule-based AI technologies during her time working with AT&T. She has also developed modern digital platforms that integrate artificial intelligence, automation, and online systems, building e-commerce solutions and AI-driven applications that connect payment platforms, hosting environments, and conversational AI tools into real-world, functional systems.

This combination of foundational understanding and practical experience allows her to translate complex AI concepts into clear, accessible language for both educators and students.

Recognizing that artificial intelligence is rapidly transforming how information is created, interpreted, and used, Hala advocates for equipping students with the ability not only to use AI tools, but to understand, question, and evaluate them. Her work emphasizes critical thinking, ethical awareness, and responsible digital citizenship.

The IntelliGloss AI Education Series supports schools in teaching key areas such as artificial intelligence foundations, algorithms, machine learning concepts, and AI ethics, as well as the broader evolution of intelligent systems—from Artificial Narrow Intelligence (ANI) to Artificial General Intelligence (AGI) and Artificial Superintelligence (ASI). These resources are designed for students in grades 6–12 and for educators seeking structured, classroom-ready approaches to AI literacy.

In addition to her work in education publishing, Hala has a strong background in entrepreneurship, having built and managed multiple businesses and educational initiatives. Her experience across industries reinforces her belief that technology education must remain grounded in human values, critical thinking, and ethical responsibility.

Her mission is clear: to ensure that the next generation understands intelligent technology—not just how to use it, but how it truly works.

Preface

Two Students. Two Paths. One Future.

Before we begin, it is important to understand why learning how artificial intelligence works—not just how to use it—matters for every student.

Imagine two students who have just graduated from high school and are preparing for a job interview. The first student knows how to use artificial intelligence tools. This student can generate answers, complete assignments quickly, and rely on AI to assist with tasks. However, this student does not understand how artificial intelligence works behind the scenes.

The second student also knows how to use AI tools, but in addition, understands the foundational concepts behind them. This student has learned about data, algorithms, tokens, models, and how intelligent systems are trained and operate. This student can think critically about AI, recognize its limitations, and adapt when needed.

At first, the first student may appear faster and more efficient. However, over time, the second student demonstrates a deeper level of understanding, independence, and problem-solving ability. The second student is not only able to use artificial intelligence but also to question it, improve it, and grow with it.

This book is written for the second student.

In a world where artificial intelligence is becoming part of everyday life, students must not only learn how to use intelligent systems—they must learn how they work. True understanding leads to confidence, responsibility, and the ability to lead in an AI-driven future.

This perspective is not just theoretical—it is personal.

There was a time when I was the first student.

I knew how to use systems. I followed processes, completed tasks, and worked within structured environments that required accuracy and consistency. At the time, I did not think of these systems as artificial intelligence. They were simply part of the job—tools that had to be learned, followed, and mastered.

But looking back, I now understand something much deeper. I was working within rule-based systems—the earliest foundation of what we now recognize as artificial intelligence.

That realization changed everything.

As I began studying modern AI, including machine learning, deep learning, and intelligent systems, I started to see a clear connection between the past and the present. The structured systems I once worked in, the logic behind decision-making, and the step-by-step processes all still exist today. They have simply evolved.

Artificial intelligence did not appear overnight. It grew from rule-based systems into systems that can now learn, adapt, and assist in ways we never imagined.

I made a decision to move from simply using systems to understanding them.

That journey—from student one to student two—is the reason these books exist.

My mission is to help others bridge that same gap.

I believe that artificial intelligence should be understandable for everyone. It should not feel intimidating or out of reach. Students should feel confident exploring it. Teachers should feel prepared to introduce it. Everyday learners should have access to clear, structured explanations that make sense.

You do not need a background in technology. You do not need to know how to code. You only need the right explanation.

A Note from the Author

AI Is a Tool — Not a Decision Maker

Artificial Intelligence is becoming part of everyday life. Students use it to complete assignments, teachers use it to support instruction, and businesses use it to improve efficiency. While these tools are powerful and useful, there is an important truth that must remain clear from the very beginning:

Artificial Intelligence does not make decisions—people do.

One of the main purposes of this book is to help readers understand how AI works, what it can do, and—just as importantly—what it cannot do. AI systems are designed to process information, identify patterns, and generate responses based on data. They can assist with thinking, but they do not think independently. They can provide answers, but they do not understand consequences. They can suggest ideas, but they do not choose actions.

Every outcome that involves AI begins and ends with human involvement. A person asks the question. A person reviews the response. A person decides what to do next. Responsibility does not transfer to the machine.

In today's world, it is easy to confuse speed with intelligence and automation with authority. Because AI can respond quickly and confidently, it may appear as though it is making decisions. In reality, it is performing a task based on patterns it has learned—not exercising judgment.

This distinction matters. When people begin to rely on AI without understanding its role, they risk misunderstanding information, misusing technology, or placing trust in a system that is not capable of accountability. Clear understanding leads to responsible use.

This book was written to remove confusion and provide clarity. It is designed to help students and educators move beyond simply using AI tools and begin understanding the structure behind them. By learning how AI supports human thinking—rather than replacing it—readers can approach technology with confidence, awareness, and responsibility.

Artificial Intelligence is a powerful assistant. It can enhance learning, support creativity, and improve productivity. But it remains a tool.

The decisions, the actions, and the responsibility will always belong to the human.

— Susie Hala

Bringing Clarity to Artificial Intelligence

During a recent meeting with a school district, it became clear that one of the biggest challenges in artificial intelligence education is not the technology itself—but the way it is explained.

In that discussion, terms such as **chatbots, generative AI, agentic AI, autonomy, tools, hallucinations, and AI usage levels** were all mentioned together. While each term represents a distinct concept, they were often blended into one conversation without clear distinctions. The result was confusion, even among those who were actively trying to understand and make informed decisions.

This experience revealed an important truth:
Without clear definitions and structure, artificial intelligence becomes difficult to teach, difficult to learn, and difficult to use responsibly.

This book is designed to provide that structure.

Understanding the Core Concepts

To build a strong foundation, it is essential to separate and define the key ideas that are often confused.

Chatbot
A chatbot is a conversational interface that allows users to interact with an AI system through questions and prompts. It responds to input but does not act beyond what is directly requested.

Generative AI (Gen AI)
Generative AI refers to systems that create new content, including text, images, audio, and code. These systems generate outputs based on patterns learned from large datasets. While powerful, generative AI does not truly understand information and may occasionally produce inaccurate results.

Agentic AI
Agentic AI describes systems that can take action toward a goal. Rather than responding to a single prompt, these systems can plan, make decisions within defined limits, and carry out multi-step tasks. This introduces a higher level of functional independence.

Autonomy
Autonomy refers to how independently an AI system operates. Some systems require constant human guidance, while others can perform multiple steps with minimal input. Autonomy is not a separate type of AI, but a measure of how much control the system has in completing tasks.

Additional Terms That Shape Understanding

AI Tools
AI tools are the applications people use to interact with artificial intelligence, such as writing assistants, design platforms, and data analysis systems. These tools make AI accessible in everyday tasks.

Hallucination
A hallucination occurs when an AI system generates information that appears correct but is inaccurate or unsupported. This is a known limitation of generative systems and highlights the need for human verification.

The AI Use Continuum

Another important concept is how AI is used at different levels. Rather than viewing AI as a single capability, it is more accurate to understand it as a continuum of use:

Assistive Use
AI supports simple tasks such as answering questions, correcting grammar, or providing suggestions.

Augmented Use
AI helps expand human capability by generating ideas, organizing content, and assisting in problem-solving.

Agentic Use
AI begins to take on multi-step responsibilities, planning and completing tasks with reduced human input.

This continuum shows that AI can range from a helpful assistant to a more independent system, depending on how it is applied.

The Moment Everything Sounded Like One Conversation

During a recent discussion on artificial intelligence, I listened closely as different experts spoke about the future of AI. One referenced advanced systems beyond human intelligence, another discussed goal-driven AI systems, and the conversation shifted quickly between topics like autonomy, tools, and system behavior. At first, it sounded like a single, unified discussion. But the more I listened, the more I realized something important.

They were not all talking about the same thing.

One part of the conversation focused on future possibilities—high-level systems that do not yet exist. Another part focused on current technologies that are already being used today. At the same time, different terms were being used to describe how AI behaves, how it makes decisions, and how much independence it may have. These ideas were layered together in a way that made them sound connected, even when they were not.

This experience revealed a major challenge in understanding artificial intelligence today. Many discussions combine different types of AI, different levels of intelligence, and different behaviors into one conversation. Without clear structure, these ideas begin to blur together. For someone trying to learn, this can feel overwhelming and confusing.

This book is built to solve that problem.

Artificial intelligence is not one single concept. It is a system made up of multiple layers. Some layers describe how intelligent a system is. Other layers describe how the system behaves. Still others describe how much control or independence the system has. When these layers are separated and explained clearly, AI becomes much easier to understand.

The goal of this book is to bring clarity where confusion often exists. Instead of mixing everything into one explanation, each concept is presented in a structured and organized way. This allows students, educators, and readers to see how the pieces fit together without losing sight of what each part actually means.

Understanding artificial intelligence begins with understanding its structure.

Once that structure is clear, the conversation becomes clearer as well.

Why Clarity Matters

When these concepts are not clearly defined, they merge into what can be described as a "conceptual blur." This can lead to misunderstandings about what AI can and cannot do, as well as unrealistic expectations or misuse in educational settings.

Clear understanding helps ensure that:

Students remain active learners, not passive users

Educators maintain control over instructional outcomes

AI is used as a support tool rather than a replacement for thinking

The Purpose of This Book

This book is built on a simple but essential principle:

Students should not only use artificial intelligence—they should understand it.

By clearly defining core concepts such as chatbots, generative AI, agentic AI, autonomy, and the continuum of AI use, this curriculum provides a structured pathway for developing both technical understanding and critical thinking.

Artificial intelligence is not a single tool or system. It is a collection of capabilities that must be understood in context.

Clarity is the foundation of responsible innovation.

Structuring Artificial Intelligence to Create Clarity and Understanding

Why Structure Is Necessary

Artificial intelligence is often presented as one unified concept. In many discussions, different ideas such as intelligence level, system behavior, and autonomy are combined into a single explanation. This can make AI appear more complex and confusing than it actually is.

Clarity begins when these ideas are separated and organized.

Structuring artificial intelligence allows each concept to be understood on its own before being connected to the larger system.

The Problem Without Structure

When AI is not structured, conversations may include multiple terms that sound related but describe entirely different things. For example, a discussion may move quickly between advanced future systems, current tools, and system behaviors without clearly distinguishing between them.

This creates the impression that all forms of AI operate at the same level and in the same way, which is not accurate.

Without structure, understanding becomes difficult.

The Solution: A Structured Approach

Artificial intelligence becomes clearer when it is organized into distinct categories.

Level explains how intelligent a system is.
Behavior explains how the system operates.
Control explains how much independence the system has.

Each category answers a different question. Together, they form a complete picture of how AI systems function.

Clarity Through Separation

A system can operate at a current level of intelligence while demonstrating different behaviors or levels of independence. For example, a system that generates responses and a system that takes steps toward completing a task may operate at the same intelligence level but differ in how they behave.

This distinction becomes clear only when structure is applied.

Instructional Insight

When teaching artificial intelligence, it is important to avoid presenting all concepts at once. Separating ideas into categories allows learners to focus on one dimension at a time, building understanding step by step.

Structured learning leads to deeper comprehension.

Key Takeaway

Artificial intelligence is not one single idea. It is a system made up of multiple parts. Structuring those parts creates clarity, improves understanding, and allows learners to see how the system truly works.

Reflection Question

How does separating intelligence level, behavior, and control make artificial intelligence easier to understand?

The IntelliGloss Instructional Approach

The IntelliGloss AI Education Series is designed to help students move beyond simply using AI tools and begin understanding artificial intelligence as a complete system.

Students learn how AI is built, how it operates, and how it connects to the real world.

A Message to Students and Readers

If you have ever felt that technology was too complicated…
If you have ever been confused by systems that were never clearly explained…

I want you to know:

You are capable of understanding artificial intelligence.

Sometimes, the challenge is not the concept itself—it is how it has been presented.

This series was created to change that.

A Message to Educators

To the educators using this material:

These books are designed to support you in introducing artificial intelligence in a way that is clear, structured, and meaningful for students.

AI is becoming part of every industry, and students deserve more than just exposure to tools—they deserve understanding.

This series aims to provide that foundation.

Final Reflection

Every experience we have—especially the challenging ones—prepares us for something greater.

The systems I once worked in taught me discipline, structure, and attention to detail. Today, those same lessons allow me to break down complex ideas and make them understandable for others.

That is what this series represents:

Turning complexity into clarity.

Why Artificial Intelligence Education Matters for Every Student

Why AI Literacy Is Essential for Every Student

Artificial intelligence is no longer a future concept or a specialized technology used only by experts. It is already part of everyday life for students of all ages. From smartphones and search engines to navigation apps, social media, streaming platforms, and educational tools, AI systems influence how information is accessed, decisions are made, and learning takes place.

Because AI is embedded in daily life, understanding it is no longer optional. It is a foundational skill, similar to digital literacy and critical thinking. Students do not need to become programmers or engineers, but they do need to understand what AI is, how it works at a basic level, and how it affects their lives.

AI education should not be limited to computer science classrooms. Every student interacts with AI systems daily. Teaching students how these systems function empowers them to become informed users rather than passive consumers of technology.

This book is designed to make artificial intelligence understandable, approachable, and relevant. It focuses on clarity, responsibility, and real-world understanding to help students prepare for a future where humans and intelligent systems work side by side.

IntelliGloss AI Education Series

Teaching how AI actually works—from hardware to power to global systems.

Why AI Education Matters

Artificial intelligence is already shaping how students learn, write, research, and solve problems.

Yet many students—and educators—are using AI tools without understanding how these systems actually work.

Schools need more than access to technology.
They need structured, responsible AI education.

Our Approach

The IntelliGloss AI Education Series is designed to help students move beyond simply using AI tools and begin understanding artificial intelligence as a complete system.

Students learn how AI is built, how it operates, and how it connects to the real world.

The IntelliGloss Framework

Our books introduce AI through a clear and connected system:

Chip Family — the hardware that powers AI

Watts Family — the rate at which AI uses power

Energy Family — the total power AI consumes over time

Infrastructure Family — the global systems that support AI

This framework helps students understand AI from the inside out.

Built for the Classroom

Each book includes:

Structured chapters aligned with semester learning

Clear explanations designed for student understanding

Reflection sections with learning objectives

Worksheets, quizzes, and answer keys

Teacher Implementation Guides

Supporting Schools and Educators

The IntelliGloss series supports:

Responsible and ethical AI use

Student data awareness and safety

Critical thinking and digital literacy

Classroom-ready instruction for grades 6–12 and beyond

What This Book Is—and What It Is Not

Many people today are becoming familiar with artificial intelligence through tools like ChatGPT, Microsoft Copilot, Canva, and other AI-powered applications. These tools can help with writing, answering questions, creating images, and completing everyday tasks.

In addition to these tools, you may also hear terms such as **AI agents, agentic AI, autonomous systems, and generative AI**. While these may sound complex, they are all part of the same evolving landscape of artificial intelligence technologies.

This book is not a guide on how to use those tools.

Instead, it explains what makes those tools possible.

Behind every AI tool is a system made up of multiple layers working together. At the most basic level, information is represented as bits and processed through powerful computer chips. That information is organized into data, broken into tokens, and then processed by algorithms and models that allow the system to recognize patterns, generate responses, and perform tasks.

These components—chips, bits, tokens, data, algorithms, and models—work together as a complete system. While users may only see the tool, the real intelligence comes from how these underlying parts interact behind the scenes.

Artificial intelligence can also be understood in terms of different levels of capability. Most of the AI systems used today fall under **Artificial Narrow Intelligence (ANI)**, which is designed to perform specific tasks, such as answering questions or generating content. More advanced forms, such as **Artificial General Intelligence (AGI)** and **Artificial Superintelligence (ASI)** represent future possibilities where AI could match or exceed human-level thinking. While these advanced levels are still theoretical, understanding the differences helps provide a broader view of where AI is today and where it may be heading.

For students, parents, and educators, this distinction is important. Learning how to use AI tools is helpful, but understanding how they work—and where they fit within the larger AI landscape—builds stronger thinking, better decision-making, and more responsible use.

Most importantly, artificial intelligence does not make decisions on its own. It does not take responsibility for actions or outcomes. AI systems generate responses based on data and patterns, but it is always the human who decides what to do with that information.

This book is designed to make these underlying systems clear and accessible, even for readers who are new to artificial intelligence.

Artificial intelligence is still in its early stages of development. As these technologies continue to grow, those who understand the foundation behind them will be better prepared to adapt, question, and use them wisely.

Who This Book Is For

This book is designed for educators, school leaders, and curriculum developers guiding students in an age of rapidly advancing technology.

Artificial intelligence is already influencing how students learn, research, and communicate. Yet many educators have not received formal training in how these systems work or how they should be addressed in the classroom.

This book helps bridge that gap by providing clear explanations and practical frameworks for understanding artificial intelligence in an educational setting.

How Schools Can Use This Book

This book supports schools in developing a structured approach to artificial intelligence literacy.

It can be used for:

- Professional development for educators
- Classroom discussions and activities
- Curriculum support across subject areas
- Policy and academic integrity conversations

Rather than focusing on specific tools, this book emphasizes lasting principles that help students understand, evaluate, and use AI responsibly.

Closing Perspective

Artificial intelligence will continue to evolve. With the right knowledge and leadership, schools can ensure that students not only use these technologies, but understand them, question them, and apply them responsibly.

IntelliGloss is more than a book series. It is a structured approach to preparing students for a future shaped by artificial intelligence.

Rather than focusing only on how to use AI tools, this series helps students understand how AI actually works—from its foundational building blocks to real-world applications.

"Before exploring the technical structure of artificial intelligence, it is equally important to understand the human principles that guide its use."

Human Values Family

Definition

The Human Values Family in artificial intelligence represents the guiding principles that shape how AI systems are created, used, and integrated into society. These values include ethics, responsibility, trust, and human well-being.

Artificial intelligence may be built on data, algorithms, and computational systems, but its true impact is measured by how it affects people. For this reason, AI is not only a technical system—it is a human-centered system.

Key Concepts

The Human Values Family exists to ensure that artificial intelligence serves humanity in a positive and responsible way. While AI systems can process information and generate outcomes, they do not possess judgment, empathy, or moral understanding.

This means that human values must guide every stage of AI development—from design to deployment.

AI reflects the intentions, decisions, and assumptions of the people who build and use it. If those values are not carefully considered, AI systems can unintentionally produce biased, harmful, or misleading results.

Understanding human values in AI is not optional—it is essential.

Core Elements of the Human Values Family

Ethics
Ethics in AI refers to making decisions that are fair, just, and respectful of human rights. This includes minimizing bias, protecting privacy, and ensuring transparency in how systems operate.

Responsibility
Responsibility means that humans remain accountable for AI systems. Developers, educators, organizations, and users must take ownership of how AI is used and the outcomes it produces.

Trust
Trust is critical for the successful adoption of AI. People must feel confident that AI systems are reliable, safe, and aligned with their best interests.

Human Well-Being
AI should enhance human life—not replace, harm, or diminish it. This includes supporting learning, improving access to information, and creating opportunities while maintaining human dignity.

Real-World Connection

Artificial intelligence is already influencing how people learn, communicate, and make decisions. From search engines to classroom tools, AI is shaping daily experiences.

Without clear human values guiding these systems, there is a risk of reinforcing misinformation, bias, or unrealistic expectations.

For students, this means learning not only how to use AI tools, but how to question them, evaluate their outputs, and understand their limitations.

Applications in Education

In the classroom, the Human Values Family helps students develop critical thinking and ethical awareness. Teachers can use this framework to guide discussions about fairness, responsibility, and the impact of technology on society.

Students can explore questions such as:

How should AI be used responsibly?

What makes an AI system fair?

How does technology influence human behavior?

This approach supports both technical understanding and responsible decision-making.

Benefits

Teaching human values in AI helps students:

Develop ethical awareness

Strengthen critical thinking

Understand the societal impact of technology

Become responsible users and future creators of AI

It ensures that learning about AI goes beyond functionality and includes responsibility

Challenges

Human values are not always universal. Different cultures, communities, and individuals may have different perspectives on what is considered fair or ethical.

Additionally, AI technology is evolving rapidly, often faster than policies and guidelines can keep up. This makes it essential for educators and students to stay informed and adaptable.

Summary

The Human Values Family reminds us that artificial intelligence is not just about machines—it is about people.

By focusing on ethics, responsibility, trust, and human well-being, students can learn to use AI thoughtfully and responsibly.

Understanding these principles helps prepare learners to navigate a world where artificial intelligence plays an increasingly important role in everyday life.

Executive Summary

IntelliGloss AI Education Series

Teaching How Artificial Intelligence Actually Works

Artificial intelligence is already shaping how students learn, write, research, and make decisions. Yet in many classrooms, students are being introduced to AI tools without understanding how these systems actually function.

This creates a critical gap.

Students may become efficient users of technology, but without foundational knowledge, they are not equipped to think critically, evaluate outputs, or use AI responsibly. As AI continues to expand across every industry, this gap will only grow more significant.

The **IntelliGloss AI Education Series** was created to address this challenge.

The Problem

Most current approaches to AI in education focus on tool usage rather than system understanding. As a result:

- Students rely on AI without understanding its limitations
- Educators lack structured frameworks for teaching AI concepts
- Key terms such as generative AI, agentic AI, and autonomy are often introduced without clear definitions
- Responsibility and ethical use are not consistently emphasized

Without clarity, artificial intelligence becomes difficult to teach, difficult to learn, and difficult to manage in a school environment.

The Solution

The IntelliGloss AI Education Series provides a structured, classroom-ready approach to artificial intelligence literacy for grades 6–12.

Rather than focusing on individual tools, this series teaches students how AI works as a complete system—from foundational components to real-world applications.

Students learn to move beyond surface-level interaction and develop true understanding.

The IntelliGloss Framework

The series introduces AI through a clear and connected structure, including:

- Foundational building blocks such as data, algorithms, tokens, and models
- System-level understanding through categories such as intelligence level, behavior, and control
- Real-world context through applications, limitations, and responsible use
- Human-centered learning through ethics, responsibility, trust, and student safety

This structured approach transforms artificial intelligence from a confusing concept into an understandable system.

Instructional Design

Each book in the series is designed for practical classroom use and includes:

- Structured chapters aligned with instructional pacing
- Clear, student-friendly explanations
- Reflection sections to reinforce understanding
- Worksheets, quizzes, and answer keys
- Teacher implementation support

No prior technical background is required for educators or students.

Guiding Principle

A central message of the IntelliGloss series is:

Artificial Intelligence is a tool—not a decision maker.

Students learn that while AI can support thinking and provide information, all decisions, actions, and responsibilities remain with humans. This principle reinforces critical thinking, accountability, and responsible technology use.

Why It Matters

AI literacy is no longer optional. It is a foundational skill.

Students who understand how AI works will be better prepared to:

Think critically about information

Adapt to emerging technologies

Use AI responsibly and ethically

Succeed in an increasingly AI-driven world

Our Goal

The IntelliGloss AI Education Series is designed to help schools move beyond simply using artificial intelligence tools and toward a deeper understanding of how these systems actually work.

By providing clear structure, defined concepts, and real-world context, this series equips students and educators with the knowledge needed to think critically, evaluate information, and use AI responsibly.

The goal is not just to introduce technology—but to build understanding, confidence, and accountability in an AI-driven world.

This is not just about learning to use AI—it is about preparing students to understand it, question it, and lead with it.

Clarity leads to confidence.
Understanding leads to responsible use.

Mission Statement

The mission of the IntelliGloss AI Education Series is to make artificial intelligence clear, structured, and accessible for every student and educator.

In a world where AI is rapidly transforming how information is created, used, and understood, this series is designed to move beyond surface-level interaction and provide a deeper understanding of how intelligent systems actually work.

Through clear explanations, organized frameworks, and real-world context, IntelliGloss equips learners with the ability to think critically, evaluate information, and engage with technology responsibly.

This mission is grounded in a simple belief:
students should not only learn how to use artificial intelligence—they should understand it.

By building both technical awareness and human-centered understanding, the IntelliGloss AI Education Series prepares students to navigate, question, and shape a future increasingly influenced by intelligent technologies.

The goal is not just to keep up with artificial intelligence—but to understand it, guide it, and use it responsibly.

Vision Statement

The vision of the IntelliGloss AI Education Series is to create a future where artificial intelligence is clearly understood, responsibly used, and thoughtfully integrated into education and everyday life.

In this future, students are not passive users of technology, but informed thinkers who understand how intelligent systems work, recognize their limitations, and apply them with purpose and responsibility.

Educators are equipped with clear frameworks and structured resources that make artificial intelligence accessible, teachable, and meaningful across all subjects—not just in technical fields.

Schools become environments where technology is not simply adopted, but understood—where students are encouraged to question, evaluate, and engage with AI in ways that support learning, creativity, and ethical awareness.

As artificial intelligence continues to evolve, this vision supports a generation that is prepared not only to adapt to change, but to lead it with knowledge, confidence, and integrity.

The future of artificial intelligence will not be defined by technology alone—but by the understanding and responsibility of those who use it.

Connecting AI Understanding to Cybersecurity Awareness

Definition

Understanding artificial intelligence is the first step toward understanding cybersecurity. While cybersecurity focuses on protecting systems, data, and users, artificial intelligence explains how those systems are built, how they function, and where they may be vulnerable.

The Connection

Every AI system is made up of components such as data, algorithms, models, and infrastructure. These same components are also the targets of cybersecurity threats.

When students understand:

How data is collected and stored

How algorithms make decisions

How AI models process information

How systems operate across frontend and backend layers

They begin to recognize where risks can exist and how systems can be misused.

Why This Matters

In today's digital world, students are not just users of technology—they are participants in complex systems powered by artificial intelligence.

Without understanding how these systems work:

Technology becomes something they trust without question

Risks become harder to recognize

Decisions are made without awareness of consequences

With understanding:

Students become more aware of how their data is used

They recognize how systems can be manipulated

They make more informed and responsible choices

Building Digital Readiness

Digital readiness is not only about using tools. It is about understanding the systems behind those tools.

By learning how AI works, students develop:

Awareness of digital environments

Confidence in navigating technology

A foundation for future learning, including cybersecurity

Conclusion

Cybersecurity begins with understanding.

Before students can protect systems, they must first understand how those systems are built and how they operate. This is why learning artificial intelligence is not only about innovation—it is also about responsibility.

The Foundation of Artificial Intelligence

Definition

The foundation of Artificial Intelligence (AI) refers to the core building blocks that allow AI systems to function. These building blocks work together to help machines learn from information, recognize patterns, and make decisions. AI is not magic—it is a system built on structured components that operate behind the scenes.

Understanding the Foundation in Simple Terms

Artificial Intelligence can be compared to a house. Before a house is complete, it must be built on a strong foundation. This foundation includes concrete, wiring, plumbing, and support structures that are not always visible but are essential for the house to function properly.

In the same way, AI systems rely on foundational components that are not visible to users but are necessary for AI tools to work. When people use AI applications such as chatbots or design tools, they are interacting with the surface. The true power of AI comes from what is underneath.

Key Components of the AI Foundation

1. Data (The Information)

Data is the starting point of all AI systems. It includes text, images, numbers, audio, and other forms of information. AI systems learn by analyzing patterns within this data.

2. Algorithms (The Instructions)

Algorithms are step-by-step instructions that tell the AI system how to process data. They guide how the system learns, identifies patterns, and produces results.

3. Models (The Trained System)

A model is created when data and algorithms are combined through a training process. The model acts as the "brain" of the AI system, allowing it to make predictions and generate responses.

4. Computing Power (The Engine)

AI systems require powerful computers to process large amounts of data. This includes specialized hardware such as processors and graphics processing units (GPUs) that allow AI to function efficiently.

5. Infrastructure (The Environment)

Infrastructure refers to the systems that support AI operations, including servers, storage, networks, and energy systems. Data centers are a key part of this infrastructure, providing the physical space where AI systems operate.

How These Components Work Together

AI systems function by combining all foundational components into a single process. Data is collected and analyzed using algorithms. This process creates a model that can recognize patterns and make decisions. The entire system is powered by computing machines and supported by infrastructure.

Why Understanding the Foundation Matters

Many people use AI tools without understanding how they work. This can lead to confusion, misuse, or over-reliance on technology. By understanding the foundation of AI, students and educators can:

Develop critical thinking skills

Use AI tools more responsibly

Recognize the limitations of AI systems

Build a deeper understanding of modern technology

Real-World Example

When a student asks a chatbot a question, the response does not come from "thinking" like a human. Instead, the AI system uses a trained model that has learned patterns from large amounts of data. It follows algorithms to predict the most appropriate answer, using powerful computers and infrastructure to deliver the response quickly.

This process is also influenced by how the question is asked. The words, structure, and clarity of a question—often referred to as a *prompt*—can affect the quality of the response. Learning how to communicate effectively with AI systems is an important skill known as prompt engineering. For further understanding, students and educators may explore *What to Say When You Talk to Yourself: A Guide to Prompt Engineering* by Susie Hala, which explains how carefully structured prompts can guide AI responses more effectively.

Conclusion

The foundation of Artificial Intelligence is built on data, algorithms, models, computing power, and infrastructure. These components work together to create systems that can learn, predict, and assist humans. Understanding this foundation helps students move beyond simply using AI tools and toward truly understanding how artificial intelligence works.

The Foundational Families of Artificial Intelligence

Introduction

Artificial intelligence is often described as a powerful technology, but in reality, it is not a single system. It is a combination of multiple components working together to create intelligent behavior.

To better understand how artificial intelligence works, it is helpful to break it down into organized groups. In the IntelliGloss framework, these groups are called **Foundational Families of Artificial Intelligence**.

Each family represents a key part of how AI systems are built and operate. Some families focus on how information is created and stored. Others focus on how machines learn, make decisions, process language, or perform tasks. Additional families represent the physical hardware, energy systems, and global infrastructure that make artificial intelligence possible.

When these families work together, they form a complete AI system.

This approach allows students and educators to move beyond simply using artificial intelligence tools and begin to understand what is happening behind the scenes. Instead of viewing AI as a mystery, learners can see it as a structured system made up of clearly defined components.

The diagram on the next page provides a visual overview of these families and how they connect to form the foundation of artificial intelligence.

By learning each family step by step, students develop a deeper understanding of how AI systems process information, learn from data, and interact with the world.

Understanding the Foundational Families of Artificial Intelligence is the first step toward true AI literacy.

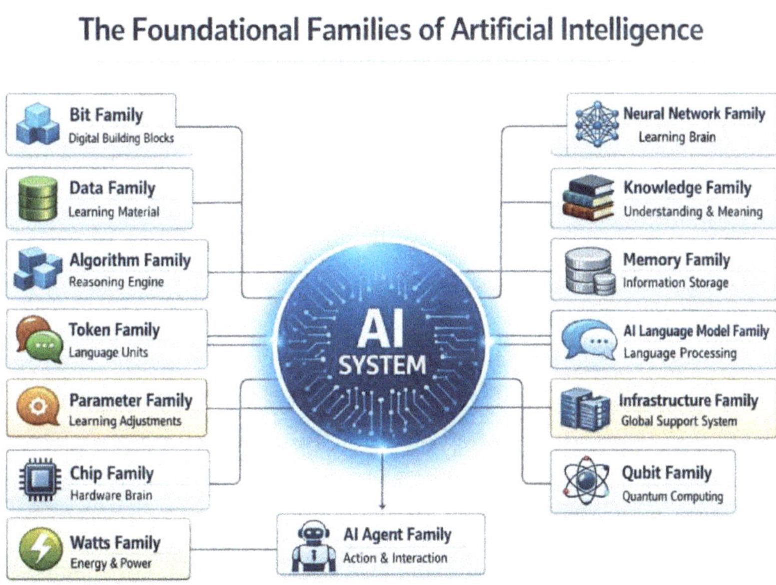

The Foundational Families of Artificial Intelligence

Family	Role	Description
Bit Family	Digital Building Blocks	The smallest unit of digital information (0 or 1). All computing systems begin with bits.
Algorithm Family	Reasoning Engine	Step-by-step instructions that tell computers how to solve problems and process information.

Family	Role	Description
Token Family	Language Units	Pieces of text used by AI models to understand and generate human language.
Parameter Family	Learning Adjustment System	Adjustable numerical values inside AI models that allow them to learn patterns from data.
Data Family	Learning Material	The information AI studies in order to learn patterns, relationships, and knowledge.
Logic Family	Decision Rules	The reasoning structures that allow AI systems to make decisions and evaluate conditions.
Memory Family	Information Storage	Systems that store and retrieve information so AI models can access past knowledge and context.
Knowledge Family	Understanding & Meaning	Structured information that allows AI to represent facts, relationships, and concepts.
Neural Network Family	Learning Brain	Interconnected layers of artificial neurons that enable AI systems to recognize patterns, learn from data, and make predictions.
AI Model Family	Intelligence Engine	The trained system that uses data, parameters, and neural networks to perform tasks such as prediction, classification, and generation.
AI Translator Architecture Family	Language Conversion System	Systems that transform input into output, enabling AI to convert text, speech, or images into meaningful responses.
AI Agent Family	Action and Task Execution System	AI systems designed to perceive information, make decisions, and carry out tasks autonomously or semi-autonomously.
Chip Family	Hardware Brain	Physical processors (GPUs, TPUs, CPUs, NPUs) that perform AI computations.
Watts Family	Energy Power	The electrical power required to run AI hardware and data centers.
AI Energy Family	Energy Source System	The total energy consumed over time to operate AI systems, including training and real-time usage.
Infrastructure Family	Global Support System	Data centers, internet networks, cloud systems, and global infrastructure that allow AI to operate and scale.
Ingredient Family	System Composition	The essential components that come together to create an AI system, including data, algorithms, models, hardware, and energy.
Qubit Family	Quantum Information Units	Quantum bits that can represent multiple states simultaneously, forming the foundation of quantum computing.

The Bit Family

Introduction

The Bit Family represents the starting point of all digital technology. Every computer system, application, and artificial intelligence model is built from bits—the smallest unit of information in computing.

A bit can hold one of two values: 0 or 1. While this may seem simple, these two values form the foundation of everything digital. When bits are combined and organized, they create larger units of data that allow computers to store text, display images, play videos, and run complex systems.

From a single bit to massive data systems, all digital information follows this same structure. This is how computers are able to represent and process the world in a form they can understand.

In artificial intelligence, bits are essential because they store the data that models learn from, process the calculations that drive decision-making, and support the systems that generate responses.

Understanding the Bit Family helps students see how simple binary signals grow into powerful technologies. It reveals that behind every advanced AI system is a foundation built from the most basic building blocks of information.

Bit Family — Visual Understanding of Data Size

How Much Data Can Each Unit Hold? (Simple Examples)

Unit	Size	Photos (Approx.)	Video (Approx. Hours)
Bit	1 bit	N/A	N/A
Byte	8 bits	1 character	N/A
Kilobyte (KB)	~1,000 bytes	Part of a paragraph	N/A
Megabyte (MB)	~1,000 KB	~1 photo	~1 minute of video
Gigabyte (GB)	~1,000 MB	~250 photos	~1–2 hours of video
Terabyte (TB)	~1,000 GB	~250,000 photos	~1,000–2,000 hours of video
Petabyte (PB)	~1,000 TB	~250 million photos	~1–2 million hours of video
Exabyte (EB)	~1,000 PB	~250 billion photos	~1–2 billion hours of video
Zettabyte (ZB)	~1,000 EB	~250 trillion photos	~1–2 trillion hours of video
Yottabyte (YB)	~1,000 ZB	~250 quadrillion photos	~1–2 quadrillion hours of video

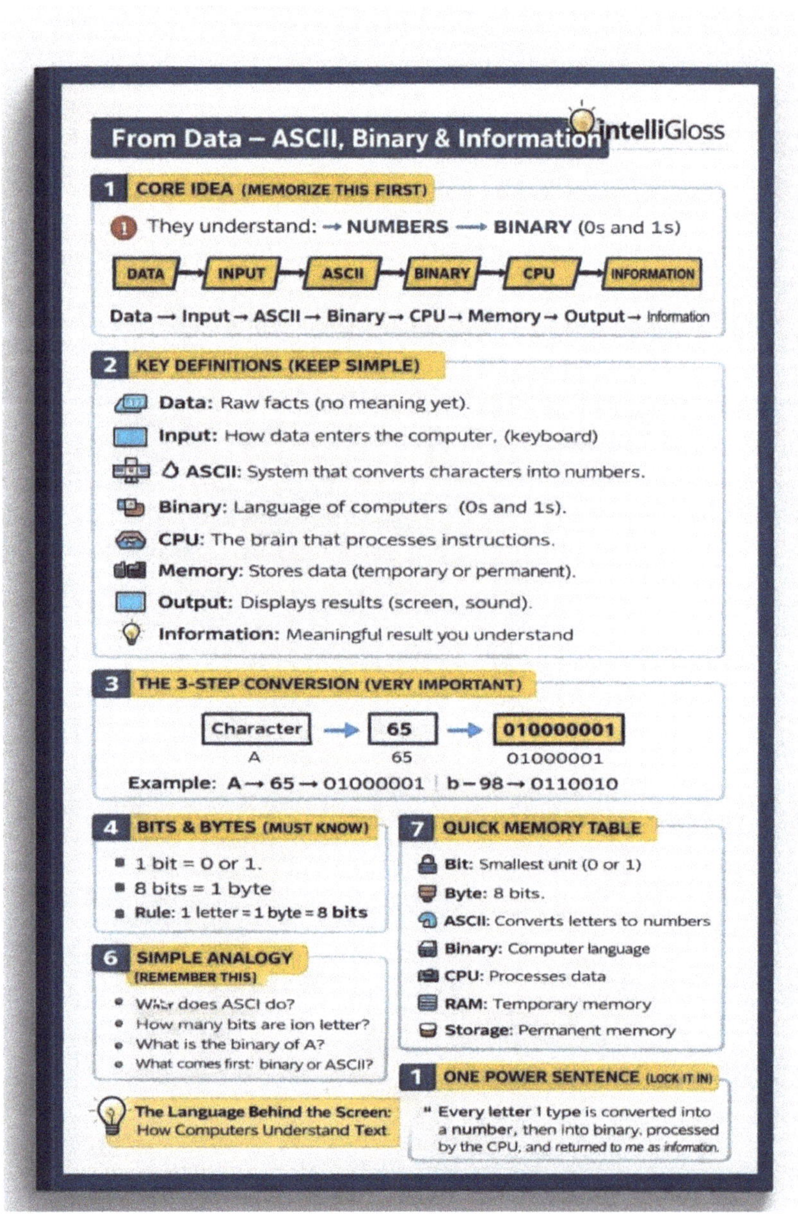

The Algorithm Family

Definition and Overview

The **Algorithm Family** represents the *thinking engine* of artificial intelligence — the set of mathematical instructions that guide how AI analyzes data, learns patterns, and makes decisions.

An **algorithm** is a sequence of steps designed to solve a problem or complete a task. In AI, algorithms tell the system *how to learn*, *how to predict*, and *how to improve* with every iteration.

In simple terms:

The Algorithm Family is the *logic of intelligence* — the invisible code that transforms data into decisions and predictions into progress.

🧠 How Algorithms Power AI

Every AI system — from simple chatbots to large-scale deep learning models — relies on algorithms as its foundation.
They determine how the model:

Processes and cleans data,

Identifies relationships between variables,

Learns from feedback, and

Improves over time.

Without algorithms, even the most powerful dataset or neural network would remain static and lifeless.

In essence, **algorithms are the teachers** that train AI how to think.

Why the Algorithm Family Matters

Algorithms are what separate automation from intelligence.
They allow machines to **reason**, **adapt**, and **learn** — not just follow commands.
For prompt engineers, understanding algorithmic behavior helps explain *why* AI sometimes misunderstands a question, repeats patterns, or changes tone after feedback.

Every AI response you receive follows an underlying process — a pattern recognition journey from input to output.

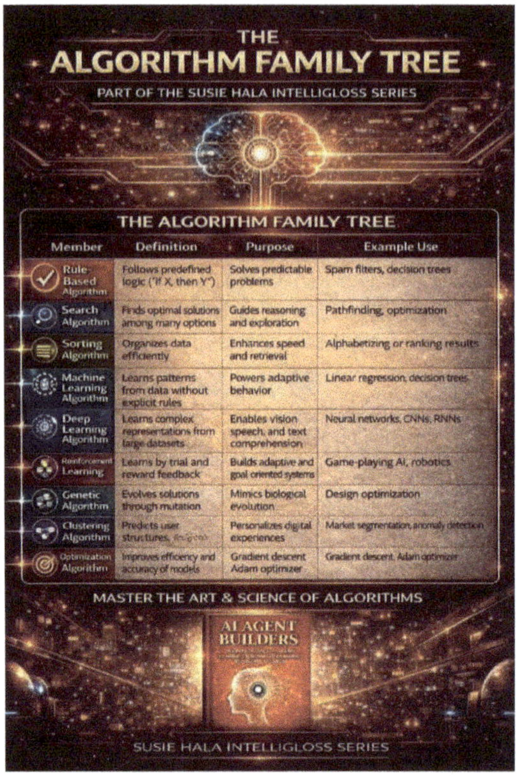

Analogy for Everyday Readers

Imagine AI as a chef in a kitchen:

The **Data Family** provides the ingredients.

The **Knowledge Family** gives the recipes.

The **Algorithm Family** is the *cooking process* — mixing, heating, tasting, and adjusting until the dish is perfect.

Just as cooking methods determine the quality of food, algorithms determine the quality of intelligence.

Algorithm Efficiency and Energy Use

Not all algorithms are equal.
Some are **fast but shallow**, while others are **deep but energy-intensive**.
Training large AI models requires algorithms that can handle billions of calculations per second — powered by the **Watts Family** (energy) and executed through the **Chip Family** (hardware).

The design of efficient algorithms directly affects sustainability in AI — minimizing power consumption while maximizing accuracy and speed.

Algorithms and Prompt Engineering

For prompt engineers, algorithms explain *how* the AI arrives at its answers.
When a model gives inconsistent or off-topic results, it's often due to:

Misinterpretation of input signals (input encoding),

Bias in training algorithms, or

Overfitting to certain data patterns.

Knowing this helps you craft prompts that guide the AI's decision-making — not just its output.

Quick Takeaway: The Algorithm Family is the reasoning heart of AI.
It transforms information into understanding and enables machines to think, learn, and evolve like digital problem-solvers.

Token Family Introduction

The Token Family represents one of the most important bridges between human language and artificial intelligence. While humans communicate using words, sentences, and meaning, AI systems do not understand language in the same way. Instead, they rely on tokens—small units of text that allow machines to process, analyze, and generate language step by step.

A token can be a word, part of a word, a character, or even punctuation. When a student types a sentence into an AI system, that sentence is not read as a whole idea. It is first broken down into tokens. These tokens become the input that the AI model uses to recognize patterns, predict outcomes, and generate responses.

The Token Family works closely with several other foundational families in artificial intelligence. It connects directly with the Data Family, which provides the text used for training, and the Neural Network Family, which processes token patterns to produce intelligent outputs. It also plays a key role in the AI Translator Architecture Family, where tokens are transformed, analyzed, and reassembled into meaningful responses.

Understanding tokens helps students see what is happening behind the scenes when they interact with AI tools. Instead of viewing AI as a "magic system," they begin to understand that every response is built from sequences of tokens processed through mathematical models.

In simple terms, if language is what humans speak, tokens are what AI understands.

Token Family Breakdown Chart

Component	Role	Description	Example
Tokenization	Input Conversion	The process of breaking text into smaller units (tokens) that AI can process	"Artificial Intelligence" → "Artificial" + "Intelligence"
Tokens	Language Units	The individual pieces of text used by AI models for understanding and generation	"AI", "learn", "ing", "."
Subword Tokens	Efficiency Units	Words split into smaller parts to handle unknown or complex vocabulary	"unbelievable" → "un", "believ", "able"
Character Tokens	Fine-Grained Units	Text broken down into individual characters for detailed processing	"AI" → "A" + "I"
Vocabulary (Token Set)	Token Library	The complete set of tokens an AI model recognizes and uses	GPT models have thousands to millions of tokens
Encoding	Token Mapping	Converting tokens into numerical representations for computation	"AI" → [1234, 5678] (example IDs)
Decoding	Output Reconstruction	Converting numerical outputs back into readable text	[1234, 5678] → "AI system"
Context Window	Memory Limit	The number of tokens an AI can process at one time	Example: 8,000 tokens ≈ several pages of text
Token Embeddings	Meaning Representation	Mathematical vectors that capture relationships between tokens	"king" and "queen" have similar embeddings
Token Prediction	Language Generation	The process of predicting the next token in a sequence	"AI is" → predicts "powerful"

The Token Family reminds us that behind every intelligent response is a structured sequence of tokens working together. What feels like natural conversation to humans is, for AI, a carefully processed stream of language units transformed into meaning.

The AI Ecosystem Family

The AI Ecosystem Family is a connected group of artificial intelligence technologies, systems, behaviors, and applications that work together to help machines perform intelligent tasks. This ecosystem includes core AI systems, AI agents, agentic AI, AI autonomy, autonomous AI workers, and generative AI. Each part plays a different role in how modern AI systems think, learn, create, make decisions, solve problems, and interact with the world.

At the center of the ecosystem is artificial intelligence itself — the broad field focused on building machines and software that can perform tasks that normally require human intelligence. AI agents act as the systems that carry out goals and actions. Agentic AI describes the ability of

AI systems to plan, reason, adapt, and pursue objectives with limited human guidance. AI autonomy represents the level of independence an AI system has while making decisions and taking actions. AI autonomous workers apply these capabilities to perform real-world tasks like digital employees or assistants. Generative AI adds the ability to create new content such as text, images, music, video, code, and designs.

The AI Ecosystem Family demonstrates that modern artificial intelligence is no longer just one single technology. Instead, it is an interconnected environment of systems, tools, intelligence, automation, creativity, and human collaboration. As AI continues to evolve, these technologies are becoming increasingly integrated into education, business, healthcare, communication, cybersecurity, research, and everyday life.

Understanding the AI Ecosystem Family helps students, educators, and readers see how the different parts of AI connect together to shape the future of intelligent systems and the digital world.

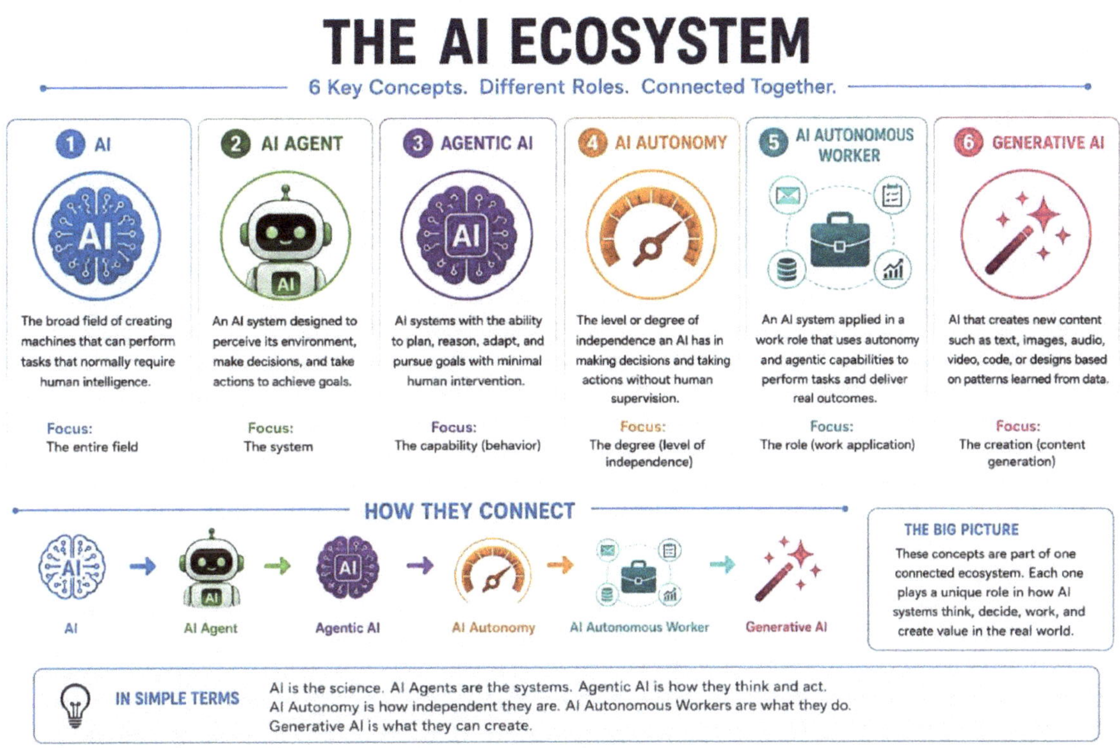

Parameter Family Introduction

The Parameter Family represents the internal learning system of artificial intelligence. While tokens provide the language and data provides the learning material, parameters are what allow AI systems to adjust, improve, and make intelligent decisions over time.

In simple terms, parameters are numerical values inside an AI model that change as the system learns. These values are not visible to users, but they play a critical role in how the model understands patterns, relationships, and meaning. Every time an AI system is trained, it adjusts its parameters to better predict outcomes and generate accurate responses.

Parameters exist throughout neural networks, where they act as the connections between artificial neurons. Each connection has a weight, which determines how important a particular piece of information is. During training, these weights are continuously adjusted based on data, allowing the system to improve its performance.

The Parameter Family works closely with the Data Family, which provides the information needed for learning, and the Neural Network Family, which organizes how parameters are structured and applied. It also supports the Token Family by helping the model interpret and predict sequences of language.

Understanding parameters helps students recognize that AI is not simply programmed with fixed rules. Instead, it learns by adjusting internal values that guide how it processes information. These adjustments are what allow AI systems to evolve from simple pattern recognition to complex reasoning and decision-making.

In essence, if data is what AI learns from, parameters are how AI learns.

Parameter Family Breakdown Chart

Component	Role	Description	Example
Parameters	Learning Values	Numerical values inside an AI model that are adjusted during training	Millions or billions of values inside a model
Weights	Connection Strength	Values that determine how strongly one neuron influences another	A higher weight = stronger influence
Bias	Adjustment Factor	A value added to help the model shift and fine-tune outputs	Helps improve accuracy in predictions
Training Process	Learning Mechanism	The process of adjusting parameters using data to improve performance	Model improves after analyzing many examples
Loss Function	Error Measurement	Measures how far the model's prediction is from the correct answer	Lower loss = better performance

Component	Role	Description	Example
Optimization Algorithm	Adjustment Strategy	Method used to update parameters efficiently	Gradient Descent adjusts weights step by step
Gradient	Direction of Change	Indicates how parameters should change to reduce error	Shows whether to increase or decrease a value
Backpropagation	Learning Process	System that sends error signals backward to update parameters	Adjusts earlier layers based on output error
Hyperparameters	Control Settings	External settings that guide how training happens (not learned)	Learning rate, batch size
Model Size	Capacity Indicator	The total number of parameters in a model	Larger models = more learning capacity

The Parameter Family is the hidden engine of learning in artificial intelligence. While users interact with outputs, it is the continuous adjustment of parameters behind the scenes that makes intelligent behavior possible.

Data Family Introduction

The Data Family represents the foundation of learning in artificial intelligence. Every AI system depends on data to develop knowledge, recognize patterns, and make decisions. Without data, artificial intelligence cannot learn, adapt, or function effectively.

Data can take many forms, including text, images, audio, video, and numerical information. These inputs provide the raw material that AI systems analyze during training. By studying large amounts of data, AI models begin to identify patterns, relationships, and structures that allow them to make predictions and generate responses.

The quality and diversity of data play a critical role in how well an AI system performs. Accurate, balanced, and relevant data helps models produce reliable results, while poor or biased data can lead to incorrect or unfair outcomes. This is why data collection, preparation, and evaluation are essential steps in the development of responsible AI systems.

The Data Family works closely with the Parameter Family, which adjusts internal values based on data, and the Neural Network Family, which processes and organizes data through layers of computation. It also supports the Token Family when dealing with language, as text data is converted into tokens for analysis.

Understanding the Data Family helps students recognize that AI does not "know" things on its own. Instead, it learns from the information it is given. The more meaningful and well-prepared the data, the more capable the AI system becomes.

In simple terms, data is the source of knowledge, and it is the starting point for all artificial intelligence.

Data Family Breakdown Chart

Component	Role	Description	Example
Data	Learning Material	Raw information used by AI systems to learn patterns and relationships	Text, images, audio, numbers
Dataset	Organized Collection	A structured group of data used for training and evaluation	A folder of labeled images
Training Data	Learning Input	Data used to teach the AI model during training	Thousands of sentences for a language model
Validation Data	Performance Check	Data used to tune the model during training without directly learning from it	Helps prevent overfitting
Test Data	Final Evaluation	Data used to measure how well the model performs after training	New unseen examples
Structured Data	Organized Format	Data arranged in tables with clear categories	Spreadsheets, databases
Unstructured Data	Flexible Format	Data without a predefined structure	Text documents, images, videos
Labeled Data	Guided Learning	Data tagged with correct answers to guide training	Image labeled "cat" or "dog"
Unlabeled Data	Self-Learning Input	Data without labels, used in unsupervised learning	Raw text without categories
Data Quality	Accuracy Measure	The reliability and correctness of data	Clean, complete, and consistent data
Data Bias	Imbalance Issue	When data does not represent all groups fairly	Skewed or incomplete datasets
Data Preprocessing	Preparation Step	Cleaning and organizing data before training	Removing errors, formatting text

The Data Family reminds us that artificial intelligence is only as strong as the information it learns from. High-quality data leads to meaningful insights, while poor data can limit or misguide intelligent systems.

Memory Family Introduction

The Memory Family represents how artificial intelligence systems store, retain, and retrieve information. Just as humans rely on memory to recall past experiences, learn new concepts, and make decisions, AI systems depend on memory to access previously processed information and maintain context.

In artificial intelligence, memory is not a single component but a collection of mechanisms that allow systems to handle information over time. Some forms of memory are short-term, holding information temporarily while a task is being completed. Other forms are long-term, storing learned knowledge that can be used across different tasks and interactions.

Memory plays a critical role in enabling AI systems to understand sequences, maintain context in conversations, and improve decision-making. For example, when a user interacts with a language model, the system uses memory to keep track of previous words, sentences, or prompts in order to generate coherent and relevant responses.

The Memory Family works closely with the Data Family, which provides the information to be stored, and the Parameter Family, which encodes learned knowledge within the model. It also supports the Neural Network Family by enabling systems to process sequences and retain important patterns over time.

Understanding the Memory Family helps students see that AI is not simply reacting to individual inputs in isolation. Instead, it relies on stored information and contextual awareness to produce meaningful and consistent outputs.

In simple terms, if data is what AI learns from, memory is how AI remembers and uses what it has learned.

Memory Family Breakdown Chart

Component	Role	Description	Example
Memory	Information Storage	The ability of an AI system to store and access information	Retaining previous inputs in a task
Short-Term Memory	Temporary Storage	Holds information for immediate processing	Keeping track of words in a sentence
Long-Term Memory	Persistent Storage	Stores learned knowledge for future use	Knowledge embedded in model parameters
Context Memory	Conversation Tracking	Maintains information within a specific interaction	Remembering earlier parts of a prompt
Working Memory	Active Processing	Handles information currently being used in computation	Processing a sequence step by step
External Memory	Extended Storage	Memory stored outside the model for retrieval	Databases, vector stores
Internal Memory	Embedded Knowledge	Information stored within the model itself	Learned patterns inside neural networks
Sequence Memory	Order Awareness	Tracks the order of inputs over time	Understanding sentence structure

Component	Role	Description	Example
Retrieval Mechanism	Access System	Retrieves stored information when needed	Searching relevant past data
Attention Mechanism	Focus System	Highlights important parts of memory for processing	Focusing on key words in a sentence
Memory Capacity	Storage Limit	The amount of information the system can handle at once	Context window size

The Memory Family shows that intelligence is not just about processing information in the moment, but about retaining, organizing, and using knowledge over time to create meaningful understanding.

Knowledge Family Introduction

The Knowledge Family represents how artificial intelligence organizes, connects, and uses information to create understanding. While data provides raw information and memory stores it, knowledge is what gives that information meaning and structure.

In artificial intelligence, knowledge is not simply a collection of facts. It is the result of identifying relationships, patterns, and connections within data. AI systems use knowledge to recognize concepts, make decisions, and generate meaningful responses. This allows machines to move beyond simple data processing and toward more intelligent behavior.

Knowledge can be represented in different ways within AI systems. Some forms are structured, such as databases and knowledge graphs, where relationships between concepts are clearly defined. Other forms are learned implicitly through neural networks, where patterns are encoded within parameters and used to guide predictions.

The Knowledge Family works closely with the Data Family, which provides the information needed to build knowledge, and the Memory Family, which stores and retrieves that information. It also connects with the Parameter Family, where learned knowledge is embedded within the model, and the Neural Network Family, which processes and organizes that knowledge.

Understanding the Knowledge Family helps students recognize that AI systems do not simply memorize information. Instead, they learn how pieces of information relate to one another, allowing them to interpret meaning, solve problems, and respond intelligently.

In simple terms, if data is information and memory stores it, knowledge is the understanding that makes it useful.

Knowledge Family Breakdown Chart

Component	Role	Description	Example
Knowledge	Understanding System	Organized information that allows AI to interpret meaning and make decisions	Recognizing relationships between concepts
Facts	Basic Information	Individual pieces of information stored within a system	“Water freezes at 0°C”
Relationships	Connection Mapping	Links between pieces of information that create meaning	“Teacher teaches student”
Knowledge Representation	Structure System	Methods used to organize and store knowledge in AI	Knowledge graphs, semantic networks
Knowledge Graph	Network Mapping	A structured representation of entities and their relationships	Google Knowledge Graph
Semantic Understanding	Meaning Interpretation	The ability to understand meaning behind words and data	Understanding synonyms and context
Inference	Reasoning Process	Drawing conclusions based on known information	If A = B and B = C, then A = C
Rules	Decision Framework	Logical guidelines used to make decisions	If temperature < 0°C → freeze
Ontology	Concept Framework	A structured system defining categories and relationships	Classification of animals
Explicit Knowledge	Direct Information	Clearly defined and stored knowledge	Rules, databases
Implicit Knowledge	Learned Patterns	Knowledge learned through experience and data	Patterns learned by neural networks
Knowledge Integration	System Coordination	Combining information from multiple sources	Merging text, images, and data

The Knowledge Family transforms information into understanding, allowing artificial intelligence to move beyond data and memory into meaningful reasoning and intelligent decision-making.

AI Model Family Introduction

The AI Model Family represents the core system within artificial intelligence that performs tasks such as prediction, classification, and content generation. It is the part of AI that users interact with, whether they are asking questions, generating images, or analyzing data.

An AI model is a trained system that has learned patterns from data. During training, the model processes large amounts of information and adjusts its internal parameters to improve accuracy. Once trained, the model can take new input and produce meaningful output based on what it has learned.

AI models can take many forms depending on their purpose. Some models are designed to recognize images, others to understand language, and others to make decisions or predictions. Large Language Models (LLMs), for example, are designed to process and generate human language by predicting sequences of tokens.

The AI Model Family works closely with the Data Family, which provides the learning material, and the Parameter Family, which stores learned patterns. It also relies on the Neural Network Family for structure and the Chip and Infrastructure Families for execution and deployment.

Understanding the AI Model Family helps students see that AI is not just a concept, but a working system that has been trained to perform specific tasks. It is the engine that transforms input into output.

In simple terms, if AI is the system, the model is the part that actually does the thinking and producing.

AI Model Family Breakdown Chart

Component	Role	Description	Example
AI Model	Core System	The trained system that performs tasks	Chatbot, image generator
Training	Learning Process	Process of teaching the model using data	Learning from datasets
Inference	Output Generation	Using the trained model to produce results	Answering a question
Model Architecture	Structural Design	Defines how the model is built	Neural networks, transformers
Parameters	Learned Values	Internal values adjusted during training	Billions of weights
Input Data	Entry Information	Data provided to the model for processing	User prompt
Output Data	Result	The response or prediction generated	AI-generated text
Model Types	Functional Categories	Different kinds of models for different tasks	Classification, generation
Fine-Tuning	Model Adjustment	Improving a model for specific tasks	Custom-trained AI
Pretrained Model	Base System	A model trained on large datasets before use	General-purpose AI
Evaluation	Performance Check	Measuring how well the model performs	Accuracy, loss metrics

The AI Model Family represents the working core of artificial intelligence, where learned patterns are transformed into meaningful actions, predictions, and responses.

Neural Network Family Introduction

The Neural Network Family represents the structural foundation of how artificial intelligence learns and processes information. Inspired by the human brain, neural networks are systems of interconnected units, often called neurons, that work together to analyze data, recognize patterns, and make decisions.

In artificial intelligence, a neural network is made up of layers. The input layer receives data, the hidden layers process that data, and the output layer produces a result. As information flows through these layers, the network applies mathematical transformations that allow it to detect patterns and relationships within the data.

Neural networks rely heavily on the Parameter Family, where weights and biases determine how strongly information flows between neurons. During training, these parameters are adjusted to improve the network's performance. The more the network learns, the better it becomes at recognizing patterns and making accurate predictions.

The Neural Network Family works closely with the Data Family, which provides the information needed for learning, and the Memory and Knowledge Families, which help store and organize learned information. It also supports the Token Family when processing language, allowing AI systems to interpret sequences of tokens in meaningful ways.

Understanding neural networks helps students see that AI is not simply following instructions. Instead, it is learning from examples and improving over time through layered processing and pattern recognition.

In simple terms, neural networks are the systems that allow AI to think, learn, and make sense of information.

Neural Network Family Breakdown Chart

Component	Role	Description	Example
Neural Network	Learning Structure	A system of interconnected neurons that processes data and learns patterns	Image recognition system
Neuron (Node)	Processing Unit	A basic unit that receives input, processes it, and passes output forward	A single calculation point

Component	Role	Description	Example
Input Layer	Data Entry Point	The first layer that receives raw data	Pixels of an image
Hidden Layers	Processing Layers	Intermediate layers that transform data and detect patterns	Feature detection layers
Output Layer	Result Generator	The final layer that produces predictions or decisions	"Cat" vs "Dog" classification
Weights	Signal Strength	Values that determine how strongly inputs influence outputs	Higher weight = stronger impact
Bias	Adjustment Value	Helps shift outputs to improve learning accuracy	Fine-tuning predictions
Activation Function	Decision Function	Determines whether a neuron should activate based on input	ReLU, Sigmoid
Forward Propagation	Data Flow	The process of passing input data through the network to produce output	Input → Hidden → Output
Backpropagation	Learning Process	Adjusts weights and biases based on error to improve performance	Correcting mistakes
Loss Function	Error Measurement	Calculates how far the output is from the correct answer	Prediction vs actual
Deep Neural Network	Advanced Structure	A network with many hidden layers for complex learning	Deep learning models

The Neural Network Family provides the structure that allows artificial intelligence to transform data into understanding, making it possible for machines to learn from experience and improve over time.

Dual Language System in Artificial Intelligence

Definition

The Dual Language System in Artificial Intelligence refers to the way AI communicates using two different forms of language at the same time: human language for interaction and machine language for internal processing.

Key Components

Human Language (Natural Language)
This is the language people use to communicate with AI, such as English, Spanish, Tongan, or Fijian. It includes words, sentences, and questions that users type or speak.

Machine Language (Numerical Representation)
This is how AI understands information internally. Words are converted into numbers called tokens and processed using mathematical models and algorithms.

How It Works (Step-by-Step)

A user enters a question in human language

The AI converts the words into numerical tokens

The AI processes the tokens using a neural network

The AI generates a response based on patterns and probabilities

The response is converted back into human language

Example

User Input:
"What is Artificial Intelligence?"

AI Process:

Converts words into numbers

Analyzes patterns from training data

Predicts the best possible answer

Output:
"Artificial Intelligence is the ability of machines to perform tasks that normally require human intelligence."

Why This Matters

Understanding the dual language system helps students realize that:

AI does not "think" like humans

AI translates language into math and back into language

Every interaction with AI is based on patterns, not emotions or understanding

Applications

Chatbots and virtual assistants

Language translation systems

Search engines

Voice recognition tools

Challenges

Misinterpretation of human language

Bias in language data

Lack of true understanding or reasoning

Summary

Artificial Intelligence works by translating human language into machine-readable data and then converting the results back into human language. This dual system allows AI to interact with people while operating through mathematical processes behind the scenes.

AI Translator Architecture Family Introduction

The AI Translator Architecture Family represents the system that transforms input into meaningful output in artificial intelligence. It acts as the bridge between what humans provide and what AI produces. Whether a user types a question, uploads an image, or speaks a command, this architecture is responsible for interpreting that input and generating a response.

In artificial intelligence, translation does not only mean converting one language to another. It refers to the broader process of transforming one form of information into another. For example, text can be translated into a response, speech can be converted into text, and images can be interpreted into descriptions. This transformation process is at the core of how modern AI systems function.

The AI Translator Architecture is built on multiple foundational families. It relies on the Token Family to break input into manageable units, the Neural Network Family to process patterns, and the Parameter Family to guide learning. It also uses knowledge and memory to maintain context and produce coherent results.

At the center of this architecture is the ability to encode and decode information. Encoding transforms input into a format the model can understand, while decoding converts processed information back into human-readable output. This continuous transformation allows AI systems to interact with users in a natural and meaningful way.

Understanding the AI Translator Architecture Family helps students see that AI is not simply responding randomly. Instead, it is systematically translating input into output through structured processes and learned patterns.

In simple terms, if tokens are the language pieces and neural networks are the brain, the AI Translator Architecture is the system that turns understanding into communication.

AI Translator Architecture Family Breakdown Chart

Component	Role	Description	Example
AI Translator Architecture	Transformation System	Converts input into meaningful output	Question → Answer
Input Processing	Data Intake	Receives and prepares user input for analysis	Text prompt entered by a user
Encoding	Input Conversion	Transforms input into numerical representations	Words → token IDs
Context Building	Meaning Formation	Organizes input into a structured understanding	Sentence context tracking
Sequence Processing	Order Handling	Maintains the correct order of information	Word sequence in a sentence
Attention Mechanism	Focus System	Identifies important parts of input data	Highlighting key words
Representation Layer	Feature Mapping	Converts data into internal representations for processing	Embeddings
Decoding	Output Generation	Converts processed data back into human-readable form	Token IDs → words
Output Generation	Response Creation	Produces the final answer or result	AI-generated response
Multimodal Translation	Cross-Format Processing	Translates between different types of data	Image → text description
Feedback Loop	Improvement Cycle	Uses results to refine future outputs	Model learning over time

The AI Translator Architecture Family shows that artificial intelligence is not just about understanding information, but about transforming it into meaningful communication that humans can use and interact with.

AI Architecture Family Introduction

The AI Architecture Family represents the overall design and structure of an artificial intelligence system. While individual families such as Data, Parameters, and Neural Networks explain how AI learns and processes information, the AI Architecture Family shows how all these components are organized and work together as a complete system.

In artificial intelligence, architecture refers to the blueprint that defines how data flows through a system, how components interact, and how decisions are produced. It determines how input is received, how it is processed, and how output is generated. A well-designed architecture allows AI systems to operate efficiently, scale to large problems, and produce reliable results.

AI architectures can vary depending on the type of system being built. Some are designed for image recognition, others for language processing, and others for decision-making or automation. Despite these differences, most architectures share common elements such as input layers, processing layers, memory components, and output mechanisms.

The AI Architecture Family connects all foundational families. It integrates the Data Family for input, the Token Family for language processing, the Neural Network Family for computation, the Parameter Family for learning, and the Memory and Knowledge Families for storing and organizing information. It also works closely with the AI Translator Architecture Family to transform input into meaningful output.

Understanding the AI Architecture Family helps students see the "big picture" of artificial intelligence. Instead of viewing AI as separate parts, they begin to understand it as a coordinated system where each component plays a specific role.

In simple terms, if individual families are the parts of AI, the AI Architecture Family is the blueprint that brings everything together into one working system.

AI Architecture Family Breakdown Chart

Component	Role	Description	Example
AI Architecture	System Blueprint	The overall design that defines how an AI system is structured and operates	ChatGPT system design
Input Layer	Data Entry Point	Receives raw input from users or external sources	Text prompt, image upload
Preprocessing Layer	Data Preparation	Cleans and organizes input data before processing	Tokenization, normalization
Processing Core	Computation Engine	The main system where data is analyzed and transformed	Neural networks, transformers
Parameter System	Learning Core	Stores adjustable values that guide learning and predictions	Model weights and biases

Component	Role	Description	Example
Memory System	Context Storage	Maintains and retrieves information during processing	Context window, external memory
Knowledge System	Understanding Layer	Organizes relationships and meaning within the system	Knowledge graphs, learned patterns
Decision Layer	Output Logic	Determines the final output based on processed data	Selecting the best response
Output Layer	Result Delivery	Presents results to the user in a usable format	Text, image, or audio response
Feedback Loop	Improvement System	Uses outcomes to refine future performance	Model updates and retraining
Scalability System	Expansion Capability	Allows the system to handle increasing data and complexity	Cloud-based AI systems
Integration Layer	System Connection	Connects AI with external tools and platforms	APIs, databases, applications

The AI Architecture Family reveals that artificial intelligence is not a single technology, but a coordinated system of interconnected components working together to transform data into intelligent outcomes.

Chip Family Introduction

The Chip Family represents the physical hardware that powers artificial intelligence systems. While software components such as data, algorithms, and neural networks define how AI works, none of these systems can function without the computing chips that perform the actual calculations.

Chips are specialized electronic components designed to process information at extremely high speeds. In artificial intelligence, these chips handle the complex mathematical operations required for training models and generating outputs. Every prediction, calculation, and response produced by an AI system is executed by hardware within the Chip Family.

Different types of chips are used depending on the needs of the system. Central Processing Units (CPUs) handle general-purpose tasks, while Graphics Processing Units (GPUs) are optimized for parallel processing, making them ideal for training neural networks. More specialized chips, such as Tensor Processing Units (TPUs) and Neural Processing Units (NPUs), are designed specifically for AI workloads, enabling faster and more efficient computation.

The Chip Family works closely with the Neural Network Family, which defines the structure of computation, and the Parameter Family, which stores the values being processed. It also connects to the Infrastructure Family, where large-scale systems of chips are organized in data centers and cloud environments.

Understanding the Chip Family helps students recognize that artificial intelligence is not purely abstract. It depends on physical machines that require power, resources, and engineering to operate. These chips are the engines that bring AI models to life.

In simple terms, if AI is the intelligence, chips are the machines that make that intelligence possible.

Chip Family Breakdown Chart

Component	Role	Description	Example
Chip (Processor)	Computation Engine	Electronic hardware that performs calculations required for AI	CPU, GPU
CPU (Central Processing Unit)	General Processor	Handles a wide range of computing tasks	Running basic applications
GPU (Graphics Processing Unit)	Parallel Processor	Processes many calculations at once, ideal for AI training	Training neural networks
TPU (Tensor Processing Unit)	AI Accelerator	Specialized chip designed for machine learning tasks	Google TPU
NPU (Neural Processing Unit)	Edge AI Processor	Optimized for running AI on devices like phones	Smartphone AI features
AI Accelerator	Performance Booster	Hardware designed to speed up AI computations	Dedicated AI chips
Memory (Hardware)	Data Storage	Stores data and instructions for processing	RAM, VRAM
Parallel Processing	Speed Mechanism	Ability to perform multiple calculations simultaneously	GPUs processing thousands of operations
Throughput	Processing Capacity	Amount of data processed over time	High-performance computing systems
Latency	Response Time	Time it takes to process a request	Faster chips = lower latency
Power Consumption	Energy Usage	Amount of energy required to run the chip	High-performance GPUs use more power
Edge Devices	Local Processing	Devices that run AI locally without cloud support	Phones, smart cameras

The Chip Family reminds us that behind every intelligent system is powerful hardware performing millions or billions of calculations, turning abstract models into real-world functionality.

Watts Family Introduction

The Watts Family represents the measurement of power used by artificial intelligence systems. While the Chip Family provides the hardware that performs computations, the Watts Family explains how much energy those systems consume while operating.

A watt is a unit of power that measures the rate at which energy is used. In artificial intelligence, watts help us understand how much electricity is required to run processors, train models, and generate responses. Every time an AI system processes data, performs calculations, or produces output, it consumes power.

Different AI systems require different levels of power depending on their size and complexity. Small systems, such as those running on mobile devices, use relatively low amounts of power. In contrast, large-scale AI models operating in data centers can require significant amounts of electricity, especially during training, where billions of calculations are performed continuously.

The Watts Family works closely with the Chip Family, which determines how efficiently computations are performed, and the Infrastructure Family, where large networks of machines operate together. It also connects to the overall design of AI systems, as more efficient models can reduce power consumption while maintaining performance.

Understanding the Watts Family helps students recognize that artificial intelligence is not only about intelligence and computation, but also about energy use and resource management. As AI continues to grow, managing power efficiently becomes an important part of building responsible and sustainable systems.

In simple terms, if chips perform the work, watts measure how much power it takes to do that work.

Watts Family Breakdown Chart

Component	Role	Description	Example
Watt (W)	Power Measurement	Unit that measures the rate of energy use	A device using 100 watts
Power Consumption	Energy Usage Rate	Amount of power used during operation	AI model running on GPUs
Energy Efficiency	Performance Balance	How effectively a system uses power to perform tasks	More output with less power
High-Performance Computing	Intensive Power Use	Systems that require large amounts of power for complex tasks	AI training clusters

Component	Role	Description	Example
Idle Power	Standby Usage	Power consumed when systems are not actively processing	Servers waiting for requests
Peak Power	Maximum Usage	Highest level of power used during heavy workloads	Training large AI models
Thermal Output	Heat Generation	Heat produced as a result of power usage	Cooling systems in data centers
Cooling Systems	Temperature Control	Systems used to manage heat from high power usage	Air or liquid cooling
Power Supply	Energy Source	Provides electricity to AI systems	Electrical grid, batteries
Edge Power Usage	Local Energy Use	Power consumption on smaller devices	Smartphones, IoT devices
Data Center Power	Large-Scale Usage	Power required for large AI operations	Server farms running AI models
Sustainable Energy	Efficiency Goal	Use of renewable energy to reduce environmental impact	Solar-powered data centers

The Watts Family highlights that intelligence comes with a cost—every AI system requires power, and understanding that power is essential for building efficient and sustainable technologies.

Watts Family (AI Power Usage Scale)

Definition

The **Watts Family** represents the real-time power usage of artificial intelligence systems, measured in watts (W). It shows how much power AI systems consume at a given moment as they process data and perform computations.

Watts Scale

1 Watt
10 Watts
100 Watts
500 Watts
1,000 Watts (1 Kilowatt)
10,000 Watts (10 Kilowatts)
100,000 Watts (100 Kilowatts)
1,000,000 Watts (1 Megawatt)
10,000,000 Watts (10 Megawatts)
100,000,000+ Watts (100+ Megawatts)

Key Characteristics

Measured in real-world electrical power

Higher watt values indicate higher processing demand

Used to represent the scale of AI systems from small devices to large infrastructures

Closely connected to the Chip Family, Energy Family, and Infrastructure Family

Examples

Low watts → small devices and basic AI functions

Medium watts → computers and advanced applications

High watts → data centers and large AI systems

Summary

The **Watts Family** provides a numerical representation of how much power artificial intelligence systems use in real time, helping to illustrate the scale and intensity of AI operations.

Student Insight

Watts show how much power AI is using right now.

AI Energy Family Introduction

The AI Energy Family represents the total amount of energy consumed by artificial intelligence systems over time. While the Watts Family measures the rate at which power is used at any given moment, the Energy Family focuses on the accumulated energy required to perform tasks, run systems, and sustain operations.

In artificial intelligence, energy is used every time a model is trained, a system processes data, or a response is generated. Large-scale AI systems, especially those operating in data centers, can consume significant amounts of energy due to the continuous processing of massive datasets and complex computations.

Energy is typically measured over time using units such as kilowatt-hours (kWh), which reflect how much power has been used during a specific period. For example, running a high-performance AI system for several hours or days results in a total energy cost that goes beyond the moment-to-moment power usage measured in watts.

The AI Energy Family works closely with the Watts Family, which provides the rate of power consumption, and the Chip Family, which determines how efficiently computations are performed. It also connects to the Infrastructure Family, where large-scale systems operate continuously and require long-term energy management.

Understanding the AI Energy Family helps students recognize that artificial intelligence has real-world resource implications. It is not only about performance and speed, but also about sustainability, efficiency, and responsible use of technology.

In simple terms, if watts measure how fast energy is used, energy measures how much is used over time.

AI Energy Family Breakdown Chart

Component	Role	Description	Example
Energy	Total Consumption	The total amount of power used over a period of time	Running an AI system for hours or days
Kilowatt-hour (kWh)	Energy Measurement	Unit used to measure energy consumption over time	1 kWh = using 1,000 watts for 1 hour
Energy Usage	Consumption Tracking	Total energy required for AI operations	Training a large model
Training Energy	Learning Cost	Energy used during model training processes	Weeks of GPU usage
Inference Energy	Response Cost	Energy used when AI generates outputs	Answering a user prompt
Energy Efficiency	Optimization Goal	Reducing energy use while maintaining performance	Efficient AI models
Energy Scaling	Growth Impact	Increase in energy use as systems grow larger	Bigger models = more energy
Data Center Energy	Infrastructure Demand	Total energy used by large AI facilities	Server farms operating 24/7
Cooling Energy	Temperature Control	Energy required to cool systems and prevent overheating	Air conditioning in data centers
Renewable Energy	Sustainability Source	Use of clean energy to power AI systems	Solar, wind-powered data centers
Carbon Impact	Environmental Effect	Emissions associated with energy consumption	AI training carbon footprint
Energy Management	Resource Control	Strategies to monitor and reduce energy use	Efficient scheduling, hardware optimization

The AI Energy Family reminds us that artificial intelligence operates within the physical world, where every computation consumes energy and every system has an impact on resources and sustainability.

Energy Family (Total Power Consumption of Artificial Intelligence)

Definition

The **Energy Family** represents the total amount of electricity used by artificial intelligence systems over time. It is measured in watt-hours (Wh) or kilowatt-hours (kWh) and shows how much energy AI systems consume while running.

Energy Scale

1 Watt-hour (Wh)
10 Watt-hours (Wh)
100 Watt-hours (Wh)
500 Watt-hours (Wh)
1,000 Watt-hours (1 Kilowatt-hour, kWh)
10,000 Watt-hours (10 kWh)
100,000 Watt-hours (100 kWh)
1,000,000 Watt-hours (1 Megawatt-hour, MWh)
10,000,000 Watt-hours (10 MWh)
100,000,000+ Watt-hours (100+ MWh)

Key Characteristics

Measured over time (not instant like watts)

Represents total electricity consumption

Increases the longer AI systems run

Directly related to cost and energy usage

Closely connected to Watts Family, Chip Family, and Infrastructure Family

Examples

Low energy → short AI tasks or small devices

Medium energy → daily AI usage on computers

High energy → training AI models and running data centers

Summary

The **Energy Family** provides a numerical representation of the total electricity consumed by artificial intelligence systems over time, helping to illustrate the overall cost and impact of AI operations.

Student Insight

Energy shows how much total power AI has used over time.

AI Infrastructure Family Introduction

The AI Infrastructure Family represents the large-scale systems and environments that support, power, and connect artificial intelligence technologies. While individual components such as chips, data, and models explain how AI works, infrastructure explains where and how these systems operate in the real world.

AI infrastructure includes data centers, cloud platforms, networking systems, and storage environments that allow artificial intelligence to function at scale. These systems provide the computing power, data access, and connectivity needed to train models, process information, and deliver results to users around the world.

Modern AI systems rely heavily on cloud-based infrastructure, where thousands of machines work together to handle massive workloads. This allows AI to scale efficiently, making it possible to process large datasets, run complex models, and serve millions of users simultaneously. Infrastructure also ensures reliability, security, and continuous availability of AI services.

The AI Infrastructure Family works closely with the Chip Family, which provides the hardware, the Watts and Energy Families, which manage power consumption, and the Data Family, which supplies the information being processed. It also supports the AI Architecture Family by providing the environment where all system components are deployed and connected.

Understanding the AI Infrastructure Family helps students recognize that artificial intelligence is not contained within a single device. Instead, it operates across global systems that require coordination, resources, and engineering to function effectively.

In simple terms, if AI is the system and chips are the engines, infrastructure is the environment that allows everything to run at scale.

AI Infrastructure Family Breakdown Chart

Component	Role	Description	Example
AI Infrastructure	System Environment	The physical and digital systems that support AI operations	Global AI platforms
Data Center	Processing Hub	Facilities that house servers and computing equipment	Large server farms
Cloud Computing	Scalable Platform	Remote systems that provide computing resources over the internet	AWS, Azure, Google Cloud
Servers	Compute Units	Machines that process data and run AI models	Rack-mounted servers
Networking	Connectivity System	Systems that allow communication between machines	Internet, fiber networks
Storage Systems	Data Management	Systems that store large volumes of data	Databases, cloud storage
Distributed Computing	Workload Sharing	Splitting tasks across multiple machines for efficiency	Parallel processing across clusters
Edge Infrastructure	Local Processing	Running AI closer to the user or device	Smart devices, IoT systems
Load Balancing	Traffic Control	Distributes workloads to prevent overload	Managing user requests
Security Systems	Protection Layer	Safeguards data and systems from threats	Encryption, firewalls
Redundancy	Reliability System	Backup systems to ensure continuous operation	Failover servers
Scalability	Growth Capability	Ability to expand resources as demand increases	Adding more servers dynamically

The AI Infrastructure Family reveals that artificial intelligence operates on a global scale, relying on interconnected systems that provide the power, storage, and connectivity needed to support intelligent technologies.

AI Agent Family Introduction

The AI Agent Family represents systems that can take action, make decisions, and perform tasks on behalf of users or other systems. Unlike traditional AI models that only respond to input, AI agents are designed to operate with a level of autonomy, allowing them to plan, execute, and adapt to achieve specific goals.

An AI agent receives input from its environment, processes that information, and takes actions based on predefined objectives or learned behaviors. These actions can include answering questions, automating workflows, retrieving information, or interacting with other systems. Some agents operate in simple environments, while others function in complex systems that require continuous decision-making.

AI agents often combine multiple foundational families. They use the Data Family to gather information, the Memory and Knowledge Families to retain and understand context, and the Neural Network and Parameter Families to process and learn from interactions. They also rely on the AI Architecture and Infrastructure Families to operate reliably at scale.

Modern AI agents can work independently or as part of larger systems. For example, a customer support agent can respond to inquiries automatically, while a more advanced agent can complete multi-step tasks such as scheduling, research, or system management.

Understanding the AI Agent Family helps students see that artificial intelligence is not only about generating responses, but also about taking meaningful action in real-world scenarios.

In simple terms, if AI models think and respond, AI agents act and execute.

AI Agent Family Breakdown Chart

Component	Role	Description	Example
AI Agent	Action System	An AI system that can make decisions and perform tasks	Virtual assistant
Environment	Operating Context	The space where the agent interacts and gathers information	Web, apps, databases
Input Perception	Data Intake	Receives information from the environment	User query or sensor input
Decision Engine	Action Selection	Determines what action to take based on input	Choosing a response or task
Action Execution	Task Performance	Carries out decisions in the environment	Sending an email, retrieving data
Goal System	Objective Setting	Defines what the agent is trying to achieve	Complete a task or solve a problem
Planning Module	Strategy Builder	Breaks down tasks into steps	Multi-step problem solving
Feedback Loop	Learning Cycle	Improves performance based on outcomes	Adjusting actions over time
Autonomy Level	Independence Scale	Degree of independence in decision-making	Fully automated vs assisted

Component	Role	Description	Example
Multi-Agent System	Collaboration Network	Multiple agents working together	Coordinated AI systems

Ingredient Family Introduction

The Ingredient Family represents the essential components that come together to create an artificial intelligence system. Just as a recipe requires specific ingredients to produce a final dish, AI systems rely on a combination of foundational elements working together to function effectively.

Artificial intelligence is not built from a single component. It requires data to learn from, algorithms to guide processing, models to perform tasks, hardware to execute computations, and energy to power the entire system. Each of these elements plays a critical role, and the absence of any one component would prevent the system from operating properly.

The Ingredient Family provides a simplified way for students to understand AI as a system made up of interconnected parts. Instead of viewing AI as complex or mysterious, learners can begin to see it as something constructed from identifiable and understandable components.

This family connects directly with all other foundational families, including Data, Algorithm, Neural Network, Parameter, Chip, and Energy Families. It serves as an overview that brings these elements together into a unified perspective.

Understanding the Ingredient Family helps students recognize that artificial intelligence is built, not magical. It is the result of carefully combining the right components in the right way.

In simple terms, if AI is the final product, the Ingredient Family represents everything needed to build it.

Ingredient Family Breakdown Chart

Component	Role	Description	Example
Data	Learning Input	Provides the information AI uses to learn patterns	Text, images, audio
Algorithms	Instruction Set	Guides how data is processed and decisions are made	Sorting, classification
AI Models	Execution System	Performs tasks such as prediction or generation	Language models
Neural Networks	Processing Structure	Organizes how data is processed through layers	Deep learning models
Parameters	Learning Adjustments	Fine-tune how the model learns and makes predictions	Weights and biases

Component	Role	Description	Example
Tokens	Language Units	Breaks text into smaller pieces for processing	Words or subwords
Hardware (Chips)	Computation Engine	Executes calculations required by AI systems	GPUs, CPUs
Energy	Power Source	Supplies the energy needed to run systems	Electricity usage
Infrastructure	Support System	Provides the environment for AI to operate at scale	Cloud systems, data centers
Memory	Storage System	Stores and retrieves information for processing	Context memory
Knowledge	Understanding Layer	Represents meaning and relationships within data	Knowledge graphs

The Ingredient Family shows that artificial intelligence is built from a combination of essential components, each playing a vital role in creating intelligent systems.

The Frontend and Backend Family of Artificial Intelligence

How AI Systems Connect User Interaction to Intelligent Processing

Introduction

Every artificial intelligence system operates through two essential layers: the frontend and the backend. These layers work together to transform human interaction into intelligent responses, allowing AI systems to function smoothly and effectively.

The frontend is the part of the system that users see and interact with. It includes screens, input tools, and the display of results. Whether a user is typing a question, speaking a command, or uploading an image, all interaction begins at the frontend.

Behind the scenes, the backend serves as the processing engine of the system. It receives input from the frontend, manages data, connects to the AI model, and performs the computations needed to generate a response. The backend is where the intelligence of the system operates, using models, algorithms, and infrastructure to interpret and respond to user requests.

This visual illustrates how these two layers work together as a complete system. It shows the flow of information from user input to AI processing and back to the user as a result. By understanding this structure, students can see that AI is not a single tool, but a coordinated system of layers working together.

In simple terms, the frontend is where interaction happens, and the backend is where intelligence is created.

Every AI system has two sides: what you see and what actually does the thinking.

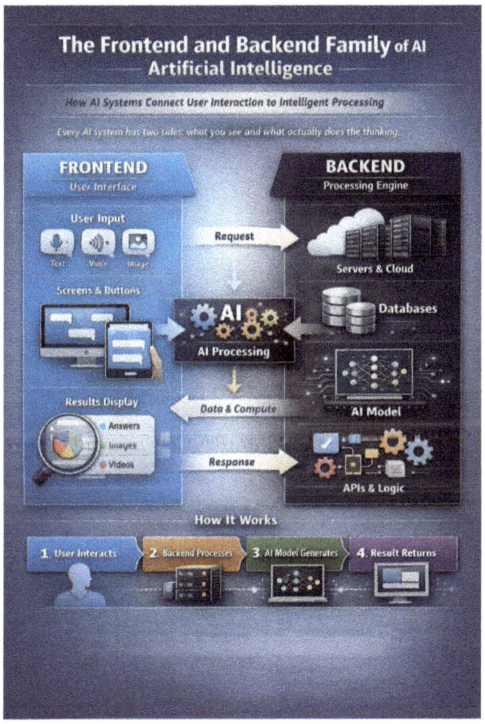

AI Qubit Family Introduction

The AI Qubit Family represents the foundation of quantum computing as it relates to artificial intelligence. While traditional computing relies on bits, which can exist as either 0 or 1, quantum computing uses qubits, which can exist in multiple states simultaneously.

A qubit is the basic unit of quantum information. Unlike classical bits, qubits can take advantage of properties such as superposition and entanglement, allowing quantum systems to process complex computations more efficiently in certain scenarios. This opens new possibilities for solving problems that are difficult or impossible for traditional computers.

In the context of artificial intelligence, qubits have the potential to accelerate learning processes, optimize large-scale systems, and improve complex simulations. Although quantum AI is still in development, it represents a future direction where computational power can expand beyond current limitations.

The AI Qubit Family connects with the Chip Family, as quantum processors are specialized hardware, and with the Algorithm Family, where new types of quantum algorithms are designed.

It also relates to the Parameter and Neural Network Families, as researchers explore quantum-enhanced learning models.

Understanding the AI Qubit Family helps students see that artificial intelligence is continuously evolving. It introduces the idea that the foundations of computing themselves can change, leading to new forms of intelligence and problem-solving.

In simple terms, if bits are the foundation of today's computing, qubits represent the foundation of tomorrow's possibilities.

AI Qubit Family Breakdown Chart

Component	Role	Description	Example
Qubit	Quantum Unit	Basic unit of quantum information	Quantum bit in a quantum computer
Superposition	Multi-State Ability	Ability to exist in multiple states at once	0 and 1 simultaneously
Entanglement	Connection Property	Linking qubits so they influence each other	Paired quantum states
Quantum Gate	Operation System	Performs operations on qubits	Quantum logic gates
Quantum Circuit	Processing Structure	Sequence of quantum operations	Quantum algorithms
Quantum Processor	Hardware Engine	Specialized chip for quantum computing	Quantum computer hardware
Quantum Algorithm	Computation Method	Algorithm designed for quantum systems	Optimization problems
Quantum Speedup	Performance Advantage	Faster processing for certain problems	Complex simulations
Quantum Noise	Stability Challenge	Errors caused by environmental interference	Qubit instability
Quantum Error Correction	Stability Solution	Techniques to reduce errors in quantum systems	Fault-tolerant computing

The AI Qubit Family introduces a new frontier in computing, where the limits of traditional systems are expanded, opening the door to more powerful and advanced forms of artificial intelligence.

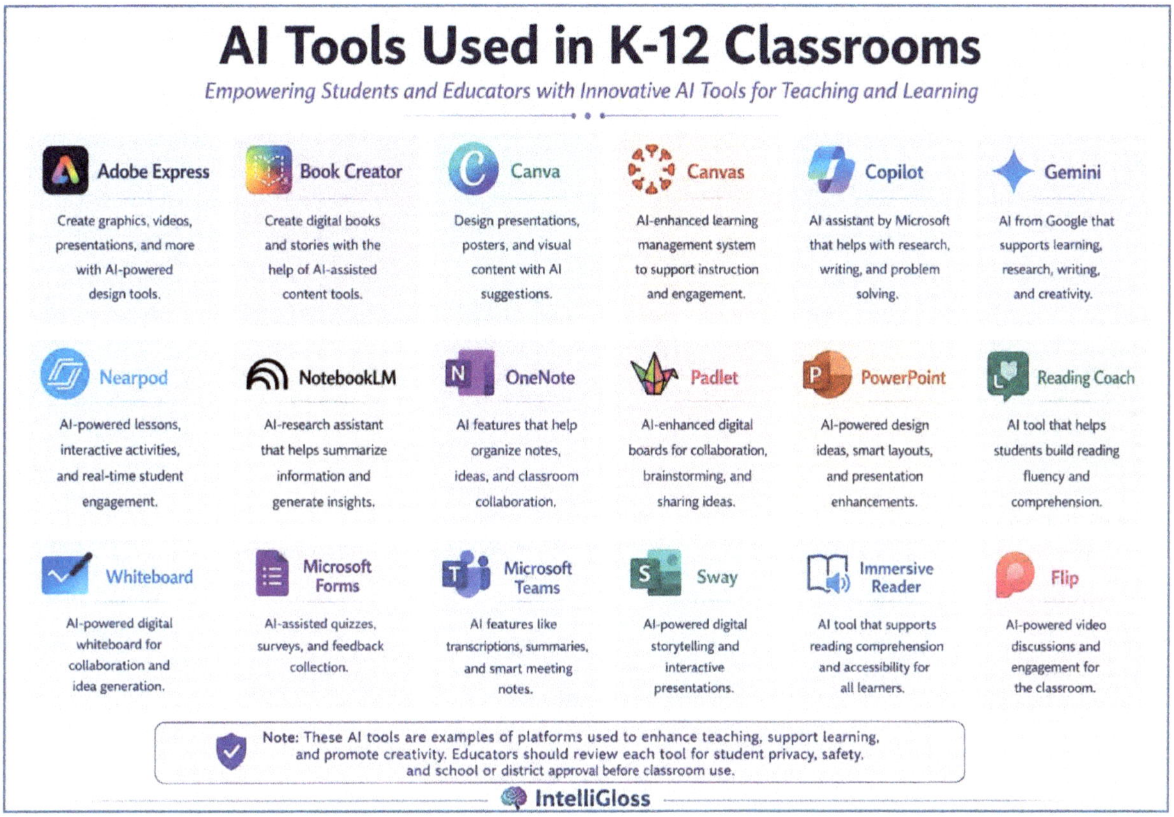
AI Tools Used in K-12 Classrooms
Empowering Students and Educators with Innovative AI Tools for Teaching and Learning
Adobe Express
Create graphics, videos, presentations, and more with AI-powered design tools.
Book Creator
Create digital books and stories with the help of AI-assisted content tools.
Canva
Design presentations, posters, and visual content with AI suggestions.
Canvas
AI-enhanced learning management system to support instruction and engagement.
Copilot
AI assistant by Microsoft that helps with research, writing, and problem solving.
Gemini
AI from Google that supports learning, research, writing, and creativity.
Nearpod
AI-powered lessons, interactive activities, and real-time student engagement.
NotebookLM
AI-research assistant that helps summarize information and generate insights.
OneNote
AI features that help organize notes, ideas, and classroom collaboration.
Padlet
AI-enhanced digital boards for collaboration, brainstorming, and sharing ideas.
PowerPoint
AI-powered design ideas, smart layouts, and presentation enhancements.
Reading Coach
AI tool that helps students build reading fluency and comprehension.
Whiteboard
AI-powered digital whiteboard for collaboration and idea generation.
Microsoft Forms
AI-assisted quizzes, surveys, and feedback collection.
Microsoft Teams
AI features like transcriptions, summaries, and smart meeting notes.
Sway
AI-powered digital storytelling and interactive presentations.
Immersive Reader
AI tool that supports reading comprehension and accessibility for all learners.
Flip
AI-powered video discussions and engagement for the classroom.
Note: These AI tools are examples of platforms used to enhance teaching, support learning, and promote creativity. Educators should review each tool for student privacy, safety, and school or district approval before classroom use.
IntelliGloss

TABLE OF CONTENTS

Introduction

KNOWLEDGE SYSTEMS

How Intelligent Machines Acquire, Organize, Store, and Apply Knowledge

By Susie Hala
IntelliGloss AI Education Series
Module 2: Artificial General Intelligence (AGI)

Artificial intelligence is often described as machines that can learn, reason, and solve problems. But before any intelligent system can make decisions, answer questions, or perform useful tasks, it must first have knowledge. Just as people rely on everything they have learned throughout their lives, intelligent machines depend on knowledge systems to understand the world around them.

Knowledge is much more than information stored in a computer. It includes facts, relationships, experiences, patterns, rules, and connections that allow an intelligent system to interpret new situations and respond appropriately. A machine that simply stores data is not intelligent. Intelligence begins when information is organized, connected, updated, and used to solve real-world problems.

Imagine asking an AI assistant a difficult question. Within seconds, it can often provide an answer, explain its reasoning, compare ideas, and even generate new content. Behind that seemingly simple interaction lies an enormous knowledge system that has learned how concepts relate to one another. Instead of treating every piece of information as isolated facts, advanced AI systems organize knowledge into meaningful structures that allow them to understand context, recognize patterns, and apply what they know in new situations.

Humans build knowledge throughout their lives. Babies begin by recognizing faces and voices. Children gradually learn language, mathematics, science, history, and social skills. Adults continue expanding their understanding through education, work, observation, and experience. Artificial intelligence follows a different path, but the goal is surprisingly similar: to continuously build a growing body of knowledge that improves performance over time.

One of the greatest challenges in artificial intelligence is not simply collecting more data. Modern AI already has access to enormous amounts of information. The real challenge is organizing that information in ways that make it useful. A knowledge system must determine which information is important, how different ideas are connected, when knowledge should be updated, and how previously learned information can be applied to new situations. These abilities move AI beyond memorization and toward genuine understanding.

As artificial intelligence advances toward Artificial General Intelligence (AGI), knowledge systems become increasingly important. AGI will require machines that can transfer knowledge between different subjects, combine ideas from multiple fields, recognize cause-and-effect relationships, and continually learn throughout their lifetime. Instead of performing only one specialized task, future intelligent systems will need broad, flexible knowledge similar to the way humans use what they have learned across many different situations.

Throughout this book, you will discover how intelligent machines gather knowledge from many sources, transform raw data into meaningful information, organize concepts into structured relationships, store knowledge efficiently, retrieve it when needed, and apply it to solve complex problems. You will also explore how modern technologies—including knowledge graphs, semantic networks, databases, vector embeddings, and large language models—work together to create increasingly capable AI systems.

You will learn that knowledge systems are not limited to computer science. They combine ideas from education, psychology, neuroscience, linguistics, mathematics, philosophy, information science, and engineering. Understanding how these fields work together provides a clearer picture of how artificial intelligence is becoming more capable every year.

This book has been written in clear, straightforward language so that students, educators, parents, and lifelong learners can understand these important concepts without needing an advanced technical background. Every chapter builds upon the previous one, introducing new ideas step by step while connecting them to real-world examples that demonstrate how knowledge systems are already influencing our daily lives.

The future of artificial intelligence will not be determined solely by faster computers or larger amounts of data. It will depend on how effectively machines can acquire, organize, store, retrieve, and apply knowledge to make better decisions, solve more complex problems, and work safely alongside people. Understanding knowledge systems is therefore one of the most important steps toward understanding the future of AGI itself.

As you begin this journey, remember that every intelligent decision—whether made by a person or a machine—starts with knowledge. The better we understand how knowledge is built and applied, the better prepared we will be to shape the next generation of intelligent technologies responsibly, ethically, and wisely.

Learn AI. Understand AI. Shape the Future.

— Susie Hala
IntelliGloss Press

Chapter 1

The Nature of Knowledge

Knowledge is one of the most valuable resources in human civilization. Every invention, scientific discovery, medical breakthrough, technological advancement, and cultural achievement has been built upon knowledge accumulated over generations. Although people use the word "knowledge" every day, few stop to think about what it truly means or why it is so essential to intelligence. Artificial General Intelligence (AGI), the next generation of intelligent machines, brings this question into sharper focus than ever before. If scientists hope to create machines capable of reasoning, learning, adapting, and solving unfamiliar problems like humans, they must first understand what knowledge is, how it is acquired, how it is organized, and how it is applied. Knowledge is not simply a collection of facts stored inside a brain or computer. It is an organized system of understanding that allows intelligent beings to interpret experiences, recognize patterns, make predictions, solve problems, and make informed decisions. Whether in humans or machines, knowledge serves as the foundation upon which intelligence is built.

Many people mistakenly believe that information and knowledge are the same thing. In reality, they are very different. Information consists of facts, numbers, observations, or data that have been collected or communicated. Knowledge, however, is created when information is understood, connected to previous experiences, and organized into meaningful relationships. Imagine opening a textbook filled with thousands of scientific terms. Simply reading every page does not automatically produce knowledge. A student develops knowledge only after understanding how those ideas relate to one another and learning how to apply them to new situations. This distinction explains why memorizing facts for an exam is very different from truly mastering a subject. A student who understands mathematical principles can solve unfamiliar problems, while a student who only memorized formulas may struggle whenever the questions change. Knowledge transforms isolated pieces of information into usable understanding.

Artificial intelligence faces a similar challenge. Today's AI systems can process enormous amounts of information at incredible speeds, but processing information alone does not necessarily produce genuine understanding. A modern AI model may analyze billions of documents, recognize millions of images, or generate pages of written text within seconds. Yet these impressive abilities do not automatically mean the machine possesses knowledge in the same way humans do. Instead, today's AI primarily discovers statistical relationships between patterns in data. Artificial General Intelligence seeks to move beyond recognizing patterns by developing structured knowledge that can be applied flexibly across many different situations. This transition from information processing to knowledge management represents one of the most important challenges facing AI researchers.

To better understand knowledge, imagine visiting a large public library. Every book represents information. Shelves contain millions of facts about science, medicine, history, mathematics, literature, engineering, and countless other subjects. However, simply walking into the library does not instantly make someone knowledgeable. A knowledgeable person understands where information belongs, how different ideas connect, which facts are reliable, when specific information should be applied, and how various concepts influence one another. In much the same way, future AGI systems must do far more than store vast amounts of information. They must organize it into interconnected structures that support reasoning, learning, planning, creativity, and decision-making. Knowledge is not defined by quantity alone but by the meaningful organization of ideas.

Knowledge also changes over time. Human understanding continues to evolve as new discoveries are made and existing beliefs are challenged. Centuries ago, people believed the Earth was the center of the universe because that explanation matched their observations. Scientific investigation gradually produced better evidence, leading to more accurate models of astronomy. Medical knowledge has evolved in similar ways as researchers learned about bacteria, viruses, genetics, and human biology. Every generation refines the knowledge inherited from previous generations. This continuous improvement illustrates an important characteristic of intelligent systems: knowledge must remain flexible rather than fixed. Future AGI systems will also need mechanisms that allow them to revise outdated conclusions, incorporate new discoveries, and adapt their understanding as circumstances change. Intelligence depends not only on acquiring knowledge but also on updating it responsibly.

Knowledge exists in many different forms. Some knowledge can be clearly explained using words, numbers, formulas, diagrams, or written instructions. This type of knowledge is often called explicit knowledge because it can be documented and shared with others. Textbooks, encyclopedias, engineering manuals, and scientific journals contain explicit knowledge that students and professionals can study. Other forms of knowledge are much more difficult to describe. A skilled musician knows exactly how to adjust finger movements while performing a complex piece of music. An experienced teacher senses when students are confused even before they ask questions. A firefighter recognizes dangerous conditions through years of practical experience. This type of practical understanding is often called tacit knowledge because it develops through experience and practice rather than written instruction. Human intelligence combines both explicit and tacit knowledge, allowing people to adapt their behavior in ways that cannot always be fully explained. Developing machines capable of acquiring both forms of knowledge remains one of the greatest ambitions of AGI research.

Human knowledge systems are remarkably sophisticated because they integrate information from many different sources simultaneously. Every day people learn through observation, conversation, reading, experimentation, education, problem solving, and personal experience. Children begin building knowledge almost immediately after birth. They learn to recognize faces, identify voices, understand language, and interact with the world long before they enter school. As they grow older, they connect new experiences with previous knowledge, gradually building increasingly complex mental models of reality. Memory allows people to retain these experiences, while reasoning helps them organize knowledge into useful frameworks. Emotions also influence learning by strengthening memories associated with important experiences. Social interactions further expand knowledge as individuals share ideas, debate opinions, and collaborate to solve problems. Human intelligence therefore emerges from a dynamic knowledge system that constantly acquires, organizes, evaluates, and applies information throughout life.

Machine knowledge systems operate quite differently. Computers do not naturally observe the world or develop understanding through life experiences in the same way humans do. Instead, they rely on carefully designed methods for representing knowledge in forms that computers can process. Early artificial intelligence systems stored knowledge using logical rules, databases, and symbolic representations created by human experts. Modern AI systems increasingly rely on machine learning, neural networks, vector representations, knowledge graphs, and large language models to organize enormous collections of information. Rather than remembering experiences exactly as humans do, machines often represent knowledge mathematically, using numerical relationships that allow algorithms to recognize patterns and make predictions. These approaches have enabled extraordinary advances in language translation, image recognition, scientific research, robotics, and autonomous systems. Nevertheless, today's AI still lacks many aspects of human knowledge, including deep common sense, flexible reasoning, and broad contextual understanding.

One of the greatest differences between humans and today's AI systems lies in common sense knowledge. Humans effortlessly understand thousands of everyday situations because they have accumulated years of lived experience. People know that ice melts when heated, objects fall when dropped, conversations depend on social context, and emotions influence behavior. Most of these ideas are never formally taught because they develop naturally through continuous interaction with the physical and social world. Artificial intelligence, however, often struggles with situations that humans consider obvious because machines typically learn from digital data rather than direct physical experience. Researchers believe that future AGI systems will require much richer knowledge systems capable of integrating language, sensory perception, memory, reasoning, and interaction with real environments. Building common sense knowledge remains one of the most important goals of AGI development.

Knowledge also provides the foundation for reasoning. Reasoning allows intelligent systems to draw conclusions, solve unfamiliar problems, predict future events, and evaluate possible actions. Without knowledge, reasoning becomes impossible because there are no meaningful concepts upon which logical thinking can operate. Imagine asking someone to solve an advanced chemistry problem without any knowledge of atoms, molecules, or chemical reactions. No amount of reasoning ability alone could compensate for the absence of foundational knowledge. Similarly, an AGI system attempting to solve complex scientific problems must first possess extensive knowledge about mathematics, physics, chemistry, biology, and many related disciplines. Knowledge supplies the building blocks, while reasoning determines how those building blocks are combined to produce new understanding.

As artificial intelligence continues to evolve, researchers increasingly recognize that knowledge systems will determine how capable future intelligent machines become. Faster processors, larger datasets, and more powerful algorithms are important, but they cannot replace well-organized knowledge. Intelligence depends on far more than computational speed. It requires understanding relationships, recognizing meaning, adapting to new situations, correcting mistakes, and applying previous learning to unfamiliar challenges. These abilities emerge from knowledge systems that are flexible, organized, continually updated, and deeply interconnected. Artificial General Intelligence will likely depend less on storing larger amounts of information and more on developing richer ways of representing, integrating, and using knowledge across many different domains.

The study of knowledge therefore stands at the center of humanity's effort to build truly intelligent machines. Every future advance in AGI will depend upon improving how machines acquire knowledge, organize concepts, build memory, reason about complex situations, revise incorrect beliefs, and apply understanding to solve new problems. Throughout this book, you will explore the remarkable systems that allow intelligent machines to transform information into meaningful knowledge. As you discover how these systems work, you will also gain a deeper appreciation for the extraordinary knowledge systems operating within the human mind—systems that continue to inspire the next generation of artificial intelligence.

Chapter 1 Summary

The Nature of Knowledge

Knowledge is the foundation of all intelligence. It allows humans and intelligent machines to understand the world, recognize patterns, solve problems, and make informed decisions. Unlike information, which consists of facts and data, knowledge is created when information is organized, connected, and understood in meaningful ways. Knowledge enables intelligence because it provides the context needed for reasoning and decision-making.

Humans acquire knowledge through observation, experience, education, communication, memory, and problem solving. Over time, people build mental models that help them interpret new situations using what they have already learned. Human knowledge is flexible and constantly evolves as new discoveries replace outdated ideas.

Artificial intelligence also depends on knowledge, but machines acquire and organize it differently. Instead of learning naturally through life experiences, AI systems rely on databases, machine learning, neural networks, knowledge graphs, and mathematical representations. While today's AI can process enormous amounts of information, Artificial General Intelligence (AGI) seeks to develop deeper understanding that more closely resembles human intelligence.

Knowledge also serves as the foundation for reasoning. Intelligent systems must possess organized knowledge before they can analyze problems, draw conclusions, or make decisions. Future AGI systems will require advanced knowledge architectures capable of continuously learning, updating information, correcting errors, and applying understanding across many different situations.

As technology advances, knowledge systems will become one of the most important building blocks of Artificial General Intelligence. Understanding how knowledge is acquired, organized, stored, and applied provides the foundation for every chapter that follows in this book.

Reflection

Knowledge shapes every decision we make throughout our lives. Every new skill, idea, and experience adds to our understanding of the world. As you learned in this chapter, intelligence is not simply about storing information—it is about understanding how ideas connect and applying them wisely.

Think about how you personally gain knowledge every day. You learn through teachers, family members, books, videos, conversations, mistakes, and personal experiences. Artificial intelligence also learns, but it uses very different methods to organize and process information. As AI continues to become part of everyday life, understanding knowledge systems helps us recognize both the strengths and limitations of intelligent machines.

One of the most exciting questions facing scientists today is whether machines can someday develop knowledge that resembles human understanding. While AI continues to improve rapidly, humans still possess unique abilities such as creativity, intuition, empathy, common sense, and personal experience that remain difficult for machines to fully replicate.

As you continue reading this book, consider how knowledge influences not only intelligent machines but also your own learning journey. Every chapter you complete becomes another piece of knowledge that helps you better understand both artificial intelligence and the world around you.

Student Worksheet

Name: ____________________________

Date: ____________________________

Part A – Vocabulary

Define each term in your own words.

1. Knowledge

____

2. Information

____

3. Artificial General Intelligence (AGI)

____

4. Knowledge System

5. Reasoning

Part B – Short Answer

1. What is the difference between information and knowledge?

2. Why does intelligence require knowledge?

3. Name three ways humans acquire knowledge.

4. How do today's AI systems acquire knowledge differently from humans?

5. Why is updating knowledge important?

Part C – Critical Thinking

Imagine you are designing the world's first true AGI system.

Describe three abilities its knowledge system would need to perform successfully.

Part D – Real-World Connection

Think about one thing you learned this week outside of school.

- Where did you learn it?
- How did it become knowledge instead of just information?
- How might AI learn the same thing differently?

Chapter 1 Quiz

Multiple Choice

1. Which statement best describes knowledge?

A. Random numbers stored in a computer

B. Organized understanding created from information

C. Pictures stored in memory

D. Internet websites

2. Information becomes knowledge when it is...

A. Deleted

B. Printed

C. Understood and connected to meaning

D. Copied

3. Which of the following is NOT a common way humans acquire knowledge?

A. Observation

B. Experience

C. Learning

D. Turning off memory

4. Modern AI systems often organize knowledge using...

A. Paper notebooks

B. Neural networks and knowledge graphs

C. Filing cabinets

D. Typewriters

5. Why is knowledge important for reasoning?

A. It provides facts and relationships needed to solve problems.

B. It slows computers down.

C. It replaces memory.

D. It removes uncertainty.

True or False

6. Information and knowledge always mean exactly the same thing.

True / False

7. Human knowledge changes as new discoveries are made.

True / False

8. Future AGI systems will need to update their knowledge over time.

True / False

9. Human intelligence relies only on memorizing facts.

True / False

10. Knowledge serves as the foundation for intelligent decision-making.

True / False

Answer Key

Vocabulary

Answers will vary but should demonstrate understanding.

Worksheet

Part B

1. Information is raw facts; knowledge is organized understanding.
2. Knowledge provides the foundation for reasoning and decision-making.
3. Possible answers:

- Observation
- Experience
- Reading
- Education
- Conversation
- Problem solving

4. AI learns using data, machine learning, algorithms, databases, and knowledge representations rather than human life experiences.
5. Because new discoveries, changing environments, and correcting mistakes improve understanding.

Quiz

1. **B**
2. **C**
3. **D**
4. **B**
5. **A**
6. **False**
7. **True**
8. **True**
9. **False**
10. **True**

Key Vocabulary

- Knowledge
- Information
- Data
- Intelligence
- Artificial General Intelligence (AGI)
- Knowledge System
- Reasoning
- Memory
- Learning
- Neural Network
- Knowledge Graph
- Machine Learning
- Pattern Recognition
- Common Sense
- Decision-Making

Learn AI. Understand AI. Shape the Future.

— Susie Hala
IntelliGloss Press

Chapter 2

From Data to Wisdom

Artificial intelligence is often described as being powered by data, but data alone does not create intelligence. Every day, billions of digital devices generate enormous amounts of data through smartphones, computers, satellites, medical equipment, scientific instruments, financial systems, vehicles, factories, and countless sensors connected to the Internet. Every online search, social media post, online purchase, weather observation, GPS location, medical scan, and scientific experiment contributes to the rapidly growing collection of digital information surrounding modern society. Yet despite this explosion of data, simply collecting more information does not automatically produce smarter decisions or deeper understanding. Human intelligence and future Artificial General Intelligence (AGI) depend upon transforming raw observations into meaningful knowledge and, ultimately, into wise decision-making. Understanding this transformation is one of the most important lessons in the study of intelligent systems because it explains why powerful computers alone cannot create truly intelligent machines.

The journey from data to wisdom is often described using the DIKW hierarchy, a framework that organizes human understanding into five connected levels: data, information, knowledge, understanding, and wisdom. Each level builds upon the one below it, adding greater meaning, context, and value. Imagine building a skyscraper. A strong foundation must be completed before additional floors can be safely constructed. In much the same way, intelligence develops by gradually transforming simple observations into increasingly sophisticated forms of understanding. Artificial intelligence researchers study this hierarchy because AGI will eventually need to move through these same stages in order to reason, learn, adapt, and solve unfamiliar problems as humans do.

At the lowest level of the hierarchy lies **data**. Data consists of individual facts, measurements, symbols, numbers, images, sounds, or observations that have not yet been interpreted. By themselves, data elements possess very little meaning. For example, the numbers "98.6," "72," "120/80," and "16" appear to be random values until someone explains that they represent body temperature, heart rate, blood pressure, and breathing rate. Similarly, a computer may record millions of pixels from a digital photograph, thousands of temperature readings from weather stations, or billions of words collected from books and websites. These raw observations are valuable because they describe reality, but without context they remain isolated pieces of information waiting to be interpreted. Modern AI systems excel at collecting and processing enormous quantities of data, yet the presence of data alone does not guarantee understanding.

When data is organized, categorized, labeled, or placed into context, it becomes **information**. Information answers basic questions such as who, what, when, and where. Consider a school attendance system that records the arrival time of every student. Individual timestamps represent data. When those timestamps are organized into attendance reports showing which students arrived on time or were absent, they become information because they communicate something meaningful. Likewise, weather sensors collect temperature, humidity, wind speed, and atmospheric pressure. Individually these measurements are simply data, but when meteorologists organize them into weather forecasts, the data becomes information that people can use to prepare for the day ahead. Artificial intelligence systems frequently perform this transformation by organizing vast collections of raw observations into searchable databases, reports, classifications, and predictions that humans can understand.

Although information is useful, it still does not represent true knowledge. **Knowledge** emerges when information is connected with experience, reasoning, relationships, and previous learning. Knowledge explains not only what happened but also why it happened and how different ideas relate to one another. A physician examining a patient's medical records does far more than read individual test results. Years of education and clinical experience allow the physician to recognize patterns, compare symptoms with previous cases, evaluate possible diagnoses, and recommend treatments. The doctor's decisions are guided by knowledge rather than isolated pieces of information. Similarly, an experienced engineer understands how mechanical systems interact, a teacher recognizes effective learning strategies, and an experienced pilot interprets hundreds of flight instruments simultaneously. In each case, knowledge transforms information into practical understanding that supports intelligent action.

Artificial intelligence is steadily improving its ability to organize information into useful knowledge. Large language models, recommendation systems, autonomous vehicles, medical diagnostic tools, and scientific research platforms all depend upon identifying meaningful relationships hidden within enormous datasets. Rather than memorizing every individual fact separately, advanced AI systems learn patterns that allow them to recognize similarities, classify objects, predict future events, translate languages, and answer complex questions. However, these systems still face an important limitation. Much of today's AI discovers statistical relationships rather than possessing genuine conceptual understanding. A language model may correctly predict the next word in a sentence because it has analyzed billions of examples, but predicting language patterns is not necessarily the same as understanding the deeper meaning behind those words. This distinction explains why AGI researchers continue searching for better methods of building richer knowledge systems.

Beyond knowledge lies **understanding**, a level that allows intelligent beings to explain relationships, interpret causes, evaluate consequences, and apply knowledge flexibly in unfamiliar situations. Understanding answers questions such as how and why. Imagine two students preparing for a physics examination. One student memorizes equations without understanding the scientific principles behind them. The other student understands the forces, energy transfers, and mathematical relationships represented by the equations. When presented with a completely new problem, the second student can adapt previous learning to solve it successfully because understanding extends beyond memorization. Human intelligence depends heavily upon this ability to apply existing knowledge creatively in new circumstances. Building similar capabilities into AGI remains one of the greatest challenges in artificial intelligence research.

Understanding also enables intelligent systems to recognize exceptions and evaluate situations that differ from previous experiences. Consider an experienced firefighter entering a burning building. Sensors may report high temperatures, smoke density, and structural conditions, but true understanding allows the firefighter to combine those observations with previous experience, training, and judgment to make rapid life-saving decisions. A machine capable of similar understanding would need far more than stored information. It would require integrated knowledge, contextual awareness, reasoning abilities, memory, and the capacity to predict how events might unfold under changing conditions. Researchers believe these higher levels of understanding will distinguish future AGI systems from today's specialized AI technologies.

At the highest level of the DIKW hierarchy stands **wisdom**, perhaps the most difficult concept to define and the most challenging ability for intelligent machines to achieve. Wisdom involves making sound judgments by combining knowledge, experience, ethical reasoning, long-term thinking, empathy, and an understanding of consequences. Wise decisions often consider not only whether something can be done but also whether it should be done. Throughout history, societies have admired individuals known for their wisdom because they consistently balanced facts with compassion, logic with ethics, and immediate needs with future consequences. Wisdom requires recognizing that complex problems rarely have simple solutions. Instead, wise decision-makers evaluate multiple perspectives before choosing actions that promote long-term well-being.

For artificial intelligence, wisdom introduces questions that extend far beyond computation. An autonomous vehicle deciding how to respond during an unavoidable accident, a medical AI recommending life-saving treatments, or an intelligent financial system allocating limited resources must all consider values that cannot be reduced to numbers alone. Future AGI systems may possess extraordinary computational abilities, but true wisdom will likely require integrating ethical reasoning, human values, social understanding, and responsible decision-making. Researchers continue debating whether machines can genuinely achieve wisdom or whether certain aspects of human judgment will always remain uniquely human. Regardless of the answer, understanding the difference between knowledge and wisdom helps students appreciate why intelligence is about far more than processing information quickly.

One of the most remarkable characteristics of the DIKW hierarchy is that each level depends upon the quality of the level below it. Poor-quality data produces unreliable information. Inaccurate information leads to flawed knowledge. Weak knowledge limits understanding, and poor understanding results in unwise decisions. This progression illustrates why modern organizations devote enormous resources to collecting accurate data, verifying information, maintaining reliable knowledge bases, and continuously improving decision-making processes. Scientists developing AGI face exactly the same challenge. The intelligence of future machines will depend not only on faster processors or larger databases but also on the quality, organization, and reliability of the knowledge they build from the information they receive.

As you continue exploring knowledge systems throughout this book, remember that intelligence is not measured simply by the amount of information an individual or machine possesses. True intelligence emerges from the ability to transform raw observations into meaningful understanding and then apply that understanding wisely in new situations. Every great scientist, physician, engineer, educator, inventor, and leader has followed this journey from data to wisdom, whether consciously or unconsciously. Artificial General Intelligence seeks to follow the same path. The challenge before researchers is not merely teaching machines to collect more data but enabling them to understand, reason, and ultimately make thoughtful decisions that benefit humanity. In the chapters ahead, you will discover the knowledge architectures and learning systems that may one day allow intelligent machines to move beyond information processing and toward genuine understanding.

Chapter 2

From Data to Wisdom (Part 2)

One of the greatest challenges facing Artificial General Intelligence (AGI) is learning how to move beyond processing data toward developing genuine understanding. Modern artificial intelligence systems are remarkably efficient at analyzing enormous amounts of information. They can search billions of web pages in seconds, recognize faces in photographs, translate dozens of languages, recommend movies, detect financial fraud, diagnose certain diseases, and even generate essays, computer programs, artwork, and scientific summaries. These accomplishments are impressive because they demonstrate the extraordinary power of modern computing and machine learning. However, despite these capabilities, today's AI systems still operate primarily by identifying patterns found within massive collections of data. They excel at recognizing statistical relationships, but they do not naturally understand the world in the same rich and flexible way that humans do. Building that deeper level of understanding represents one of the defining goals of AGI research.

To appreciate why understanding is so difficult, imagine teaching two students about the water cycle. The first student memorizes a sequence of words: evaporation, condensation, precipitation, and collection. During an exam, the student correctly repeats each term in order and receives a high score. The second student, however, understands why the Sun heats water, how water vapor rises into the atmosphere, why clouds form, how temperature changes create rainfall, and how rivers eventually return water to oceans. If presented with a new environmental problem, such as predicting how climate change might affect rainfall patterns, the second student is far more likely to reason through the situation successfully. This difference illustrates the distinction between memorization and understanding. Intelligence is measured not by how many facts can be recalled, but by how effectively those facts can be applied to solve new and unfamiliar problems.

Artificial intelligence researchers frequently describe this ability as **generalization**. Generalization allows knowledge learned in one situation to be applied successfully in another. Human beings demonstrate this ability constantly. A child who learns how to ride one bicycle can usually learn to ride another without starting from the beginning. A musician who understands rhythm can often adapt to playing a new instrument more quickly than someone with no musical experience. A physician who studies one infectious disease can often use that knowledge to understand a newly emerging illness. These examples illustrate that intelligence depends upon transferring knowledge rather than simply storing isolated facts. Future AGI systems must develop similar capabilities if they are to function effectively across many different domains instead of performing only narrow specialized tasks.

Building intelligent understanding also requires recognizing relationships between ideas. Human knowledge is not stored as isolated pieces of information scattered randomly throughout the brain. Instead, concepts become connected through an enormous network of associations. When someone hears the word "forest," they may immediately think about trees, wildlife, rivers, climate, ecosystems, conservation, camping, seasons, and even personal memories of hiking with family members. These relationships allow people to retrieve relevant knowledge almost instantly when solving problems or making decisions. Scientists hope future AGI systems will organize knowledge in similar ways by connecting concepts into dynamic knowledge networks rather than maintaining isolated databases of unrelated facts. The stronger these relationships become, the more flexible and intelligent the system's reasoning can be.

Context plays an equally important role in transforming information into understanding. Consider the simple word "bank." Without context, the word has multiple meanings. It may refer to a financial institution, the side of a river, a maneuver performed by an airplane, or even storing something for future use. Humans rarely struggle to identify the intended meaning because surrounding words, previous conversations, and personal experiences provide context. Artificial intelligence must also learn to interpret context accurately. Modern language models have made remarkable progress in contextual understanding, yet they occasionally misunderstand complex situations because they rely heavily on patterns found in training data rather than possessing genuine awareness of real-world circumstances. Developing richer contextual understanding remains an essential objective for AGI research.

Understanding also depends upon identifying **cause-and-effect relationships**. Throughout daily life, humans constantly ask questions beginning with "why." Why do seasons change? Why do bridges remain standing? Why does exercise improve health? Why do businesses succeed or fail? These questions require much more than collecting facts because they involve explaining relationships between events. Scientists seek causes that explain observations, while engineers predict how changing one part of a system affects the whole. Physicians identify the causes of illnesses before recommending treatments. Teachers analyze why some learning methods are more effective than others. Artificial General Intelligence must eventually develop similar abilities to explain why events occur rather than merely recognizing that certain events often appear together. This shift from correlation to causation represents one of the most significant advances required for truly intelligent machines.

Another important characteristic of intelligent understanding is the ability to recognize uncertainty. Human beings rarely possess complete information before making decisions. Doctors often evaluate patients before every laboratory result becomes available. Business leaders make investments despite uncertain economic conditions. Emergency responders act quickly during natural disasters without knowing every detail of the situation. Good decision-makers learn to balance available evidence, estimate risks, and revise conclusions as new information becomes available. Future AGI systems must demonstrate similar flexibility by recognizing uncertainty rather than presenting every answer with absolute confidence. An intelligent system should understand when evidence is incomplete, when additional information is needed, and when multiple possible explanations deserve consideration. Such humility may become one of the defining characteristics of trustworthy AGI.

The transformation from data to wisdom also depends upon continuous learning. Human knowledge is never finished. Students continue learning throughout elementary school, high school, college, professional careers, and everyday life. Every conversation, book, experiment, success, and mistake contributes to expanding or refining understanding. Scientists revise theories when new discoveries emerge. Engineers improve designs after identifying weaknesses. Teachers adjust instructional strategies based on student performance. This lifelong process of learning allows human intelligence to remain flexible in an ever-changing world. AGI systems will require similar capabilities. Instead of relying solely on knowledge acquired during initial training, they must continually incorporate new discoveries, update outdated information, correct errors, and adapt to changing environments while preserving previously learned knowledge.

Learning from mistakes is particularly important because intelligence grows through self-correction. Consider how children learn to walk. They fall repeatedly, adjust their balance, strengthen muscles, and gradually improve through practice. Scientists perform experiments that sometimes fail, yet those failures often reveal valuable information leading to future breakthroughs. Athletes review mistakes to improve performance. Writers revise early drafts before publication. Intelligent systems become stronger not because they avoid mistakes entirely, but because they recognize errors, understand why they occurred, and modify future behavior accordingly. Artificial General Intelligence will likely require sophisticated self-correction mechanisms capable of evaluating previous decisions, identifying weaknesses, and improving performance without requiring constant human supervision.

Wisdom adds another dimension to this learning process because it introduces ethical judgment. Two people may possess identical knowledge yet reach different decisions depending upon their values, responsibilities, and understanding of consequences. For example, an AI system might identify the fastest route for an emergency vehicle, but a wise system must also consider pedestrian safety, road conditions, traffic laws, and the protection of human life. Similarly, a medical AI recommending treatment options should balance statistical success rates with patient preferences, quality of life, and ethical standards established by healthcare professionals. Wisdom requires integrating factual knowledge with moral reasoning, long-term thinking, and an appreciation for human values. Many researchers believe this integration will become one of the greatest challenges in building AGI that benefits society.

As knowledge systems become increasingly sophisticated, collaboration between humans and intelligent machines will become more important than ever. Rather than replacing human intelligence, future AGI is more likely to complement it by rapidly analyzing enormous datasets, identifying hidden patterns, generating possible solutions, and supporting human decision-makers. Scientists may use AGI to accelerate medical discoveries. Engineers may use intelligent systems to design safer buildings and transportation systems. Educators may personalize instruction based on each student's learning needs. Environmental researchers may better understand climate systems through advanced simulations. In every case, the most successful outcomes will arise when human wisdom guides machine intelligence rather than allowing technology to operate without meaningful oversight.

The journey from data to wisdom ultimately represents the journey from observation to understanding, from memorization to reasoning, and from information processing to intelligent decision-making. Every level of the DIKW hierarchy contributes something essential to this progression. Data provides the raw observations. Information organizes those observations into meaningful patterns. Knowledge connects ideas through learning and experience. Understanding explains relationships and supports flexible reasoning. Wisdom applies all of these elements responsibly while considering ethics, consequences, and long-term goals. Artificial General Intelligence must eventually master every stage of this hierarchy if it is to approach the broad adaptability of human intelligence.

As you continue reading this book, remember that intelligence is not measured by the amount of data a machine stores or the speed at which it performs calculations. True intelligence emerges when knowledge becomes meaningful, understanding becomes flexible, and decisions reflect thoughtful judgment. The future of AGI will depend not only on building larger computers or collecting bigger datasets but on creating knowledge systems capable of learning continuously, reasoning deeply, adapting wisely, and working responsibly alongside humanity. The transformation from data to wisdom is therefore not simply a technical challenge—it is the pathway toward building intelligent systems that can contribute positively to the future of our world.

Learn AI. Understand AI. Shape the Future.

— Susie Hala
IntelliGloss Press

Chapter 2 Summary

From Data to Wisdom

Artificial intelligence begins with data, but intelligence cannot exist through data alone. Data consists of raw facts, numbers, measurements, images, sounds, and observations that have little meaning until they are organized and interpreted. When data is arranged into meaningful patterns, it becomes information. Information becomes knowledge when it is connected to experience, reasoning, and previously learned concepts. As understanding grows, knowledge can be applied to solve unfamiliar problems. Finally, wisdom allows intelligent beings to make responsible decisions by considering ethics, long-term consequences, and human values.

This progression is known as the **DIKW Hierarchy**—Data, Information, Knowledge, Understanding, and Wisdom. Each level builds upon the one before it. Poor-quality data can lead to inaccurate information, flawed knowledge, poor understanding, and unwise decisions. Therefore, the quality of every stage is essential for building reliable intelligence.

Humans naturally move through the DIKW hierarchy throughout their lives. They gather experiences, recognize patterns, develop understanding, and apply wisdom when making decisions. Modern AI systems are extremely effective at processing large amounts of data and identifying statistical patterns, but they still face challenges in developing true understanding and wisdom. Artificial General Intelligence (AGI) seeks to overcome these limitations by creating systems capable of learning continuously, transferring knowledge across different situations, reasoning about cause and effect, and adapting to unfamiliar environments.

One of the most important goals of AGI research is enabling machines to transform information into meaningful understanding rather than simply recognizing patterns. Future AGI systems will require advanced knowledge systems that can organize concepts, retrieve information efficiently, revise outdated beliefs, learn from mistakes, and make thoughtful decisions while considering uncertainty and ethical responsibilities.

The journey from data to wisdom is not only the foundation of human intelligence but also one of the greatest challenges in developing truly intelligent machines.

Reflection

Every day, people are surrounded by enormous amounts of data. News articles, social media posts, search engines, videos, scientific discoveries, conversations, and classroom lessons all provide information. However, becoming intelligent is not about collecting the largest amount of information—it is about learning how to organize, understand, evaluate, and wisely apply what we learn.

Think about your own education. Every subject you study follows the same journey described in the DIKW hierarchy. You first collect facts. Then you organize those facts into information. Through practice and experience, you develop knowledge. As you solve more difficult problems, your understanding grows. Eventually, you develop the wisdom to make thoughtful decisions using everything you have learned.

Artificial intelligence is following a similar path. Today's AI systems can process enormous amounts of information, but future AGI will require much more than powerful computers. It must develop flexible understanding, recognize uncertainty, learn continuously, and make responsible decisions that benefit society.

As technology becomes increasingly integrated into everyday life, understanding the journey from data to wisdom will help you become not only a more informed learner but also a more responsible user, designer, and leader of future AI technologies.

Student Worksheet

Name: ____

Date: ____

Part A – Vocabulary

Define each term in your own words.

1. Data

2. Information

3. Knowledge

4. Understanding

5. Wisdom

6. DIKW Hierarchy

Part B – Short Answer

1. What is the difference between data and information?

2. Why is knowledge more valuable than information alone?

3. Explain why understanding is different from memorization.

4. Why must AGI move beyond simply processing data?

---

5. Why is wisdom considered the highest level of the DIKW hierarchy?

Part C – Matching

Match each level with its correct description.

Letter	Description	Number
A	Data	___ Makes responsible decisions
B	Information	___ Raw observations
C	Knowledge	___ Organized facts
D	Understanding	___ Applies learning to new situations
E	Wisdom	___ Connects ideas and experience

Part D – Critical Thinking

Imagine you are designing an AGI system that will help doctors diagnose diseases.

Describe how the system would move through each level of the DIKW hierarchy before making a medical recommendation.

Data

Information

Knowledge

Understanding

Wisdom

Part E – Real-World Application

Choose one activity you perform every day (driving, cooking, studying, sports, music, etc.).

Explain how you use:

- Data
- Information
- Knowledge
- Understanding
- Wisdom

during that activity.

Chapter 2 Quiz

Multiple Choice

1. Which level of the DIKW hierarchy comes first?

A. Wisdom

B. Information

C. Data

D. Knowledge

2. Information becomes knowledge when it is...

A. Deleted

B. Connected to experience and understanding

C. Printed

D. Memorized only

3. Which level explains why something happens?

A. Data

B. Information

C. Understanding

D. Storage

4. Which statement best describes wisdom?

A. Memorizing large amounts of data

B. Making thoughtful decisions using knowledge and ethical judgment

C. Reading faster

D. Saving information

5. One major goal of AGI is to...

A. Store unlimited data only

B. Move beyond pattern recognition toward genuine understanding

C. Replace all human thinking

D. Eliminate learning

True or False

6. Data always has meaning by itself.

True / False

7. The DIKW hierarchy shows how intelligence develops from raw observations.

True / False

8. Modern AI already possesses human-level wisdom.

True / False

9. Understanding allows knowledge to be applied to unfamiliar situations.

True / False

10. Poor-quality data can lead to poor decisions.

True / False

Answer Key

Vocabulary

Answers will vary but should demonstrate accurate understanding.

Worksheet

Part B

1. Data consists of raw facts, while information is organized data with meaning.
2. Knowledge connects information through experience, reasoning, and understanding.
3. Memorization recalls facts, while understanding explains relationships and applies learning.
4. Because AGI must reason, adapt, solve unfamiliar problems, and understand context.
5. Wisdom combines knowledge, understanding, ethics, judgment, and long-term thinking.

Part C – Matching

A → Raw observations

B → Organized facts

C → Connects ideas and experience

D → Applies learning to new situations

E → Makes responsible decisions

Part D

Answers will vary but should demonstrate progression through:

- Collecting patient measurements (Data)
- Organizing medical records (Information)
- Comparing diseases and symptoms (Knowledge)
- Explaining likely diagnoses (Understanding)
- Recommending ethical, patient-centered treatment (Wisdom)

Part E

Answers will vary.

Quiz Answers

1. **C**
2. **B**
3. **C**

4. **B**
5. **B**
6. **False**
7. **True**
8. **False**
9. **True**
10. **True**

Key Vocabulary

- Data
- Information
- Knowledge
- Understanding
- Wisdom
- DIKW Hierarchy
- Context
- Generalization
- Pattern Recognition
- Cause and Effect
- Decision-Making
- Critical Thinking
- Artificial General Intelligence (AGI)
- Continuous Learning
- Ethical Reasoning

Chapter Takeaway

Knowledge transforms information into understanding, but wisdom transforms understanding into responsible action. The future of Artificial General Intelligence depends not only on collecting more data but on learning how to think, reason, adapt, and make ethical decisions using knowledge.

Learn AI. Understand AI. Shape the Future.

— Susie Hala
IntelliGloss Press

Chapter 3

How Humans Acquire Knowledge

Part 1

From the moment a baby opens its eyes for the first time, the process of learning begins. Long before children can speak, read, or write, they are already collecting information about the world around them. They observe faces, recognize voices, respond to sounds, feel different textures, and begin discovering how their actions influence their surroundings. Every experience becomes part of a lifelong journey of acquiring knowledge. Unlike computers, which must be programmed or trained using carefully prepared datasets, humans are naturally designed to learn continuously throughout their lives. Every conversation, every mistake, every success, every question, and every new experience contributes to building a rich and interconnected understanding of the world. This remarkable ability to learn from everyday life is one of the defining characteristics of human intelligence and serves as an important source of inspiration for scientists working to develop Artificial General Intelligence (AGI). To build machines that think more like humans, researchers must first understand how people acquire, organize, remember, and apply knowledge.

Human knowledge acquisition begins with **observation**. Observation is the process of gathering information by using the senses to interact with the environment. Vision, hearing, touch, taste, and smell all provide continuous streams of information that help people understand what is happening around them. Imagine walking into a classroom for the first time. Before anyone speaks, your brain has already noticed the arrangement of desks, the lighting, the colors on the walls, the expressions of classmates, the teacher standing at the front of the room, and perhaps even the temperature or smell of the classroom. Much of this information is collected automatically without conscious effort. The brain constantly observes, filters, and organizes incoming sensory information, allowing people to respond appropriately to changing situations. Observation provides the raw material from which knowledge begins to grow.

Observation alone, however, is not enough. Humans also learn through **experience**, which gives meaning to what they observe. Experience occurs when people interact directly with the world and see the results of their actions. A child may observe that a stove is hot, but touching a hot surface teaches a much more powerful lesson about heat and safety. A student learning to ride a bicycle cannot become skilled simply by reading instructions. Balance, coordination, and confidence develop through repeated practice. Every success and every mistake strengthens understanding because experience connects information with real-world consequences. These experiences create lasting memories that influence future decisions. Scientists often describe experience as one of the most powerful teachers because it transforms abstract information into practical knowledge that can be applied in many different situations.

As people grow older, they begin to combine observation and experience into increasingly complex mental models. A mental model is an internal representation that helps explain how something works. For example, children gradually develop mental models of gravity after repeatedly observing that objects fall when dropped. They form mental models of language by hearing words used in conversation. They build mental models of friendship through interactions with family members, classmates, and neighbors. These internal models become more detailed and accurate as new experiences are added. Human intelligence depends heavily upon these mental models because they allow people to predict outcomes, solve problems, and adapt to unfamiliar situations. When researchers discuss world models in AGI, they are attempting to create similar internal representations that allow intelligent machines to understand how the world operates.

One of the most remarkable tools humans use for acquiring knowledge is **language**. Language allows people to learn not only from their own experiences but also from the experiences of others. Every conversation becomes an opportunity to receive knowledge accumulated by parents, teachers, scientists, historians, engineers, physicians, and countless individuals throughout history. Without language, each generation would need to rediscover nearly everything from the beginning. Instead, language allows knowledge to accumulate and expand across centuries. Books preserve scientific discoveries. Teachers explain mathematical concepts developed long ago. Parents share life lessons with their children. Researchers publish new findings that become the foundation for future discoveries. Language acts as a bridge connecting individual minds into a collective human knowledge system.

Reading represents one of the greatest examples of language-based learning. A student studying astronomy can learn about distant galaxies without ever leaving Earth. A medical student can study the discoveries of scientists who lived hundreds of years ago. An engineering student can understand complex bridge designs created by experts from different countries. Through reading, individuals gain access to knowledge that would be impossible to acquire through personal experience alone. Modern education depends upon this extraordinary ability to transfer knowledge across time and distance. Artificial intelligence systems also rely heavily on language because written documents provide enormous collections of human knowledge for machine learning models to analyze. However, understanding language requires much more than recognizing words. Human readers naturally interpret context, identify implied meanings, recognize humor, understand metaphors, and adjust interpretations based on previous experiences. These abilities remain difficult challenges for modern AI systems.

Conversation adds another important dimension to knowledge acquisition because it allows learning to become interactive. Unlike books, conversations provide immediate feedback. Students ask questions, teachers explain difficult concepts differently, classmates offer alternative perspectives, and discussions encourage critical thinking. Through dialogue, people refine their understanding by comparing ideas, challenging assumptions, and exploring different viewpoints. Many scientific breakthroughs have emerged from collaborative discussions rather than isolated work. Universities, research laboratories, and classrooms encourage conversation because exchanging ideas often leads to deeper understanding than studying alone. Future AGI systems may eventually need similar collaborative abilities, allowing multiple intelligent agents to exchange knowledge, solve problems together, and build shared understanding through communication.

Another essential component of human learning is **memory**. Every experience, observation, and conversation would quickly disappear without the brain's remarkable ability to store information for future use. Memory allows people to retain knowledge, recognize familiar situations, and connect new experiences with previous learning. Imagine trying to learn mathematics if every lesson disappeared from memory overnight. Students would need to relearn addition before attempting subtraction, multiplication, or algebra every single day. Memory provides continuity, allowing knowledge to grow steadily over time rather than constantly starting from the beginning. Without memory, intelligence would be impossible because learning depends upon building new understanding on top of previously acquired knowledge.

Scientists classify human memory into several different forms, each serving a unique purpose. **Sensory memory** briefly stores information received through the senses, often lasting only a fraction of a second. This temporary storage allows the brain to determine which information deserves further attention. **Working memory**, sometimes called short-term memory, holds small amounts of information that people actively use while solving problems, reading sentences, or following conversations. For example, students use working memory while performing mental arithmetic or remembering the beginning of a sentence until they reach its conclusion. Although working memory has limited capacity, it plays a critical role in reasoning, learning, and decision-making.

Information that proves important can eventually become part of **long-term memory**, where it may remain for years or even an entire lifetime. Long-term memory stores facts, experiences, skills, vocabulary, personal events, and countless other forms of knowledge. A person may remember childhood vacations, the multiplication table learned in elementary school, how to ride a bicycle, or the face of a lifelong friend decades after those memories were first formed. Long-term memory is not simply a storage container. Each time people recall memories, the brain strengthens connections, updates details, and sometimes reorganizes information based on new experiences. This dynamic process allows human knowledge to remain flexible rather than fixed.

Emotions also influence how memories are formed. Experiences connected with strong emotions—whether joy, excitement, fear, or sadness—are often remembered more vividly than ordinary events. Students frequently remember an inspiring science experiment, an unforgettable field trip, or an important personal achievement because emotional experiences strengthen memory formation. This relationship between emotion and memory highlights another difference between humans and current AI systems. Machines can store enormous quantities of information with remarkable accuracy, but they do not experience emotions that naturally influence learning and memory in the same way humans do. Researchers continue exploring whether future AGI systems might require mechanisms that prioritize information based on importance, relevance, or long-term goals rather than emotional experiences.

Learning also depends upon repetition and practice. Few people master complex skills after a single lesson. Musicians improve through hours of practice. Athletes strengthen their abilities through repeated training. Scientists conduct numerous experiments before making important discoveries. Students review lessons, solve practice problems, and revise essays because repetition strengthens neural connections within the brain. Every successful repetition makes future recall easier and more reliable. Modern machine learning systems follow a similar principle by repeatedly analyzing enormous datasets during training. Although the mechanisms differ greatly, both humans and machines improve performance through repeated exposure, correction, and refinement. This similarity provides valuable insights for researchers attempting to design learning systems that become increasingly intelligent over time.

As knowledge accumulates, the human brain becomes remarkably efficient at organizing information into interconnected networks rather than isolated facts. New ideas are linked with previous experiences, allowing people to retrieve relevant information quickly when solving problems or making decisions. These growing networks of knowledge become the foundation for reasoning, creativity, critical thinking, and lifelong learning. Understanding how these knowledge networks develop provides valuable clues for scientists designing future AGI systems capable of learning continuously, adapting to new situations, and building increasingly sophisticated models of the world.

(End of Part 1 — Part 2 will continue with Pattern Recognition, Cognitive Development, Lessons for Artificial Intelligence, and a powerful conclusion.)

Chapter 3

How Humans Acquire Knowledge

Part 2

As humans continue learning throughout childhood and adulthood, the brain begins to recognize that the world is filled with repeating structures. Every language contains grammar, every mathematical problem follows certain rules, every season brings familiar weather changes, and every social interaction contains recognizable behaviors. Instead of treating every new experience as completely different, the brain searches for similarities that connect present experiences with previous ones. This remarkable ability is known as **pattern recognition**, and it is one of the most important characteristics of human intelligence. Pattern recognition allows people to identify faces in a crowded room, recognize familiar voices over the telephone, predict the ending of a sentence before it is completed, and understand complex situations using knowledge gained from earlier experiences. Without pattern recognition, every experience would appear completely new, making learning slow, inefficient, and almost impossible.

Pattern recognition begins very early in life. Infants gradually recognize the faces of parents and family members long before they understand spoken language. Young children notice that certain sounds consistently represent specific words. As they grow older, they recognize letters, numbers, colors, shapes, and objects. Eventually, they begin identifying increasingly complex patterns found in mathematics, music, literature, science, and human behavior. A child who learns that adding one more object increases the total quantity has begun recognizing mathematical relationships. A student reading novels recognizes patterns in storytelling. A biology student learns that living organisms share similar structures and life processes. An experienced physician recognizes patterns of symptoms associated with particular diseases. Throughout life, human intelligence becomes stronger because it continually identifies relationships hidden within enormous amounts of information.

One reason pattern recognition is so powerful is that it reduces mental effort. Imagine trying to read if every word had to be interpreted as a completely new collection of individual letters. Reading would become painfully slow because the brain would never recognize familiar words or grammatical structures. Instead, experienced readers instantly recognize entire words, phrases, and sentence patterns, allowing them to focus on meaning rather than individual letters. Skilled drivers no longer consciously think about every movement required to operate a vehicle because repeated practice has transformed those actions into recognizable patterns. Musicians recognize musical structures instead of individual notes. Scientists identify patterns in research data that guide future experiments. Pattern recognition allows the brain to work efficiently by organizing knowledge into meaningful structures that can be retrieved and applied quickly.

Modern artificial intelligence relies heavily on pattern recognition as well. Machine learning systems analyze enormous datasets searching for mathematical relationships that help classify objects, recognize speech, detect diseases, recommend products, translate languages, and generate text. A facial recognition system identifies patterns among millions of facial features. A language model discovers statistical relationships among billions of words. A medical AI identifies patterns associated with specific diseases by analyzing thousands of medical images. Although these systems often perform pattern recognition with extraordinary accuracy, there remains an important difference between recognizing patterns and understanding their meaning. Humans naturally combine pattern recognition with reasoning, memory, context, emotions, and lived experience. Artificial General Intelligence seeks to integrate these abilities so machines can move beyond identifying patterns toward building genuine understanding of the world.

As knowledge continues to expand, human intelligence develops through a process known as **cognitive development**. Cognitive development refers to the gradual improvement of thinking, learning, reasoning, memory, language, and problem-solving abilities throughout life. Human intelligence does not appear fully developed at birth. Instead, it grows through continuous interaction with family members, teachers, classmates, communities, and the surrounding environment. Every stage of life introduces new experiences that reshape the brain's understanding of reality. Children learn basic language before studying literature. They master arithmetic before learning algebra. They understand simple observations before developing abstract scientific reasoning. Each new stage builds upon previous learning, creating increasingly sophisticated knowledge systems capable of solving more complex problems.

Educational psychologists have long observed that learning occurs most effectively when new information connects with existing knowledge. Students rarely understand advanced concepts if foundational knowledge is missing. A student cannot successfully study calculus without first understanding arithmetic, algebra, and geometry. Similarly, learning about artificial intelligence becomes easier after understanding computers, algorithms, data, and machine learning. This cumulative nature of learning demonstrates why education is often organized into carefully planned sequences that gradually increase in complexity. Artificial intelligence researchers recognize this principle as well. Future AGI systems may need developmental learning processes that allow increasingly complex knowledge to emerge from simpler foundations rather than attempting to learn everything simultaneously.

Curiosity plays an equally important role in cognitive development. Humans possess a natural desire to ask questions about the world. Young children repeatedly ask "Why?" because they seek explanations rather than simply accepting observations. Why is the sky blue? Why do birds fly? Why do people become sick? Why do plants need sunlight? These questions encourage exploration, experimentation, and discovery. Curiosity motivates individuals to search for information, test ideas, and challenge existing assumptions. Throughout history, many of humanity's greatest scientific breakthroughs have begun with simple questions asked by curious minds. Albert Einstein once remarked that curiosity was more important than knowledge because it drives the search for understanding. Future AGI systems may also require forms of artificial curiosity that encourage exploration, hypothesis generation, and continuous learning rather than merely responding to predefined instructions.

Human beings also learn through **mistakes**. Errors often become some of the most valuable learning experiences because they reveal weaknesses in existing knowledge. A student solving a mathematics problem incorrectly receives feedback that helps identify misunderstandings. A scientist whose experiment fails often discovers new information that leads to improved theories. Engineers revise prototypes after identifying design flaws. Athletes analyze unsuccessful performances to improve future competitions. Rather than viewing mistakes as failures, intelligent learners recognize them as opportunities to strengthen understanding. This ability to evaluate errors and adjust future behavior is one of the defining characteristics of human learning. Scientists developing AGI hope to create systems capable of similar self-correction, allowing machines to improve continuously without requiring complete retraining after every mistake.

Social interaction significantly accelerates knowledge acquisition. Humans rarely learn in isolation. Families teach children language, values, traditions, and social behaviors. Teachers guide students through increasingly advanced subjects. Friends exchange ideas, debate opinions, and introduce new perspectives. Professionals collaborate to solve difficult scientific and engineering challenges. Entire civilizations progress because knowledge is shared across generations rather than remaining limited to individual experiences. This collective learning process explains why humanity has achieved remarkable advances in medicine, transportation, communication, agriculture, and technology. Every generation inherits knowledge accumulated by previous generations and then contributes new discoveries for future learners. Artificial General Intelligence may eventually participate in similar collaborative knowledge ecosystems, exchanging information among multiple intelligent systems while working alongside human experts.

One of the most fascinating characteristics of human intelligence is the ability to transfer knowledge from one situation to another. This ability, often called **generalization**, allows people to solve unfamiliar problems by applying principles learned in different contexts. A student who understands fractions can later understand probability. An engineer who designs bridges may use similar structural principles when designing skyscrapers. A musician who learns one instrument often learns another more easily because underlying concepts transfer across different situations. This flexibility distinguishes general intelligence from narrow expertise. Current AI systems often perform exceptionally well within specific tasks but struggle when asked to apply their knowledge outside their original training environments. Developing robust generalization remains one of the central goals of AGI research.

Another lesson AI researchers have learned from studying human cognition is that knowledge is constantly reorganized. Every new experience has the potential to strengthen, modify, or replace previous beliefs. Students who once believed that heavier objects fall faster eventually revise their understanding after studying gravity. Scientific theories evolve as new evidence emerges. Medical guidelines change as researchers discover better treatments. Human intelligence remains effective because it welcomes correction rather than resisting change. Future AGI systems must demonstrate similar flexibility by continuously updating knowledge bases, revising conclusions, and integrating new discoveries while maintaining consistency across previously learned information.

Researchers studying the human brain increasingly recognize that intelligence emerges not from any single ability but from the interaction of many interconnected systems working together. Observation gathers information. Memory preserves experiences. Language communicates ideas. Pattern recognition identifies relationships. Reasoning explains causes. Curiosity motivates exploration. Social interaction expands understanding. Emotional experiences strengthen important memories. Self-correction improves future performance. Together, these systems form an extraordinary knowledge architecture capable of adapting to an ever-changing world. Artificial General Intelligence seeks to replicate many of these capabilities, not by copying the human brain exactly, but by understanding the principles that allow intelligent behavior to emerge from interconnected learning systems.

The lessons humans provide for artificial intelligence extend far beyond algorithms and computer hardware. They demonstrate that intelligence is a lifelong process of observation, exploration, communication, reflection, and continuous improvement. Knowledge is not accumulated all at once but grows gradually through countless experiences that become connected over time. Every question answered leads to new questions. Every problem solved opens new opportunities for discovery. Every generation builds upon the knowledge of those who came before. These principles provide a roadmap for developing future AGI systems capable of learning continuously rather than remaining limited to fixed programming.

As you continue through this book, remember that the greatest teacher humanity has ever known is the process of learning itself. The human mind has evolved extraordinary methods for acquiring, organizing, remembering, and applying knowledge across every aspect of life. Scientists developing Artificial General Intelligence continue studying these remarkable abilities because they believe the future of intelligent machines depends upon understanding how humans learn so naturally. The more researchers uncover about human knowledge acquisition, the closer they move toward creating intelligent systems capable of adapting, reasoning, collaborating, and growing throughout their own lifetimes. In many ways, the story of AGI is also the story of understanding ourselves, for the better we understand how humans learn, the better prepared we are to design intelligent machines that serve humanity with wisdom, responsibility, and purpose.

Learn AI. Understand AI. Shape the Future.

— Susie Hala
IntelliGloss Press

Chapter 3 Summary

How Humans Acquire Knowledge

Human knowledge begins developing from the moment we are born. Through observation, experience, language, memory, and interaction with the world, people gradually build an understanding of how their environment works. Unlike computers that require programming or training datasets, humans naturally learn throughout their entire lives by continuously connecting new experiences with previous knowledge.

Observation is the starting point of learning. Our senses constantly gather information about the world around us. Experience gives meaning to those observations by allowing us to interact with our environment and learn from both successes and mistakes. Over time, these experiences form mental models that help us predict outcomes, solve problems, and make informed decisions.

Language greatly expands human learning by allowing knowledge to be shared across generations. Books, conversations, classrooms, and digital communication enable people to learn from the discoveries and experiences of others without personally experiencing every event. Memory preserves these experiences, allowing knowledge to accumulate rather than disappear. Different forms of memory—including sensory memory, working memory, and long-term memory—work together to support learning and intelligent thinking.

Pattern recognition enables people to identify relationships between ideas, objects, and events. Instead of treating every situation as completely new, the human brain recognizes familiar structures and applies previous learning to new challenges. Cognitive development builds upon these abilities by gradually increasing reasoning, problem-solving, language, and critical thinking skills throughout life.

Curiosity motivates exploration, while mistakes become valuable opportunities for learning and improvement. Human intelligence also grows through collaboration, communication, and social interaction. These abilities allow individuals to transfer knowledge across different situations and continuously update their understanding as new information becomes available.

Scientists studying Artificial General Intelligence (AGI) examine these human learning processes because they provide valuable insights into how future intelligent machines might acquire, organize, remember, and apply knowledge. Understanding how humans learn is one of the most important foundations for building machines capable of lifelong learning, flexible reasoning, and adaptive intelligence.

Reflection

Learning is one of the most remarkable abilities humans possess. Every conversation, every book, every classroom lesson, every challenge, and every experience contributes to building the knowledge that shapes our understanding of the world. Unlike machines that often rely on carefully prepared datasets, humans naturally learn through curiosity, observation, exploration, practice, and reflection.

Think about how much you have learned since you were a young child. You learned to speak, read, solve problems, make friends, understand emotions, and develop new skills without realizing how extraordinary your brain truly is. Every mistake helped you improve. Every question expanded your understanding. Every experience became another building block in your lifelong knowledge system.

Artificial intelligence researchers continue studying human learning because our brains remain one of the greatest examples of adaptive intelligence ever known. As future AGI systems become more advanced, they may increasingly resemble the lifelong learning process that humans naturally perform every day.

As you continue your education, remember that knowledge is not simply collected—it is built over time through curiosity, effort, reflection, and continuous growth. Every lesson you learn today becomes the foundation for tomorrow's discoveries.

Student Worksheet

Name: ________________________________

Date: ________________________________

Part A – Vocabulary

Define each term in your own words.

1. Observation

2. Experience

3. Pattern Recognition

4. Cognitive Development

5. Mental Model

6. Generalization

Part B – Short Answer

1. Why is observation considered the beginning of learning?

2. How does experience strengthen knowledge?

3. Explain why language is one of humanity's greatest learning tools.

4. Describe the importance of long-term memory.

5. Why do scientists study human learning when developing AGI?

Part C – Matching

Letter	Human Learning Process	Number
A	Observation	___ Stores information for future use
B	Experience	___ Uses the senses to gather information
C	Memory	___ Learns by interacting with the world
D	Pattern Recognition	___ Finds similarities and relationships
E	Language	___ Shares knowledge across generations

Part D – Critical Thinking

Imagine you are designing an AGI robot that will attend school alongside human students.

Describe how the robot should:

- Observe its environment
- Learn through experience
- Remember information
- Recognize patterns
- Continue improving every day

Part E – Personal Reflection

Think about one skill you have learned (riding a bicycle, playing sports, reading, music, coding, cooking, etc.).

Explain how each of the following contributed to learning that skill:

- Observation
- Practice
- Mistakes
- Memory
- Pattern Recognition

____
____
____
____
____
____

Chapter 3 Quiz

Multiple Choice

1. Human knowledge begins primarily through...

A. Observation

B. Computers

C. Memorization only

D. Testing

2. Which of the following allows humans to learn from previous generations?

A. Sleeping

B. Language

C. Guessing

D. Luck

3. Pattern recognition helps people...

A. Forget information

B. Identify relationships and similarities

C. Eliminate memory

D. Avoid learning

4. Cognitive development refers to...

A. Losing information

B. The gradual growth of thinking and reasoning abilities

C. Computer programming

D. Data storage

5. One important lesson AGI researchers learn from humans is that intelligence should...

A. Never change

B. Learn continuously throughout life

C. Depend only on data

D. Avoid mistakes

True or False

6. Humans only learn during school.

True / False

7. Experience helps transform information into knowledge.

True / False

8. Memory allows people to build knowledge over time.

True / False

9. Mistakes can become valuable learning opportunities.

True / False

10. Artificial General Intelligence researchers study human learning to improve future intelligent systems.

True / False

Answer Key

Vocabulary

Answers will vary but should demonstrate accurate understanding.

Worksheet

Part B

1. Observation gathers information through the senses.
2. Experience connects information with real-world actions and outcomes.
3. Language allows knowledge to be shared across people and generations.
4. Long-term memory stores knowledge, experiences, and skills for future use.
5. Because human learning provides a model for building more flexible and adaptive AI systems.

Part C – Matching

A → Uses the senses to gather information

B → Learns by interacting with the world

C → Stores information for future use

D → Finds similarities and relationships

E → Shares knowledge across generations

Part D

Answers will vary but should demonstrate understanding of lifelong learning, observation, memory, pattern recognition, and continuous improvement.

Part E

Answers will vary based on each student's personal experiences.

Quiz Answers

1. **A**
2. **B**
3. **B**
4. **B**
5. **B**
6. **False**
7. **True**
8. **True**
9. **True**
10. **True**

Key Vocabulary

- Observation
- Experience
- Knowledge
- Learning

- Memory
- Long-Term Memory
- Working Memory
- Pattern Recognition
- Cognitive Development
- Mental Model
- Curiosity
- Generalization
- Lifelong Learning
- Artificial General Intelligence (AGI)
- Knowledge Acquisition

Chapter Takeaway

Every human being is born with the remarkable ability to learn. Through observation, experience, language, memory, curiosity, and continuous practice, people transform everyday experiences into lifelong knowledge. Understanding how humans acquire knowledge provides one of the most important roadmaps for building the next generation of Artificial General Intelligence.

Learn AI. Understand AI. Shape the Future.

— Susie Hala
IntelliGloss Press

Chapter 4

Knowledge Representation

Part 1

Knowledge is only valuable if it can be organized in a way that allows it to be understood and used. Imagine walking into the world's largest library where millions of books have been removed from their shelves and scattered randomly across the floor. Every book is still present, but finding the information you need would become almost impossible. The knowledge has not disappeared; it has simply lost its organization. Artificial intelligence faces a similar challenge. Collecting enormous amounts of data is not enough to create intelligence. Information must be organized into meaningful structures that allow an intelligent system to locate, understand, relate, and apply knowledge whenever it is needed. This process is known as **knowledge representation**, and it serves as one of the most important foundations of Artificial General Intelligence (AGI). Without effective knowledge representation, even the most powerful AI system would struggle to reason, solve problems, or learn efficiently because it would have no organized way of understanding the information it possesses.

Knowledge representation refers to the methods used to organize information so that it becomes meaningful and useful for intelligent reasoning. Human beings naturally organize knowledge throughout their lives. People do not remember every individual experience as an isolated event. Instead, the brain groups similar ideas together, forms categories, builds relationships between concepts, and creates mental structures that simplify learning and decision-making. When someone hears the word "bird," they immediately think about feathers, wings, nests, eggs, flight, and perhaps familiar birds such as robins, eagles, or parrots. The brain automatically connects related concepts without consciously searching through every memory. These organized mental structures allow humans to understand language, recognize objects, predict outcomes, and solve unfamiliar problems quickly. Artificial intelligence researchers seek to develop similar organizational systems that allow machines to represent knowledge in ways that support intelligent behavior.

One of the simplest methods of representing knowledge involves the use of **symbols**. A symbol is something that represents another object, idea, action, or relationship. Human civilization depends heavily upon symbolic thinking. Letters represent sounds. Numbers represent quantities. Traffic signs communicate instructions. Mathematical equations describe scientific relationships. Maps represent geographical locations. Computer programming languages use symbols to instruct machines how to perform specific tasks. Symbols allow complex ideas to be communicated efficiently because they stand for something larger than themselves. Early artificial intelligence systems relied heavily on symbolic reasoning by representing knowledge using words, logical statements, and mathematical rules. These systems performed well in structured environments where knowledge could be described precisely, such as solving algebra problems or following carefully defined procedures.

Symbols become even more powerful when they are organized into **concepts**. A concept represents a general idea formed by combining many related experiences into a single mental category. For example, people understand the concept of a "chair" even though chairs come in many different shapes, sizes, colors, and materials. Some chairs have four legs, while others have only one. Some are made of wood, others of metal or plastic. Some are used in classrooms, while others are found in restaurants or offices. Despite these differences, the human brain recognizes all of them as chairs because it has formed a general concept based on shared characteristics. This ability to create concepts allows humans to think abstractly rather than memorizing every individual object separately. Future AGI systems must develop similar conceptual representations if they are to understand the world with the flexibility demonstrated by human intelligence.

Concepts also allow people to organize knowledge into categories and hierarchies. Consider the concept of transportation. Within this broad category exist smaller concepts such as automobiles, trains, airplanes, bicycles, and ships. Each of these categories contains even more detailed concepts. Automobiles include sedans, trucks, sports cars, electric vehicles, and autonomous vehicles. Electric vehicles may include passenger cars, delivery vans, and buses. This hierarchical organization allows knowledge to expand naturally while remaining well organized. Instead of storing millions of unrelated facts, the brain builds structured networks where general ideas branch into increasingly specific concepts. Artificial intelligence systems use similar approaches when organizing information into taxonomies, ontologies, and hierarchical knowledge structures that support efficient retrieval and reasoning.

As knowledge grows, relationships between concepts become just as important as the concepts themselves. Human intelligence depends upon understanding how ideas connect rather than simply memorizing isolated facts. Students studying biology learn that plants require sunlight, water, carbon dioxide, and nutrients to grow. These ideas are connected because changes in one element influence the others. Economists study how supply affects prices and how prices influence consumer behavior. Historians examine how political decisions shape future events. Scientists investigate how changes in climate influence ecosystems. Knowledge becomes increasingly valuable as these relationships become clearer because understanding connections allows people to explain causes, predict consequences, and solve complex problems. Artificial intelligence researchers therefore design knowledge representation systems that emphasize relationships rather than isolated pieces of information.

One method used to organize these relationships is the creation of **semantic structures**. The word "semantic" refers to meaning. Semantic structures organize knowledge according to the meanings and relationships among concepts rather than simply storing words or numbers. For example, a semantic representation may indicate that a dog is an animal, that animals are living organisms, that dogs can be pets, and that pets often live with humans. These relationships allow an intelligent system to draw logical conclusions. If it knows that all mammals breathe air and that dogs are mammals, it can correctly conclude that dogs breathe air even if that exact statement was never stored separately. This ability to infer new knowledge from existing relationships represents one of the defining characteristics of intelligent reasoning.

Human language demonstrates the importance of semantic knowledge every day. Consider the sentence, "The teacher placed the book on the desk because it was full." Humans immediately understand that "it" most likely refers to the desk being full rather than the book. This interpretation depends upon semantic understanding rather than grammatical rules alone. Context, experience, and relationships among concepts help people identify the intended meaning. Artificial intelligence systems must develop increasingly sophisticated semantic representations to interpret language accurately, answer questions, summarize information, and communicate naturally with humans.

Knowledge representation also involves organizing experiences into **schemas**. A schema is a mental framework that helps people understand familiar situations by organizing previous knowledge into reusable patterns. Imagine entering a restaurant. Without thinking about every step individually, you already know that someone may greet you, provide a menu, take your order, prepare the food, deliver the meal, and eventually provide the bill. This organized expectation exists because your brain has developed a restaurant schema through previous experiences. Similar schemas exist for classrooms, airports, hospitals, grocery stores, birthday parties, sporting events, and countless other situations. Schemas reduce mental effort because they allow people to predict what is likely to happen next while remaining flexible enough to handle unexpected events.

Artificial intelligence researchers study schemas because they provide an efficient method for organizing knowledge about recurring situations. Instead of treating every experience as entirely unique, an AGI system could recognize familiar patterns and activate the appropriate knowledge structure automatically. A medical AI might activate a clinical diagnosis schema when evaluating patients. An autonomous vehicle might activate a driving schema while navigating city streets. An educational AI tutor could activate an instructional schema when teaching mathematics. These organized frameworks help intelligent systems retrieve relevant knowledge quickly while adapting to changing circumstances.

Closely related to schemas are **frames**, another important method of representing knowledge. A frame is a structured representation that describes an object, event, or concept by organizing its important characteristics into predictable categories. Consider the frame for a classroom. It may include a teacher, students, desks, whiteboards, computers, textbooks, assignments, discussions, and assessments. Not every classroom contains exactly the same features, but the frame provides a general structure that helps intelligent systems recognize and understand similar environments. Frames allow machines to store complex knowledge in organized formats while leaving room for variation and exceptions. Rather than memorizing thousands of unrelated facts, AI systems can retrieve entire knowledge structures whenever a familiar concept is encountered.

These methods of organizing knowledge demonstrate an important principle: intelligence depends not only on how much information is stored but also on how effectively that information is represented. Human intelligence succeeds because the brain organizes knowledge into interconnected concepts, relationships, semantic meanings, schemas, and frames that work together to support reasoning and learning. Artificial General Intelligence will require similarly sophisticated knowledge representations capable of expanding continuously while maintaining organization, consistency, and flexibility. In the next part of this chapter, you will explore how knowledge is encoded into machine-readable forms, how computers transform human understanding into computational structures, and why effective knowledge representation serves as one of the most important building blocks of future AGI.

(End of Part 1 — Part 2 will continue with Knowledge Encoding, Machine-Readable Knowledge, Modern Representation Architectures, AGI Applications, and a powerful chapter conclusion.)

Chapter 4

Knowledge Representation

Part 2

As artificial intelligence has evolved, researchers have discovered that representing knowledge is far more difficult than simply storing large amounts of information inside a computer. Human knowledge is flexible, constantly changing, and deeply connected to experience. Computers, however, require information to be represented in precise formats that algorithms can process mathematically. The challenge is not merely teaching a machine facts but teaching it how those facts relate to one another, when they apply, and how they should be used in different situations. This process is known as **knowledge encoding**, and it serves as the bridge between human understanding and machine intelligence. Knowledge encoding transforms concepts, relationships, observations, and experiences into structured representations that computers can analyze, retrieve, update, and reason about. Without effective encoding methods, even the most advanced AI system would possess enormous quantities of information but very little usable intelligence.

In the earliest days of artificial intelligence, knowledge encoding depended almost entirely on human experts. Scientists, engineers, physicians, and mathematicians manually described knowledge by writing thousands of logical rules that computers could follow. An expert medical system, for example, might contain rules stating that if a patient has a fever, cough, and positive laboratory test, then a particular disease is likely. Engineers carefully entered these rules into specialized knowledge bases, allowing computers to solve well-defined problems. These systems performed surprisingly well within limited domains because every decision followed logical reasoning based on carefully constructed rules. However, they also revealed an important limitation. Human knowledge is far too large, dynamic, and constantly changing for experts to manually encode every possible fact, relationship, and situation. As knowledge expanded, maintaining these systems became increasingly difficult, motivating researchers to develop more flexible methods for representing knowledge.

Modern artificial intelligence addresses this challenge by allowing computers to learn many knowledge representations automatically from data rather than relying entirely on manually written rules. Machine learning algorithms analyze enormous collections of text, images, videos, sounds, scientific publications, and sensor measurements to discover meaningful patterns without explicit programming. Instead of storing every fact separately, these systems learn mathematical relationships that capture similarities among concepts. Large language models, for example, represent words, phrases, and ideas as complex numerical patterns called **embeddings**. These mathematical representations allow computers to recognize that words such as "teacher," "student," "classroom," and "education" are closely related even though they consist of different letters. The computer does not simply memorize definitions; it learns relationships by observing how concepts appear together across billions of examples. This approach has dramatically expanded the ability of AI systems to organize and retrieve knowledge efficiently.

Machine-readable knowledge differs significantly from the way humans naturally think. People often rely on stories, emotions, experiences, images, conversations, and intuition when organizing ideas. Computers require knowledge to be represented using numerical values, logical structures, vectors, graphs, probabilities, and algorithms that software can manipulate mathematically. Imagine looking at a photograph of a family standing in front of a house. A human instantly recognizes smiling faces, relationships among family members, the season of the year, and perhaps even emotions expressed within the image. A computer, however, initially sees only millions of numerical values representing colored pixels. Through advanced knowledge representation techniques, those numerical patterns gradually become meaningful concepts such as "person," "tree," "house," "sky," "child," or "dog." This transformation demonstrates the importance of knowledge representation because it converts raw computational information into meaningful structures that support intelligent reasoning.

One of the greatest advances in modern AI has been the development of **distributed knowledge representations**. Rather than storing every concept in a single location, information is distributed across large mathematical networks. This approach resembles the human brain, where memories are not stored in one individual neuron but emerge from interactions among billions of interconnected neurons. Distributed representations allow AI systems to recognize similarities between concepts, tolerate incomplete information, and adapt to new situations more effectively than earlier symbolic systems. For example, if an AI system understands concepts related to bicycles, motorcycles, and automobiles, it may more easily learn about electric scooters because many characteristics overlap. Knowledge is not isolated but shared across interconnected representations, allowing learning to become more flexible and efficient.

Another important development involves combining multiple methods of knowledge representation into unified architectures. Modern intelligent systems often integrate symbolic reasoning, machine learning, knowledge graphs, vector databases, logical inference, and probabilistic reasoning within a single framework. Each representation method contributes unique strengths. Symbolic systems excel at logical reasoning and following explicit rules. Machine learning recognizes complex patterns within enormous datasets. Knowledge graphs organize relationships among concepts. Vector databases support semantic search and contextual retrieval. Probabilistic models estimate uncertainty and evaluate multiple possible outcomes. By combining these approaches, AI systems become far more capable than relying on any single representation method alone. Researchers believe future AGI systems will require even more integrated architectures capable of combining perception, memory, reasoning, planning, language, and learning into unified knowledge systems.

Knowledge representation also plays a central role in communication between intelligent systems. Consider autonomous vehicles operating within a smart city. Each vehicle continuously collects information using cameras, radar, lidar, GPS, and environmental sensors. To cooperate safely, these vehicles must represent traffic conditions, road hazards, construction zones, weather conditions, and pedestrian movements using common knowledge structures that other vehicles can understand. Similarly, medical AI systems may exchange patient information, diagnostic knowledge, treatment recommendations, and research findings across hospitals around the world. Scientific research platforms may share experimental results among laboratories studying climate change, genetics, or renewable energy. Shared knowledge representations allow intelligent systems to collaborate efficiently because information remains organized in consistent formats that multiple machines can interpret accurately.

Knowledge representation becomes even more important when intelligent systems encounter unfamiliar situations. Human beings constantly apply previous knowledge to new experiences by recognizing similarities and adapting existing mental models. Imagine an experienced teacher moving from teaching elementary school to high school. Although the students are older and the subject matter becomes more advanced, many educational principles remain applicable because the teacher transfers previous knowledge into a new environment. Future AGI systems must demonstrate similar adaptability. Rather than requiring complete retraining whenever circumstances change, they should reorganize existing knowledge, identify relevant relationships, and build new understanding by extending previous learning. Flexible knowledge representation makes this type of transfer learning possible because concepts remain interconnected rather than isolated.

Researchers also recognize that knowledge representation must remain dynamic throughout an intelligent system's lifetime. Knowledge is never truly finished because the world continues changing. Scientific discoveries replace outdated theories. Medical treatments improve. Languages evolve. Technologies advance. Social norms shift. Environmental conditions change. Human beings continually revise their understanding as new evidence becomes available. Future AGI systems must demonstrate similar adaptability by updating knowledge representations without destroying valuable previous learning. This challenge, often called **knowledge maintenance**, requires balancing stability with flexibility. Intelligent systems must preserve reliable knowledge while remaining open to new discoveries that improve understanding. Achieving this balance represents one of the most important research areas in AGI development.

Ethics also influences knowledge representation in significant ways. Intelligent systems are only as reliable as the knowledge they represent. If training data contains incomplete information, historical inaccuracies, cultural biases, or unfair assumptions, those weaknesses may become embedded within the AI's knowledge structures. Researchers therefore emphasize the importance of building knowledge systems that are accurate, diverse, transparent, and continuously evaluated for fairness. Knowledge representation is not merely a technical problem but also a social responsibility because the decisions made by intelligent systems increasingly affect healthcare, education, employment, finance, transportation, and public safety. Future AGI systems will require knowledge architectures capable of supporting not only intelligent reasoning but also responsible and ethical decision-making.

The study of knowledge representation reveals an important truth about intelligence itself. Intelligence does not arise simply because information exists. It emerges because information is organized into meaningful structures that support understanding, reasoning, learning, communication, and adaptation. Human beings naturally build these structures throughout their lives by connecting experiences, language, memory, and observation into rich networks of knowledge. Artificial intelligence researchers seek to develop computational systems capable of organizing information with similar flexibility and depth. Every improvement in knowledge representation brings intelligent machines one step closer to reasoning more effectively, learning more continuously, and collaborating more naturally with human beings.

As Artificial General Intelligence continues to evolve, knowledge representation will remain one of its most essential foundations. Future intelligent systems will require knowledge architectures that integrate symbols, concepts, semantic relationships, frames, schemas, vector representations, logical reasoning, memory systems, and continuous learning into unified models capable of understanding the complexity of the real world. These knowledge systems will not simply store information; they will organize it into living structures that grow, adapt, revise themselves, and support increasingly sophisticated forms of intelligence. The better scientists understand how knowledge should be represented, the closer humanity moves toward building machines capable of learning, reasoning, and solving problems with a flexibility approaching that of the human mind.

In many ways, knowledge representation serves as the language through which intelligence communicates with itself. It allows experiences to become memories, memories to become understanding, and understanding to become intelligent action. Whether inside the human brain or within the future architectures of Artificial General Intelligence, knowledge representation transforms scattered information into organized understanding that makes learning, reasoning, creativity, and discovery possible. Every future advance in AGI will depend upon this remarkable ability to represent knowledge in ways that are not only computationally efficient but also meaningful, adaptable, and aligned with the ever-changing world it seeks to understand.

Learn AI. Understand AI. Shape the Future.

— Susie Hala
IntelliGloss Press

Chapter 4 Summary

Knowledge Representation

Knowledge is only useful when it is organized in a way that allows it to be understood, retrieved, and applied. Knowledge representation is the process of organizing information into meaningful structures that support reasoning, learning, problem-solving, and decision-making. It serves as one of the most important foundations of Artificial General Intelligence (AGI) because intelligent systems must know not only facts but also how those facts relate to one another.

Humans naturally organize knowledge by creating concepts, categories, relationships, mental models, schemas, and frames. These structures allow the brain to recognize patterns, retrieve information quickly, and apply previous learning to new situations. Rather than remembering isolated facts, humans build interconnected networks of knowledge that continue growing throughout life.

Artificial intelligence must also represent knowledge in organized ways. Early AI systems relied primarily on symbolic reasoning and manually written rules created by human experts. While effective in limited situations, these systems became difficult to maintain as knowledge expanded. Modern AI increasingly uses machine learning, semantic representations, embeddings, vector databases, and knowledge graphs to organize information automatically by discovering relationships within enormous datasets.

Knowledge representation also involves encoding information into formats that computers can process mathematically. Unlike humans, who naturally understand stories, emotions, and experiences, machines require structured numerical representations, logical relationships, and computational models. These representations allow AI systems to retrieve information efficiently, recognize similarities among concepts, and perform intelligent reasoning.

Researchers continue developing more advanced knowledge architectures by combining symbolic reasoning, neural networks, semantic networks, vector representations, and probabilistic models into unified systems. Future AGI will require flexible knowledge representations capable of continuous learning, updating information, correcting errors, transferring knowledge across different domains, and supporting ethical decision-making.

Knowledge representation is much more than storing information. It is the framework that transforms data into organized understanding, allowing intelligent systems to think, learn, communicate, and solve problems in increasingly human-like ways.

Reflection

Think about everything you know today. You recognize thousands of objects, understand multiple subjects, remember important experiences, and solve problems without consciously searching through every memory. Your brain accomplishes this because it organizes knowledge into meaningful relationships instead of storing isolated facts.

Artificial intelligence faces the same challenge. Simply storing billions of pieces of information does not create intelligence. Intelligent systems must organize information so they can retrieve the right knowledge at the right time, connect related ideas, recognize patterns, and apply previous learning to unfamiliar situations.

As AGI continues to develop, knowledge representation will become increasingly important because it determines how effectively intelligent systems understand the world. Every improvement in organizing knowledge brings AI one step closer to reasoning more like humans.

As you continue your education, remember that successful learning is not about memorizing disconnected facts. It is about building connections between ideas, organizing knowledge into meaningful structures, and using that understanding to solve new problems throughout your life.

Student Worksheet

Name: ____________________________________

Date: _____________________________________

Part A – Vocabulary

Define each term using your own words.

1. Knowledge Representation

2. Symbol

3. Concept

4. Semantic Structure

5. Schema

6. Frame

7. Knowledge Encoding

Part B – Short Answer

1. Why is knowledge representation important for intelligent systems?

2. Explain the difference between symbols and concepts.

3. How do schemas help humans understand familiar situations?

---

4. Why must AI encode knowledge into machine-readable formats?

---

5. Why is continuous knowledge updating important for future AGI?

Part C – Matching

Letter	Knowledge Representation Method	Number
A	Symbol	___ Represents a familiar situation
B	Concept	___ Represents an object or idea
C	Semantic Structure	___ Organizes meaning and relationships
D	Schema	___ General mental category
E	Frame	___ Describes characteristics of an object or event

Part D – Critical Thinking

Imagine you are designing an AGI assistant for a hospital.

Explain how the assistant should organize knowledge about:

- Patients

- Diseases

- Treatments

- Medical Equipment

- Emergency Situations

How would effective knowledge representation improve patient care?

Part E – Real-World Application

Choose one place you visit often (school, grocery store, library, sports field, workplace, etc.).

Describe the **schema** your brain uses to understand what normally happens there.

Chapter 4 Quiz

Multiple Choice

1. Knowledge representation helps intelligent systems...

A. Forget information

B. Organize and use knowledge effectively

C. Eliminate memory

D. Store only numbers

2. A concept is...

A. A random collection of facts

B. A general mental category representing similar objects or ideas

C. A computer program

D. A database

3. Semantic structures organize knowledge according to...

A. Alphabetical order

B. Meaning and relationships

C. File size

D. Memory location

4. A schema helps people...

A. Predict familiar situations

B. Delete memories

C. Replace learning

D. Avoid reasoning

5. Modern AI often represents knowledge using...

A. Embeddings and vector representations

B. Only paper documents

C. Filing cabinets

D. Typewriters

True or False

6. Knowledge representation is only about storing information.

True / False

7. Humans naturally organize knowledge into connected ideas.

True / False

8. Machine-readable knowledge allows AI systems to process information.

True / False

9. Future AGI will require flexible knowledge representation systems.

True / False

10. Knowledge representation plays no role in reasoning.

True / False

Answer Key

Vocabulary

Answers will vary but should demonstrate accurate understanding.

Worksheet

Part B

1. It organizes information so intelligent systems can reason, learn, retrieve knowledge, and make decisions.
2. Symbols represent ideas or objects, while concepts organize many related examples into one general category.

3. Schemas organize previous experiences into reusable mental frameworks that help predict familiar situations.
4. Computers process numerical and logical structures rather than human experiences or emotions.
5. Because knowledge changes over time and intelligent systems must adapt to new discoveries.

Part C – Matching

A → Represents an object or idea

B → General mental category

C → Organizes meaning and relationships

D → Represents a familiar situation

E → Describes characteristics of an object or event

Part D

Answers will vary but should demonstrate organized knowledge structures and reasoning.

Part E

Answers will vary.

Quiz Answers

1. **B**
2. **B**
3. **B**
4. **A**
5. **A**
6. **False**
7. **True**
8. **True**
9. **True**

10. **False**

Key Vocabulary

- Knowledge Representation
- Symbol
- Concept
- Category
- Semantic Structure
- Schema
- Frame
- Knowledge Encoding
- Embedding
- Vector Representation
- Knowledge Graph
- Machine-Readable Knowledge
- Logical Reasoning
- Artificial General Intelligence (AGI)
- Knowledge Architecture

Chapter Takeaway

Knowledge becomes intelligence only when it is organized into meaningful relationships. Whether inside the human brain or an Artificial General Intelligence system, knowledge representation transforms scattered information into connected understanding, making learning, reasoning, communication, and intelligent decision-making possible.

Learn AI. Understand AI. Shape the Future.

— Susie Hala
IntelliGloss Press

Chapter 5

Knowledge Graphs and Semantic Networks

Part 1

Knowledge is much more than a collection of isolated facts. The true power of intelligence comes from understanding how ideas connect with one another. Imagine trying to understand the history of the United States by memorizing thousands of separate dates without knowing how the events influenced one another. You might remember that the Declaration of Independence was signed in 1776, that the Constitution was adopted in 1787, and that the Civil War began in 1861, but without understanding the relationships among these events, history would become little more than disconnected pieces of information. The same principle applies to every field of knowledge. Scientists understand ecosystems because they recognize relationships among plants, animals, climate, and natural resources. Physicians diagnose diseases because they understand how symptoms, organs, medications, and biological systems interact. Engineers design bridges because they understand the relationships among materials, forces, gravity, and structural design. Intelligence emerges not from isolated facts but from the network of relationships that connect them. Artificial General Intelligence (AGI) depends on building these interconnected knowledge structures, and two of the most powerful tools developed for this purpose are **knowledge graphs** and **semantic networks**.

Human beings naturally organize knowledge into connected webs of ideas. When someone hears the word "school," dozens of related concepts immediately become active in the mind. Students may think about teachers, classrooms, homework, books, learning, friends, science, mathematics, sports, cafeterias, libraries, and graduation. None of these ideas exist independently because every concept is connected to many others through previous experiences and learning. The brain constantly activates these relationships without conscious effort, allowing people to retrieve information quickly, recognize patterns, solve problems, and understand new situations. Cognitive scientists often describe human memory as a vast network of interconnected concepts rather than a collection of isolated facts stored like files inside a cabinet. Artificial intelligence researchers seek to build similar knowledge structures that allow machines to reason by following meaningful connections between ideas instead of relying only on memorized information.

One of the most effective methods for organizing these relationships is through a **knowledge graph**. A knowledge graph is a structured representation of information that connects concepts using meaningful relationships. Instead of storing facts separately, a knowledge graph links related ideas together into a network that resembles a map of knowledge. Every concept becomes a **node**, while every relationship between concepts becomes a **connection**, often called an **edge**. Together, these nodes and edges create a graph that allows intelligent systems to navigate knowledge by following relationships from one concept to another. Unlike traditional databases that simply store records, knowledge graphs capture the meaning behind information by showing how different ideas influence one another.

Imagine creating a simple knowledge graph about the solar system. The Sun would become one node. Earth would become another node. A connection between them might state that "Earth orbits the Sun." Another node might represent the Moon, connected by the relationship "Moon orbits Earth." Additional nodes could include Mars, Jupiter, gravity, planets, stars, and galaxies. As more concepts are added, the graph grows into an increasingly rich network of knowledge. Rather than memorizing individual facts separately, an intelligent system can follow these relationships to answer questions, discover new connections, and perform logical reasoning. For example, if the graph indicates that all planets orbit stars and that Earth is a planet, the system can infer that Earth orbits a star even if that exact statement was never stored independently.

Knowledge graphs become especially powerful because they allow intelligent systems to combine information from many different sources into one unified structure. Consider a healthcare knowledge graph. One section may connect diseases with symptoms. Another may connect medications with treatments. A third may describe organs, body systems, genetics, medical procedures, laboratory tests, and research studies. Physicians constantly rely on these relationships when diagnosing illnesses and selecting treatments. An AI system using a knowledge graph can quickly identify related concepts, compare medical evidence, suggest possible diagnoses, and explain how different conditions may be connected. Because every concept remains linked within a larger network, new information can be added without reorganizing the entire system.

Knowledge graphs are already used throughout modern technology. Internet search engines rely on knowledge graphs to understand relationships among people, places, organizations, historical events, books, scientific concepts, and countless other subjects. When someone searches for a famous scientist, the search engine does more than locate documents containing that person's name. It also identifies related discoveries, universities, awards, collaborators, publications, and historical contributions because these concepts are connected within its knowledge graph. Digital assistants use similar techniques when answering questions, recommending information, or interpreting conversations. Recommendation systems used by streaming services, online retailers, and educational platforms also benefit from knowledge graphs because they understand relationships among products, movies, books, music, courses, and user preferences.

Closely related to knowledge graphs are **semantic networks**. Although the two concepts share many similarities, semantic networks place greater emphasis on representing the meanings of concepts and the relationships among them. The word **semantic** refers to meaning. A semantic network therefore focuses on organizing knowledge according to what concepts represent rather than simply storing their names. Human understanding depends heavily on semantic relationships because words often have multiple meanings depending on context. For example, the word "apple" may refer to a fruit, a technology company, or even part of a person's eye in certain scientific discussions. Humans determine the correct meaning by examining surrounding information, previous conversations, and contextual clues. Semantic networks help AI systems perform similar reasoning by representing multiple meanings and the relationships that distinguish them.

Consider the concept of "bird" within a semantic network. The network may indicate that a bird is an animal, that animals are living organisms, that birds have feathers, lay eggs, possess wings, and usually fly. Additional relationships may describe exceptions, such as penguins that cannot fly or ostriches that run instead of flying. Because semantic networks represent these relationships explicitly, intelligent systems can answer questions, draw logical conclusions, and recognize exceptions more effectively than systems that simply memorize isolated facts. Semantic knowledge allows AI to understand not only what something is but also how it relates to countless other concepts within a larger network of understanding.

Semantic networks also help intelligent systems interpret natural language. Imagine hearing the sentence, "The scientist placed the microscope on the laboratory table because it was stable." Humans immediately understand that "it" most likely refers to the table rather than the microscope because tables are expected to provide stable support. This interpretation depends upon semantic relationships among concepts rather than grammar alone. Artificial intelligence systems increasingly rely on semantic networks to resolve such ambiguities by examining how words relate to one another within larger knowledge structures. These capabilities improve language translation, question answering, document summarization, and conversational AI.

One of the greatest strengths of knowledge graphs and semantic networks is their ability to support reasoning. Instead of simply retrieving stored information, intelligent systems can discover new knowledge by following existing relationships. Suppose a knowledge graph indicates that dolphins are mammals, mammals breathe air, and dolphins live in the ocean. When asked whether dolphins breathe air despite living underwater, the AI can combine multiple relationships to produce a correct explanation rather than relying upon memorization alone. This ability to infer new knowledge from existing relationships represents an essential characteristic of intelligent reasoning and serves as one of the major goals of Artificial General Intelligence.

As knowledge continues expanding, maintaining these networks becomes increasingly important. Millions of new scientific discoveries, technological innovations, medical treatments, and educational resources appear every year. Knowledge graphs provide an organized framework for integrating this growing information while preserving meaningful relationships among concepts. Rather than creating disconnected collections of facts, they allow intelligent systems to build continuously expanding maps of human knowledge that remain organized, searchable, and understandable. In the next part of this chapter, you will explore how graph databases store these relationships, how modern AI uses knowledge graphs to support reasoning and decision-making, and why these technologies are expected to become essential components of future Artificial General Intelligence.

(End of Part 1 — Part 2 will continue with Graph Databases, Real-World Applications, Building Machine Understanding, AGI Integration, and a powerful chapter conclusion.)

Chapter 5

Knowledge Graphs and Semantic Networks

Part 2

As knowledge graphs continue to expand, they require specialized methods for storing and managing the enormous number of relationships that exist between concepts. Traditional databases were designed primarily to organize structured records into rows and columns. For example, a school database might contain one table listing students, another listing teachers, and another listing courses. Each table stores valuable information, but discovering complex relationships often requires multiple searches and complicated queries. While traditional databases remain extremely useful for many business and organizational tasks, they were not originally designed to represent the rich web of interconnected knowledge that intelligent systems require. This limitation led computer scientists to develop **graph databases**, a technology specifically designed to store and manage relationships as efficiently as the information itself.

A graph database organizes knowledge using the same principles found in knowledge graphs. Every object, person, location, event, or idea becomes a **node**, while every relationship becomes an **edge** connecting two nodes. Instead of searching through separate tables to determine how concepts relate to one another, graph databases allow intelligent systems to follow relationships directly. Imagine planning a trip between two cities. Rather than examining thousands of separate records, a graph database can quickly identify roads, airports, train stations, hotels, restaurants, weather conditions, and transportation options because all of these elements are connected within the same network. This ability to move efficiently through connected information makes graph databases particularly valuable for artificial intelligence, where reasoning often depends upon understanding complex relationships rather than retrieving isolated facts.

One advantage of graph databases is their flexibility. Human knowledge is constantly changing as new discoveries are made, technologies evolve, and societies grow. If researchers discover a new species of animal, identify a new planet, or develop a new medical treatment, these concepts can be added to a graph database simply by creating new nodes and relationships. Existing knowledge remains intact while the network continues to expand naturally. This flexibility resembles the way humans learn throughout life. Every new experience becomes connected to previous knowledge instead of replacing everything already learned. Scientists believe that future AGI systems will require this same ability to continuously expand their knowledge structures without disrupting existing understanding.

Relationships themselves carry valuable information. Consider a family tree. Knowing that two people exist is useful, but understanding that one person is a parent, sibling, grandparent, or cousin of another provides much deeper knowledge. Knowledge graphs capture these relationships explicitly, allowing intelligent systems to answer questions that would otherwise require complex reasoning. An educational knowledge graph, for example, may connect students to teachers, teachers to schools, schools to districts, districts to states, and states to educational standards. From these relationships, an AI system can answer questions about enrollment, curriculum, teacher assignments, graduation requirements, or academic performance with remarkable efficiency. The value lies not only in the individual facts but also in the meaningful connections among them.

Modern artificial intelligence increasingly depends on graph databases to support intelligent decision-making. Financial institutions use graph technology to detect fraud by identifying hidden relationships among accounts, transactions, businesses, and individuals. Instead of examining each transaction independently, AI systems analyze entire networks of financial activity to identify suspicious patterns that may indicate criminal behavior. Cybersecurity professionals use graph databases to trace how attackers move through computer networks by following relationships among devices, users, software applications, and security events. Scientists use graph technologies to study biological systems, where genes, proteins, diseases, medications, and environmental factors interact in highly complex ways. In every case, understanding relationships provides insights that would be difficult to discover by examining isolated pieces of information.

Healthcare offers one of the most powerful examples of knowledge graphs in action. Imagine a physician treating a patient with several medical conditions at the same time. The patient may have diabetes, high blood pressure, kidney disease, and a history of heart problems while taking multiple medications prescribed by different specialists. Each condition influences the others, and each medication may interact differently depending on the patient's medical history. A healthcare knowledge graph connects diseases, symptoms, medications, laboratory results, genetic information, allergies, treatment guidelines, and scientific research into one integrated network. Artificial intelligence can then analyze these relationships to identify possible diagnoses, recommend treatment options, detect dangerous drug interactions, and support physicians in making informed clinical decisions. Rather than replacing medical professionals, knowledge graphs help organize complex medical knowledge into forms that support safer and more effective patient care.

Education also benefits from knowledge graphs and semantic networks. Traditional textbooks present information chapter by chapter, but human learning often involves connecting ideas across multiple subjects. A student studying the American Revolution may also need knowledge of geography, economics, political philosophy, mathematics, and scientific developments occurring during the same historical period. Educational knowledge graphs connect these related concepts, allowing intelligent tutoring systems to personalize instruction based on each student's existing knowledge. If a student struggles with algebra because of weaknesses in fractions, the system can identify prerequisite concepts and recommend targeted review materials. If another student demonstrates advanced understanding, the system can suggest more challenging topics that build upon existing strengths. This adaptive learning approach becomes possible because knowledge graphs reveal how educational concepts relate to one another.

Scientific research increasingly depends upon semantic networks to accelerate discovery. Modern scientists produce millions of research papers every year, making it impossible for any individual to read everything published within even a single field. Artificial intelligence systems use semantic networks to connect research findings across disciplines, revealing relationships that human researchers might overlook. For example, discoveries in molecular biology may provide insights relevant to cancer treatment, environmental science, agriculture, or pharmaceutical development. By organizing scientific knowledge into interconnected semantic networks, AI systems help researchers identify emerging trends, generate new hypotheses, and discover connections across previously unrelated fields. This capability has become especially valuable in areas such as drug discovery, climate research, and materials science, where progress often depends on integrating knowledge from multiple scientific disciplines.

Building genuine machine understanding requires more than creating larger knowledge graphs. Intelligent systems must also understand the meaning behind the relationships they store. For example, knowing that "water freezes at zero degrees Celsius" is useful, but understanding why water freezes, how temperature affects molecular movement, and how freezing influences ecosystems, engineering, and weather demonstrates much deeper knowledge. Human beings naturally integrate factual knowledge with experience, reasoning, and common sense. Future AGI systems must develop similar capabilities by combining knowledge graphs with memory systems, reasoning engines, world models, and continuous learning architectures. Knowledge graphs provide the structure, but understanding emerges when intelligent systems learn how to interpret and apply those structures flexibly across many different situations.

Another challenge involves managing uncertainty. Human knowledge is rarely complete or perfectly certain. Scientists often revise theories when new evidence becomes available. Physicians may consider multiple possible diagnoses before reaching a final conclusion. Historians interpret evidence that sometimes contains conflicting accounts. Future AGI systems must represent uncertainty within their knowledge graphs instead of assuming that every relationship is absolutely correct. Some connections may carry higher confidence than others, allowing intelligent systems to weigh evidence, compare competing explanations, and revise conclusions as new information emerges. This ability to manage uncertainty will become increasingly important as AGI systems participate in scientific discovery, healthcare, education, engineering, and public policy.

Knowledge graphs also encourage collaboration among intelligent systems. Imagine multiple AI agents working together to respond to a natural disaster. One system analyzes weather forecasts, another monitors transportation networks, another evaluates hospital capacity, while another tracks emergency supplies. Each system contributes specialized knowledge to a shared knowledge graph, allowing all participants to understand the broader situation. Emergency managers receive integrated information rather than isolated reports, enabling faster and more informed decision-making. Similar collaborative knowledge systems may eventually support scientific research, environmental monitoring, global health, and space exploration, where solving complex problems requires combining knowledge from many different domains.

As researchers move closer to developing Artificial General Intelligence, knowledge graphs and semantic networks are expected to become even more sophisticated. Future AGI systems will likely build their own knowledge graphs automatically, continuously updating relationships as they observe the world, communicate with humans, perform experiments, and learn from experience. These evolving knowledge structures may eventually resemble living maps of human understanding, expanding continuously while maintaining logical organization and consistency. Rather than remaining static collections of facts, future knowledge graphs will become dynamic systems that grow, adapt, reason, and refine themselves throughout an AGI's lifetime.

The study of knowledge graphs and semantic networks demonstrates one of the most important principles of intelligence: understanding grows through relationships. Facts become meaningful only when connected to other facts. Ideas become valuable when linked with experience, reasoning, and context. Human civilization itself has advanced because generations have built networks of shared knowledge that continue expanding over time. Artificial General Intelligence follows the same path. By organizing concepts into rich, interconnected networks, future intelligent systems will gain the ability to reason more effectively, communicate more naturally, solve increasingly complex problems, and collaborate more successfully with people around the world.

Knowledge graphs and semantic networks therefore represent far more than computer technologies. They reflect the very structure of intelligent thought. Whether inside the human brain or within future AGI architectures, intelligence depends upon recognizing that every idea exists within a larger web of relationships. The stronger and more meaningful those connections become, the greater the ability to understand the world, generate new knowledge, and apply intelligence responsibly for the benefit of humanity.

Learn AI. Understand AI. Shape the Future.

— Susie Hala
IntelliGloss Press

Chapter 5 Summary

Knowledge Graphs and Semantic Networks

Knowledge becomes more valuable when ideas are connected rather than stored as isolated facts. Knowledge graphs and semantic networks organize information into interconnected structures that allow both humans and artificial intelligence systems to understand relationships among concepts. These connections support reasoning, learning, problem-solving, and intelligent decision-making.

A **knowledge graph** represents information as a network of **nodes** and **edges**. Nodes represent objects, people, places, events, or concepts, while edges describe the relationships between them. Instead of storing information separately, knowledge graphs organize ideas into meaningful networks that allow AI systems to retrieve information, discover new relationships, and make logical inferences.

Semantic networks focus on the meanings of concepts and how those meanings relate to one another. They help AI understand language, recognize context, interpret multiple meanings of words, and connect similar ideas. These semantic relationships improve natural language processing, question answering, document summarization, and conversational AI.

Graph databases provide an efficient way to store and manage knowledge graphs. Unlike traditional databases that organize information into tables, graph databases are specifically designed to manage complex relationships among connected concepts. This makes them especially useful in fields such as healthcare, education, finance, cybersecurity, transportation, and scientific research.

Knowledge graphs also support intelligent reasoning by allowing AI systems to infer new information from existing relationships. Rather than simply memorizing facts, AI can follow connections across multiple concepts to answer questions and solve problems more effectively. Modern search engines, recommendation systems, digital assistants, fraud detection platforms, and medical decision-support systems already use knowledge graphs to improve their performance.

Future Artificial General Intelligence (AGI) will likely depend heavily on advanced knowledge graphs that continuously grow, update themselves, integrate information from multiple sources, and support increasingly human-like understanding. These evolving knowledge networks will help intelligent machines connect ideas, transfer knowledge across different situations, collaborate with other AI systems, and make better decisions.

Knowledge graphs and semantic networks demonstrate that intelligence is built upon relationships. The stronger and more meaningful those relationships become, the greater the ability to understand, reason, learn, and create new knowledge.

Reflection

Every subject you study is connected to many others. Mathematics supports engineering. Biology connects with chemistry. History influences politics. Language strengthens communication. The more connections you build between ideas, the deeper your understanding becomes.

Your brain naturally creates a knowledge graph throughout your life. Every new experience becomes connected to previous memories, allowing you to recognize patterns, solve problems, and understand unfamiliar situations. Instead of storing isolated facts, your mind builds an ever-growing network of relationships that becomes richer every day.

Artificial intelligence is learning to organize knowledge in similar ways. Knowledge graphs and semantic networks help AI move beyond memorizing information by understanding how ideas relate to one another. As AGI continues to develop, these knowledge structures will become increasingly important because they provide the foundation for reasoning, collaboration, and intelligent decision-making.

As you continue learning, try to connect new ideas with what you already know. Every new connection strengthens your personal knowledge network and helps you become a more effective learner and problem solver.

Student Worksheet

Name: ________________________________

Date: ________________________________

Part A – Vocabulary

Define each term using your own words.

1. Knowledge Graph

____

2. Node

____

3. Edge

____

4. Semantic Network

____

5. Graph Database

____

6. Relationship

____

7. Inference

____

____

Part B – Short Answer

1. Why are relationships important in knowledge graphs?

2. How do semantic networks improve language understanding?

3. What is the difference between a traditional database and a graph database?

4. Give two real-world examples where knowledge graphs are used.

5. Why are knowledge graphs important for future AGI?

Part C – Matching

Letter	Concept	Number
A	Node	___ Organizes connected knowledge
B	Edge	___ Represents a concept or object
C	Knowledge Graph	___ Describes relationships
D	Semantic Network	___ Focuses on meaning
E	Graph Database	___ Stores connected information efficiently

Part D – Critical Thinking

Imagine you are creating a knowledge graph for your school.

Describe five nodes that would be included.

Describe at least five relationships connecting those nodes.

Explain how this knowledge graph could help students and teachers.

Part E – Real-World Application

Choose one topic you enjoy learning about.

Examples:

- Sports
- Space
- Animals
- Music
- History
- Video Games

Create a simple knowledge graph by listing:

Five nodes:

1. __________
2. __________
3. __________
4. __________
5. __________

Describe how each node connects to another.

Chapter 5 Quiz

Multiple Choice

1. A knowledge graph primarily organizes...

A. Pictures only

B. Connected concepts and relationships

C. Computer hardware

D. Internet cables

2. In a knowledge graph, a node represents...

A. A relationship

B. A concept, object, or idea

C. A computer program

D. A password

3. An edge represents...

A. A document

B. A relationship between nodes

C. A processor

D. A webpage

4. Semantic networks help AI understand...

A. Electricity

B. Word meanings and relationships

C. Battery life

D. Screen resolution

5. Which technology is specifically designed to manage connected information?

A. Spreadsheet

B. Graph Database

C. Calculator

D. Printer

True or False

6. Knowledge graphs organize information into connected networks.

True / False

7. Search engines often use knowledge graphs.

True / False

8. Semantic networks focus on the meanings of concepts.

True / False

9. Future AGI will likely depend on advanced knowledge graphs.

True / False

10. Relationships between ideas are unimportant for intelligence.

True / False

Answer Key

Vocabulary

Answers will vary but should demonstrate understanding.

Worksheet

Part B

1. Relationships connect concepts and allow intelligent reasoning.
2. They organize meanings and contextual relationships among concepts.
3. Traditional databases organize rows and columns, while graph databases organize connected relationships.
4. Possible answers:

- Search engines
- Healthcare
- Education
- Fraud detection
- Cybersecurity
- Recommendation systems
- Scientific research

5. They allow AGI to organize, retrieve, reason, and continuously expand knowledge.

Part C – Matching

A → Represents a concept or object

B → Describes relationships

C → Organizes connected knowledge

D → Focuses on meaning

E → Stores connected information efficiently

Part D

Answers will vary.

Students should demonstrate understanding of nodes, relationships, and knowledge organization.

Part E

Answers will vary.

Quiz Answers

1. **B**
2. **B**
3. **B**
4. **B**
5. **B**
6. **True**
7. **True**
8. **True**
9. **True**
10. **False**

Key Vocabulary

- Knowledge Graph
- Semantic Network
- Node
- Edge
- Relationship
- Graph Database
- Semantic Meaning
- Knowledge Organization
- Connected Intelligence
- Reasoning
- Inference
- Natural Language Processing
- Artificial General Intelligence (AGI)
- Context
- Knowledge Architecture

Chapter Takeaway

Knowledge becomes truly intelligent when ideas are connected. Knowledge graphs and semantic networks transform isolated facts into meaningful relationships, allowing humans and future Artificial General Intelligence systems to reason, learn, communicate, and solve complex problems through interconnected understanding rather than simple memorization.

Learn AI. Understand AI. Shape the Future.

— Susie Hala
IntelliGloss Press

Chapter 6

Memory Systems for Intelligent Machines

Part 1

Memory is one of the defining characteristics of intelligence. Without memory, learning would be impossible because every experience would disappear almost immediately after it occurred. Imagine waking up each morning unable to remember your family, your school, your language, or even your own name. Every conversation would feel like the first conversation you had ever experienced. Every lesson taught in school would have to begin from the very beginning because nothing learned yesterday would remain available today. Under these conditions, knowledge could never accumulate, skills could never improve, and intelligent decision-making would become impossible. Human intelligence depends on memory because memory preserves experiences, organizes knowledge, connects ideas, and allows previous learning to guide future actions. Artificial General Intelligence (AGI) faces the same challenge. If intelligent machines are expected to reason, solve unfamiliar problems, collaborate with humans, and continue learning throughout their operational lives, they must possess memory systems capable of storing, retrieving, updating, and applying knowledge with flexibility and accuracy.

Human memory is often compared to a library, but this comparison only captures a small part of its complexity. A library stores books exactly as they were written, waiting for readers to retrieve them when needed. The human brain, however, continuously reorganizes memories as new experiences occur. Every new lesson becomes connected with previous learning. Every conversation may strengthen or revise existing beliefs. Every problem solved creates additional relationships that influence future reasoning. Memory is therefore not simply a storage system but an active and constantly evolving knowledge architecture. Scientists studying artificial intelligence recognize that future AGI systems will require similar dynamic memory systems capable of growing throughout their lifetimes while maintaining consistency across enormous collections of knowledge.

One of the first types of memory encountered in both biological and artificial systems is **working memory**. Working memory refers to the temporary storage of information needed to perform immediate tasks. Imagine solving a complex mathematics problem. You temporarily remember several numbers while performing calculations, mentally compare different possibilities, and gradually work toward a solution. Once the problem is completed, many of those temporary details disappear because they are no longer needed. Similarly, while reading a paragraph in this textbook, your brain remembers the beginning of each sentence until you reach its conclusion, allowing ideas to connect naturally into meaningful understanding. Working memory acts as the mind's active workspace where reasoning, planning, decision-making, and problem-solving occur.

Working memory has limited capacity, which explains why people sometimes struggle to remember long lists of numbers, multiple instructions given simultaneously, or complicated directions delivered too quickly. Teachers often divide difficult lessons into smaller sections because working memory functions most effectively when information is presented in manageable amounts. This educational principle also influences modern artificial intelligence. Large language models, for example, process information within limited context windows that function somewhat like working memory. Only the information currently available within that context influences immediate reasoning. Future AGI systems will likely require much larger and more flexible working memory architectures capable of managing multiple complex tasks simultaneously while maintaining coherent reasoning across extended conversations and long-term projects.

Closely related to working memory is **short-term memory**, which temporarily stores information for brief periods before it is either forgotten or transferred into long-term memory. Imagine meeting someone new at a conference. You may remember the person's name long enough to continue the conversation, but unless the interaction becomes meaningful or is repeated later, the name may quickly fade from memory. Students experience this phenomenon when preparing for examinations. Facts memorized only the night before an exam often disappear shortly afterward because they never became fully integrated into long-term knowledge. Human brains naturally filter enormous amounts of incoming information, preserving only experiences judged important enough to retain. Without this filtering process, memory would become overwhelmed by countless unimportant details encountered every day.

Artificial intelligence also requires methods for managing temporary information efficiently. An autonomous vehicle continuously receives enormous streams of data from cameras, radar, lidar, GPS receivers, traffic sensors, and weather systems. Much of this information remains useful only for a few seconds before becoming outdated. The vehicle must temporarily store nearby traffic conditions while driving through an intersection but can safely discard those details once the intersection has been crossed. Similar temporary memory systems exist in intelligent manufacturing robots, medical monitoring equipment, financial trading systems, and conversational AI assistants. Efficient short-term memory allows intelligent systems to focus on current tasks without permanently storing every observation they encounter.

The most familiar form of human memory is **long-term memory**, where knowledge, experiences, skills, and personal history are preserved over extended periods. Long-term memory allows people to remember childhood experiences, recognize family members, understand language, recall scientific concepts, and perform complex skills learned years earlier. Unlike working memory, which actively manages information during immediate tasks, long-term memory serves as the foundation upon which intelligence continues growing throughout life. Every subject studied in school contributes to long-term memory. Every language learned, every friendship developed, every skill practiced, and every lesson experienced gradually becomes part of an individual's expanding knowledge system.

Long-term memory demonstrates one of the most remarkable characteristics of human intelligence: cumulative learning. Knowledge acquired years earlier continues supporting future learning because previous experiences remain available whenever needed. A student who mastered multiplication during elementary school can later study algebra, physics, engineering, economics, or computer science because those earlier mathematical concepts remain stored within long-term memory. A physician continues relying on anatomy learned in medical school throughout an entire professional career. An experienced pilot remembers flight procedures developed through thousands of hours of practice. This ability to build increasingly sophisticated knowledge over time distinguishes intelligent learners from systems that simply respond to immediate situations without preserving previous experiences.

Scientists developing AGI recognize that long-term memory must function differently from conventional computer storage. Traditional computer files remain unchanged unless someone deliberately edits them. Human memories, however, become stronger, weaker, or reorganized each time they are recalled. New experiences modify previous understanding by creating additional connections among related concepts. Researchers therefore seek memory architectures capable of continuously reorganizing knowledge rather than simply storing static information. Future AGI systems may automatically strengthen frequently used knowledge, reorganize related concepts into richer networks, and update outdated information whenever new discoveries become available. Such adaptive memory systems would allow intelligent machines to grow continuously rather than remaining fixed after initial training.

Another important characteristic of long-term memory is organization. Human beings rarely retrieve isolated facts independently. Instead, recalling one memory often activates many related memories simultaneously. Hearing the word "ocean" may trigger thoughts about beaches, marine animals, vacations, weather, sailing, environmental conservation, and childhood experiences. This interconnected organization makes memory retrieval remarkably efficient because related knowledge becomes available together. Artificial intelligence researchers increasingly design memory architectures that resemble these interconnected knowledge networks rather than isolated databases. Combining long-term memory with knowledge graphs, semantic networks, and reasoning systems allows intelligent machines to retrieve relevant information more naturally and apply it more effectively to complex problems.

Memory also influences creativity. Creative thinking often occurs when existing knowledge from different domains combines in new and unexpected ways. An inventor may connect engineering principles with biological observations to create innovative technologies inspired by nature. A composer combines musical knowledge with emotional experiences to create original works. Scientists frequently solve difficult problems by recognizing relationships between ideas that previously appeared unrelated. Memory therefore serves not only as a storage system but also as the foundation for imagination, innovation, and discovery. Future AGI systems capable of genuine creativity will likely depend upon memory architectures that support flexible combinations of knowledge across many different disciplines rather than simply retrieving isolated information.

As intelligent systems become increasingly capable, memory will play an even greater role in supporting continuous learning, adaptive reasoning, and collaboration with humans. Working memory enables immediate problem-solving. Short-term memory manages temporary information during ongoing tasks. Long-term memory preserves knowledge accumulated across months, years, or even decades of learning. Together, these memory systems provide the foundation upon which intelligence develops, expands, and evolves. In the next part of this chapter, you will explore **episodic memory**, **semantic memory**, advanced memory architectures for AGI, and how future intelligent machines may develop lifelong learning systems that continually improve through experience while preserving everything they have learned.

(End of Part 1 — Part 2 will continue with Episodic Memory, Semantic Memory, Memory Architectures for AGI, Lifelong Learning, and a powerful chapter conclusion.)

Chapter 6

Memory Systems for Intelligent Machines

Part 2

As scientists have learned more about the human brain, they have discovered that memory is not a single system but a collection of specialized systems working together to support intelligent behavior. Each type of memory performs a unique function while contributing to the brain's remarkable ability to learn, reason, solve problems, and adapt to changing environments. Among the most important forms of long-term memory are **episodic memory** and **semantic memory**. These two memory systems work together continuously, allowing people to remember both personal experiences and general knowledge about the world. Understanding how these systems operate has become one of the most valuable sources of inspiration for researchers attempting to build Artificial General Intelligence (AGI). Future intelligent machines will likely require memory systems that resemble these human capabilities if they are to learn continuously and interact naturally with people.

Episodic memory stores personal experiences that occur at specific times and places. It allows people to remember events they have personally experienced rather than simply recalling facts. You may remember your first day of school, a family vacation, an important graduation ceremony, a memorable science experiment, or a conversation with a close friend. These memories contain more than information; they include context, location, sequence, and often emotions connected to the experience. Episodic memory helps people answer questions such as, "What happened yesterday?" or "Where did I leave my backpack?" It creates the personal history that shapes individual identity and allows people to learn from previous experiences.

One remarkable feature of episodic memory is its ability to connect events across time. Imagine learning to drive a car. Your first lesson may have felt confusing as you attempted to coordinate steering, braking, mirrors, traffic signals, and surrounding vehicles. After many hours of practice, those individual experiences gradually combine into a coherent understanding of safe driving. Each lesson becomes another episode contributing to improved performance. Humans rely on episodic memory whenever they reflect on successes, recognize previous mistakes, or compare current situations with similar experiences from the past. Scientists believe future AGI systems may require similar capabilities so they can remember previous interactions, evaluate completed tasks, and improve future performance based on accumulated experience rather than beginning every task as though it were entirely new.

Unlike episodic memory, **semantic memory** stores general knowledge about the world independent of personal experience. Semantic memory includes vocabulary, mathematical principles, historical facts, scientific theories, geographical information, and countless other concepts learned throughout life. You know that water freezes at zero degrees Celsius, that Earth orbits the Sun, and that plants require sunlight for photosynthesis, even if you cannot remember exactly when or where you first learned these facts. Semantic memory forms the foundation of education because it allows knowledge to accumulate across generations. Every textbook, classroom lesson, encyclopedia, and scientific publication contributes to expanding semantic memory by transferring knowledge from one person to another.

Artificial intelligence systems already demonstrate impressive forms of semantic memory. Large language models are trained using enormous collections of books, articles, websites, scientific publications, and educational resources. Through this training, they develop mathematical representations of language and knowledge that allow them to answer questions, summarize information, generate explanations, and assist with many different tasks. However, today's AI generally lacks true episodic memory because most systems do not naturally remember every interaction they have with users over extended periods. Future AGI systems will likely combine semantic memory with episodic memory, enabling machines to integrate general knowledge with personal experiences accumulated through continuous interaction with the world.

The relationship between episodic and semantic memory demonstrates an important principle of intelligence. Experiences often become general knowledge over time. Consider a child learning that touching a hot stove causes pain. Initially, this lesson exists as a specific episode connected to one personal experience. As the child grows older, repeated experiences gradually produce a broader understanding that hot objects can cause burns and should be handled carefully. Individual experiences therefore contribute to general knowledge, while general knowledge helps interpret future experiences. Human intelligence constantly moves information between these two memory systems, strengthening understanding through continuous learning. Researchers hope future AGI architectures will demonstrate similar abilities by converting repeated experiences into increasingly sophisticated knowledge that supports future reasoning.

Memory systems must also retrieve information efficiently. Storing enormous amounts of knowledge serves little purpose if the correct information cannot be found when needed. Imagine a physician attempting to diagnose a patient while searching randomly through millions of medical records. Even with extensive knowledge available, diagnosis would become slow and unreliable. Human memory solves this problem through association. One idea naturally activates related ideas, allowing people to retrieve relevant knowledge almost instantly. Thinking about "ocean" may trigger memories of beaches, marine animals, weather systems, sailing, and environmental conservation. This associative retrieval allows humans to solve problems rapidly because connected knowledge becomes available together. Artificial intelligence researchers increasingly design memory systems using knowledge graphs, semantic networks, and vector databases that support similar forms of associative retrieval.

Efficient retrieval becomes especially important when intelligent systems perform complex reasoning. Consider an autonomous rescue robot responding to an earthquake. The robot must immediately retrieve knowledge about damaged buildings, structural engineering, medical emergencies, evacuation procedures, navigation, communication, and environmental hazards. Waiting several minutes to search through unrelated information could place lives at risk. Future AGI systems will therefore require highly organized memory architectures capable of rapidly retrieving relevant knowledge while ignoring unnecessary details. Scientists continue developing retrieval algorithms that balance speed, accuracy, and contextual understanding so intelligent machines can respond effectively in dynamic environments.

Another major challenge involves protecting previously learned knowledge while continuing to acquire new information. Humans generally retain important childhood memories even while learning thousands of new concepts throughout adulthood. Artificial intelligence systems, however, sometimes experience a problem known as **catastrophic forgetting**, where learning new tasks causes previously learned information to disappear. Imagine studying French for several years only to completely forget the language after beginning to study Spanish. Most people retain much of their French knowledge while adding Spanish vocabulary over time. Future AGI systems must demonstrate similar lifelong learning abilities by preserving existing knowledge while continuously incorporating new experiences. Solving catastrophic forgetting has therefore become one of the most active areas of research in artificial intelligence.

Scientists believe future AGI systems will require sophisticated **memory architectures** that integrate multiple specialized memory systems into one unified framework. Working memory will manage immediate reasoning tasks. Short-term memory will temporarily store recent observations. Episodic memory will preserve personal experiences. Semantic memory will organize general knowledge. Knowledge graphs will connect related concepts. Retrieval systems will locate relevant information. Reasoning engines will apply memory to solve problems. Together, these components will function as an integrated cognitive architecture rather than independent storage systems. Intelligence emerges because these memory systems cooperate continuously, allowing knowledge to flow naturally among perception, reasoning, planning, decision-making, and learning.

Memory also supports communication between intelligent agents. Imagine several autonomous scientific research systems collaborating to develop treatments for emerging diseases. One system analyzes genetic information, another studies protein structures, a third evaluates clinical trials, while a fourth monitors global health data. Shared memory architectures allow each system to contribute discoveries to a common knowledge base while benefiting from the findings of the others. Instead of working independently, the systems develop collective intelligence through shared memory and continuous knowledge exchange. Similar collaborative memory systems may eventually support smart cities, environmental monitoring, disaster response, education, manufacturing, and space exploration, where solving complex problems requires cooperation among multiple intelligent agents.

The future of AGI depends heavily upon developing memory systems capable of lifelong learning. Unlike today's AI models, which often require complete retraining to incorporate significant new knowledge, future intelligent machines should learn continuously through daily interaction with their environments. Every conversation, experiment, observation, task, and problem solved should become part of an expanding memory system that strengthens future performance. Lifelong learning allows intelligence to grow naturally over time, much like human knowledge develops from childhood through adulthood. Scientists envision AGI systems whose memories become richer, more organized, and more accurate with every new experience rather than remaining largely fixed after initial training.

Ethics also plays an important role in designing memory systems. Intelligent machines capable of remembering conversations, personal preferences, medical histories, educational records, financial information, and daily activities must protect sensitive information responsibly. Future AGI systems will require secure memory architectures that preserve privacy, respect legal protections, prevent unauthorized access, and allow individuals appropriate control over personal information. Responsible memory management will become just as important as technical performance because society must trust intelligent systems before allowing them to participate in healthcare, education, government, business, and everyday life.

Memory is therefore far more than a storage device. It is the foundation that allows intelligence to develop across time. Every lesson learned, every experience remembered, every relationship recognized, and every problem solved contributes to an ever-expanding network of knowledge that supports future reasoning and decision-making. Human intelligence demonstrates that learning is not a single event but a continuous process of remembering, connecting, updating, and applying knowledge throughout life. Artificial General Intelligence seeks to build similar capabilities, enabling machines to preserve valuable experiences while continuously adapting to an ever-changing world.

As you continue exploring the study of knowledge systems, remember that intelligence is measured not by how much information can be stored but by how effectively that information can be remembered, organized, retrieved, and applied. Memory transforms isolated experiences into lifelong understanding. It allows knowledge to accumulate across generations, supports creativity and innovation, strengthens reasoning, and enables intelligent systems to improve with experience. For both humans and future AGI, memory is not simply a record of the past—it is the foundation upon which the future of intelligence is built.

Learn AI. Understand AI. Shape the Future.

— Susie Hala
IntelliGloss Press

Chapter 6 Summary

Memory Systems for Intelligent Machines

Memory is one of the most important foundations of intelligence because it allows knowledge to accumulate over time. Without memory, humans and intelligent machines would have to relearn everything each time they encountered a new situation. Memory preserves experiences, stores knowledge, connects ideas, and allows previous learning to guide future decisions. Artificial General Intelligence (AGI) will require advanced memory systems capable of learning continuously throughout its lifetime.

Human memory consists of several specialized systems that work together. **Working memory** temporarily stores information needed for immediate tasks such as solving problems, reading, or making decisions. **Short-term memory** holds information briefly before it is either forgotten or transferred into long-term memory. These systems help people manage current activities while preventing the brain from becoming overwhelmed with unnecessary information.

Long-term memory stores knowledge, experiences, skills, and important life events over extended periods. It allows people to remember language, mathematics, scientific concepts, personal experiences, and practical skills developed throughout life. Unlike computer storage, human long-term memory continually reorganizes itself by strengthening connections among related ideas.

Long-term memory includes **episodic memory** and **semantic memory**. Episodic memory stores personal experiences that occur at specific times and places, while semantic memory stores general knowledge about the world, including facts, vocabulary, scientific principles, and concepts learned through education. Together, these memory systems allow people to connect personal experiences with general understanding.

Artificial intelligence researchers study these memory systems because future AGI will need similar capabilities. Modern AI already demonstrates forms of semantic memory by learning from enormous collections of data, but future AGI must also develop episodic memory, lifelong learning, efficient retrieval systems, and memory architectures capable of continuously updating knowledge without forgetting previous learning.

Scientists are also working to solve challenges such as catastrophic forgetting, where AI loses previously learned knowledge while learning new tasks. Future memory architectures may integrate working memory, episodic memory, semantic memory, knowledge graphs, retrieval systems, and reasoning engines into unified cognitive systems that more closely resemble human learning.

Memory is much more than storage. It is the foundation that supports learning, reasoning, creativity, adaptation, and intelligent decision-making. As AGI continues to evolve, advanced memory systems will become one of its most essential components.

Reflection

Think about everything you have learned since you were born. You remember your family, your friends, your language, your education, and many important life experiences. Every new lesson builds upon knowledge you already possess because memory allows learning to continue throughout your lifetime.

Memory also helps you solve problems. When faced with a new challenge, your brain automatically searches previous experiences for similar situations. You use what you have learned before to make better decisions today. This ability makes humans lifelong learners.

Artificial intelligence is moving toward similar capabilities. Today's AI can store enormous amounts of information, but future AGI must learn continuously without forgetting previous knowledge. It must remember conversations, apply earlier experiences to new situations, and organize knowledge into systems that become stronger over time.

As technology continues advancing, understanding how memory works will help you appreciate both the incredible abilities of the human brain and the challenges scientists face while building intelligent machines. Every lesson you learn today becomes part of the knowledge that will help shape your future decisions tomorrow.

Student Worksheet

Name: ______________________________________

Date: _______________________________________

Part A – Vocabulary

Define each term using your own words.

1. Working Memory

____

2. Short-Term Memory

____

3. Long-Term Memory

____

4. Episodic Memory

____

5. Semantic Memory

____

6. Lifelong Learning

____

7. Catastrophic Forgetting

____

Part B – Short Answer

1. Why is memory essential for intelligence?

____
____

2. Explain the difference between working memory and long-term memory.

____
____

3. How does episodic memory differ from semantic memory?

____
____

4. Why is efficient memory retrieval important for AGI?

____
____

5. What is catastrophic forgetting, and why is it a challenge for AI?

____
____
____

Part C – Matching

Letter	Memory Type	Number
A	Working Memory	___ Stores personal experiences

Letter	Memory Type		Number
B	Short-Term Memory	___	Temporary problem-solving workspace
C	Long-Term Memory	___	Stores knowledge over many years
D	Episodic Memory	___	Holds information briefly
E	Semantic Memory	___	Stores facts and concepts

Part D – Critical Thinking

Imagine you are designing the memory system for an AGI assistant that works in a hospital.

Describe how the assistant would use:

Working Memory

____

Long-Term Memory

____

Episodic Memory

____

Semantic Memory

____

Why would combining all four memory systems improve patient care?

____

____

____

Part E – Personal Connection

Think about learning to ride a bicycle, play an instrument, participate in a sport, cook, or develop another skill.

Describe how each memory system helped you learn.

Working Memory

____

Long-Term Memory

Experience (Episodic Memory)

Knowledge (Semantic Memory)

Chapter 6 Quiz

Multiple Choice

1. Which memory system temporarily stores information needed for immediate tasks?

A. Long-Term Memory

B. Working Memory

C. Episodic Memory

D. Semantic Memory

2. Which memory stores personal experiences?

A. Semantic Memory

B. Working Memory

C. Episodic Memory

D. Graph Memory

3. Semantic memory stores...

A. Personal memories only

B. Facts, concepts, and general knowledge

C. Temporary information

D. Computer programs

4. Catastrophic forgetting refers to...

A. Forgetting your homework

B. AI losing previous knowledge while learning new information

C. Computer shutdowns

D. Memory chip failure

5. Future AGI memory systems should...

A. Never learn new information

B. Continuously learn while preserving previous knowledge

C. Store only recent information

D. Replace all human memory

True or False

6. Long-term memory stores knowledge accumulated throughout life.

True / False

7. Working memory acts like the brain's active workspace.

True / False

8. Human memory remains completely unchanged after experiences occur.

True / False

9. Future AGI will likely require multiple memory systems working together.

True / False

10. Memory plays no role in creativity or reasoning.

True / False

Answer Key

Vocabulary

Answers will vary but should demonstrate accurate understanding.

Worksheet

Part B

1. Memory allows knowledge to accumulate, supports learning, reasoning, and decision-making.
2. Working memory manages immediate tasks, while long-term memory stores knowledge and experiences over long periods.
3. Episodic memory stores personal experiences; semantic memory stores general facts and concepts.
4. Efficient retrieval allows intelligent systems to quickly locate relevant knowledge when solving problems.
5. Catastrophic forgetting occurs when AI loses previously learned information while learning new tasks.

Part C – Matching

A → Temporary problem-solving workspace

B → Holds information briefly

C → Stores knowledge over many years

D → Stores personal experiences

E → Stores facts and concepts

Part D

Answers will vary but should demonstrate understanding of the different memory systems and their roles.

Part E

Answers will vary based on each student's personal learning experience.

Quiz Answers

1. **B**
2. **C**
3. **B**
4. **B**
5. **B**
6. **True**
7. **True**
8. **False**
9. **True**
10. **False**

Key Vocabulary

- Memory
- Working Memory
- Short-Term Memory
- Long-Term Memory
- Episodic Memory
- Semantic Memory

- Memory Retrieval
- Lifelong Learning
- Catastrophic Forgetting
- Knowledge Architecture
- Cognitive Architecture
- Artificial General Intelligence (AGI)
- Continuous Learning
- Reasoning
- Memory Systems

Chapter Takeaway

Memory is the foundation of learning and intelligence. By preserving experiences, organizing knowledge, retrieving information, and supporting continuous learning, memory allows both humans and future Artificial General Intelligence systems to grow, adapt, reason, and make increasingly intelligent decisions throughout their lifetimes.

Learn AI. Understand AI. Shape the Future.

— Susie Hala
IntelliGloss Press

Chapter 7

Knowledge Storage and Retrieval

Part 1

Imagine trying to find a single book inside the world's largest library if every book had been placed randomly on the floor with no shelves, labels, catalog, or organizational system. Although the information would still exist, locating the right book at the right moment would be nearly impossible. The same challenge exists for both humans and intelligent machines. Collecting enormous amounts of knowledge has little value unless that knowledge can be stored efficiently and retrieved whenever it is needed. Intelligence depends not only on learning new information but also on remembering where knowledge is stored, recognizing when it is relevant, and accessing it quickly enough to solve problems. Artificial General Intelligence (AGI) will require knowledge systems capable of storing billions of interconnected concepts while retrieving the most appropriate information within fractions of a second. The science of knowledge storage and retrieval therefore represents one of the most important foundations of future intelligent systems.

Throughout human history, societies have continually developed better methods for preserving knowledge. Ancient civilizations carved important information into stone tablets, painted symbols on cave walls, and later recorded ideas on papyrus, parchment, and paper. Libraries organized books into carefully arranged collections so scholars could locate information efficiently. The invention of computers transformed knowledge storage once again by allowing enormous quantities of information to be stored electronically. Today, cloud computing, distributed databases, and digital archives preserve knowledge on a scale unimaginable only a few decades ago. Yet despite these technological advances, the underlying challenge remains the same: knowledge is only valuable when it can be found and used at the moment it is needed. Artificial intelligence faces this identical challenge, except on a scale involving trillions of relationships among concepts rather than millions of printed pages.

One of the primary tools used to organize digital knowledge is the **database**. A database is an organized collection of information designed to store, manage, and retrieve data efficiently. Unlike a simple folder of documents, a database organizes information according to carefully designed structures that allow computers to locate specific records almost instantly. Schools use databases to store student records, attendance, grades, schedules, and enrollment information. Hospitals maintain databases containing medical histories, laboratory results, prescriptions, and treatment plans. Banks organize financial transactions within secure databases that support millions of customers every day. Businesses, governments, scientific laboratories, and educational institutions all rely on databases because they provide fast, reliable access to enormous amounts of organized information.

Traditional databases are especially effective when information follows consistent structures. Imagine a school maintaining a student database. Each student record contains similar categories such as name, student identification number, grade level, courses, attendance, and contact information. Because every record follows the same format, computers can quickly search for students, calculate averages, generate reports, and organize information according to many different criteria. These structured databases have served organizations successfully for decades and remain essential components of modern information systems. However, Artificial General Intelligence requires knowledge storage that extends beyond simple rows and columns because intelligent reasoning depends on understanding complex relationships among ideas rather than merely retrieving individual records.

Human knowledge rarely exists in perfectly organized tables. Consider the concept of "climate change." This single topic connects to atmospheric science, chemistry, biology, economics, engineering, politics, agriculture, renewable energy, international policy, environmental conservation, and countless other fields. These relationships cannot easily be represented within a traditional database without becoming extremely complicated. Future AGI systems therefore require more flexible storage methods capable of representing concepts that connect naturally across many different domains. Instead of treating knowledge as isolated records, intelligent systems increasingly organize information into interconnected structures that support reasoning, inference, and continuous learning.

One of the most important developments supporting modern artificial intelligence is **vector storage**. Unlike traditional databases that organize information according to fixed categories, vector storage represents knowledge mathematically using high-dimensional numerical representations called **vectors**. Although the mathematics behind vectors is highly sophisticated, the basic idea is surprisingly intuitive. Instead of remembering only exact words or phrases, vector storage captures the meaning behind concepts. Words, sentences, documents, images, sounds, and even videos can all be converted into mathematical representations that preserve their semantic relationships. Concepts with similar meanings become located near one another within a multidimensional mathematical space, allowing AI systems to retrieve information based on meaning rather than exact wording.

Imagine asking two students to explain the water cycle. One student writes, "Water evaporates into the atmosphere and later falls as rain." Another writes, "The Sun heats water, creating vapor that eventually returns to Earth through precipitation." Although the wording differs significantly, both students describe the same scientific process. Traditional keyword searches might treat these answers as different because they contain different vocabulary. Vector storage, however, recognizes that both descriptions share similar meanings. By representing knowledge mathematically according to semantic relationships rather than exact words, intelligent systems retrieve information more naturally, much like humans recognize similar ideas even when expressed differently.

This ability becomes especially important as knowledge continues expanding across multiple languages, scientific disciplines, and communication styles. Human beings rarely ask questions using exactly the same words found in textbooks. A student might ask, "How do plants make food?" while a biology textbook discusses "photosynthesis." A physician may describe a medical condition using technical terminology while a patient explains the same symptoms using everyday language. Modern AI systems rely on vector storage to bridge these differences by recognizing conceptual similarity rather than depending upon identical vocabulary. As a result, intelligent systems provide more accurate answers because they search for meaning instead of merely matching keywords.

Vector storage has transformed many technologies people use every day. Search engines increasingly rely on semantic retrieval rather than simple keyword matching. Recommendation systems identify books, movies, songs, and educational resources based on conceptual similarity rather than identical descriptions. Digital assistants interpret spoken questions despite differences in wording, accents, or sentence structure. Scientists searching research literature can locate relevant discoveries even when different authors use different terminology. These advances demonstrate how representing knowledge according to meaning significantly improves the ability of intelligent systems to retrieve useful information.

Knowledge storage alone, however, does not produce intelligence. Equally important is the ability to retrieve the right information at precisely the right moment. This process is known as **retrieval**, and it represents one of the defining characteristics of intelligent reasoning. Human beings constantly retrieve relevant knowledge without consciously thinking about the process. A teacher answering a student's question immediately recalls previous lessons, educational principles, and classroom experiences. A physician evaluating symptoms retrieves medical knowledge developed through years of education and clinical practice. An experienced engineer recalls mathematical principles, design standards, and previous projects while solving technical problems. These examples demonstrate that intelligence depends as much upon retrieval as it does upon storage.

Modern AI systems increasingly rely on specialized **retrieval systems** that search enormous knowledge collections before generating responses. Rather than depending entirely on information learned during initial training, retrieval systems locate relevant documents, research papers, databases, or knowledge graphs whenever new questions arise. This approach allows AI to incorporate current information, reduce errors, and provide more reliable answers because it supplements learned knowledge with retrieved evidence. Future AGI systems will likely combine lifelong memory with advanced retrieval architectures that continuously search, evaluate, compare, and integrate knowledge from multiple sources before making decisions.

An effective retrieval system must balance both speed and accuracy. Retrieving irrelevant information wastes valuable computational resources, while overlooking important knowledge may produce incorrect conclusions. Human brains solve this problem through association. Thinking about one concept naturally activates related memories that may become useful during reasoning. Scientists developing AGI seek similar capabilities by designing retrieval algorithms that identify the most relevant information based on context, semantic similarity, previous experiences, and current goals rather than simply searching for matching words. These intelligent retrieval strategies will become increasingly important as future AGI systems manage knowledge collections containing trillions of interconnected concepts.

Knowledge storage and retrieval therefore function together as complementary components of intelligence. Storage preserves information, while retrieval transforms stored knowledge into useful understanding by making it available precisely when needed. In the next part of this chapter, you will explore how intelligent systems perform advanced searches, manage context across long conversations and complex tasks, develop efficient recall strategies, and build retrieval architectures capable of supporting lifelong learning and Artificial General Intelligence.

(End of Part 1 — Part 2 will continue with Search Mechanisms, Context Management, Efficient Recall Strategies, Retrieval-Augmented Intelligence, and a powerful chapter conclusion.)

Chapter 7

Knowledge Storage and Retrieval

Part 2

As knowledge collections continue expanding, intelligent systems must do far more than simply retrieve information quickly. They must retrieve the **right** information at the **right time** and within the **right context**. Human intelligence demonstrates this ability constantly. A physician does not recall every medical fact ever learned while examining a patient. Instead, the brain automatically retrieves the knowledge most relevant to the patient's symptoms, medical history, age, medications, and current condition. Likewise, a teacher explaining fractions to elementary students selects examples appropriate for their age rather than presenting advanced university mathematics. This remarkable ability to retrieve knowledge selectively allows humans to think efficiently instead of becoming overwhelmed by everything they know. Artificial General Intelligence (AGI) must develop similar capabilities so it can identify the most relevant knowledge while ignoring information that is unrelated to the current task.

This process depends heavily on **search mechanisms**. Search mechanisms are the methods intelligent systems use to locate information within their knowledge stores. Early computer search systems relied primarily on exact keyword matching. If a person searched for the word "automobile," the system would return documents containing that exact word while overlooking documents that used terms such as "car," "vehicle," or "electric transportation." Although this approach worked reasonably well for simple databases, it often failed when people expressed ideas using different vocabulary. Human communication is naturally flexible because the same idea can be described in many different ways. Future AGI systems therefore require search mechanisms that understand meaning rather than simply matching individual words.

Modern artificial intelligence has made enormous progress by developing **semantic search**, a method that retrieves information based on meaning rather than exact language. Instead of asking whether two sentences contain identical words, semantic search asks whether they communicate similar ideas. Imagine two students researching renewable energy. One searches for "solar power," while another searches for "electricity generated from sunlight." Although the wording differs, both students seek the same knowledge. Semantic search recognizes this conceptual similarity because it examines relationships among ideas rather than focusing solely on vocabulary. This capability allows intelligent systems to locate more accurate and relevant information while reducing the limitations of traditional keyword searches.

Semantic search also improves communication between humans and AI because people rarely ask questions in identical ways. One person may ask, "How do airplanes stay in the air?" while another asks, "What creates lift during flight?" A third might simply ask, "Why don't airplanes fall?" Although these questions use different words, they all seek knowledge about the same scientific principles. Intelligent retrieval systems recognize these similarities and retrieve information explaining aerodynamics, lift, thrust, drag, and gravity regardless of the specific wording used by the individual. This flexibility makes AI systems more useful because they respond to meaning instead of memorized phrases.

As retrieval systems become more sophisticated, they must also manage **context** effectively. Context refers to the surrounding information that gives meaning to ideas, conversations, and decisions. Human beings depend on context throughout daily life. Consider the simple word "cell." In a biology classroom, it refers to the basic unit of life. During a discussion about prisons, it refers to a jail cell. In conversations about smartphones, it often refers to cellular communication technology. The correct meaning depends entirely upon context. Human brains identify these differences almost instantly because previous knowledge, surrounding words, and current situations provide additional information. Artificial intelligence must develop similar contextual understanding to communicate naturally and reason accurately.

Context management becomes especially important during extended conversations. Imagine asking an AI assistant to help plan a science fair project. During the conversation, you discuss renewable energy, select solar panels as your topic, ask about electricity generation, request help creating graphs, and later ask, "Can you explain how it works?" A well-designed retrieval system understands that "it" refers to the solar panel discussed earlier rather than another unrelated topic. Maintaining this contextual awareness requires sophisticated memory systems capable of tracking previous conversations, identifying relevant details, and retrieving information that supports the ongoing discussion. Future AGI systems will likely manage context across conversations lasting hours, days, or even years while preserving continuity and personal relevance.

Context management also allows intelligent systems to personalize their responses. Consider two students asking the same question about fractions. One student is in third grade, while the other is studying advanced engineering. Although the question may be identical, the most appropriate explanation differs significantly depending on each student's background knowledge. Effective retrieval systems consider the learner's age, educational level, previous lessons, and learning goals before selecting information. This ability to adapt knowledge retrieval according to individual needs represents one of the most promising applications of AGI in education because it supports personalized instruction rather than one-size-fits-all teaching.

Another important aspect of intelligent retrieval involves **efficient recall strategies**. Human memory does not search randomly through every stored experience whenever a question arises. Instead, related ideas automatically activate one another through associations developed over years of learning. Hearing the word "forest" may immediately trigger memories of trees, wildlife, ecosystems, hiking, conservation, seasons, and climate. These associations reduce the time required to locate relevant knowledge because the brain follows well-established connections among related concepts. Artificial intelligence researchers seek to replicate similar recall strategies by organizing knowledge into semantic networks, knowledge graphs, vector databases, and associative memory systems that retrieve information through meaningful relationships rather than exhaustive searches.

Efficient recall also depends on prioritization. Not every memory deserves equal attention. A physician treating a patient with chest pain immediately recalls knowledge about the cardiovascular system rather than information about ancient civilizations. An engineer designing a bridge retrieves principles of physics, structural mechanics, and materials science rather than recipes for baking bread. Human intelligence automatically prioritizes knowledge according to current goals, allowing decision-making to remain focused and efficient. Future AGI systems must demonstrate similar prioritization by evaluating relevance, confidence, urgency, and contextual importance before selecting which knowledge to retrieve.

Modern AI increasingly combines retrieval systems with language models through approaches often called **retrieval-augmented intelligence**. Instead of relying solely on knowledge acquired during initial training, these systems search external knowledge sources while generating responses. Imagine a scientist asking about a newly discovered exoplanet announced only yesterday. A language model trained months earlier may not possess this information. However, a retrieval-augmented system can search current scientific databases, retrieve the latest research, evaluate reliable sources, and incorporate updated information into its response. This combination allows AI to remain current without requiring complete retraining whenever new discoveries occur. Researchers believe retrieval-augmented architectures will play a major role in future AGI because they combine long-term learning with continuous access to expanding knowledge.

Retrieval systems also help reduce one of the most widely discussed challenges in artificial intelligence: incorrect or unsupported responses. When AI generates answers based solely on statistical patterns learned during training, it may occasionally produce inaccurate information. Retrieval systems improve reliability by locating supporting evidence from trusted sources before generating responses. Much like a student consulting textbooks while writing a research paper, intelligent systems verify information through retrieval before presenting conclusions. This evidence-based approach becomes especially important in fields such as healthcare, law, engineering, scientific research, and education, where accurate information directly influences important decisions.

Future AGI systems will likely integrate knowledge storage, retrieval, reasoning, planning, and learning into unified cognitive architectures. Storage preserves information across years of experience. Retrieval identifies the most relevant knowledge for current tasks. Context management ensures information remains meaningful within ongoing conversations and situations. Reasoning combines retrieved knowledge to solve unfamiliar problems. Learning updates memory based on new discoveries and experiences. Rather than functioning as separate technologies, these components cooperate continuously, allowing intelligent systems to think, adapt, and improve throughout their operational lifetimes.

Researchers also envision retrieval systems that extend beyond digital information into physical experiences. Imagine an autonomous household robot that remembers where kitchen utensils are stored, recalls family preferences, recognizes previous maintenance issues with household appliances, and learns daily routines over many years. Instead of retrieving only documents from databases, the robot retrieves experiences accumulated through continuous interaction with its environment. These experiential retrieval systems move AI closer to the way humans remember previous events and apply those memories to future situations. Such capabilities may eventually become essential for AGI systems designed to work alongside people in homes, hospitals, schools, factories, and scientific laboratories.

Knowledge storage and retrieval also play a critical role in collaboration among intelligent agents. Imagine multiple AI systems managing a modern hospital. One system monitors patient vital signs, another schedules operating rooms, another analyzes laboratory results, while another manages pharmaceutical inventories. Each system retrieves specialized knowledge while contributing new information to shared knowledge repositories. Together, they form an integrated intelligence capable of responding more effectively than any individual system working alone. Similar collaborative retrieval architectures may support smart cities, environmental monitoring, disaster response, manufacturing, agriculture, transportation, and space exploration, where complex challenges require knowledge drawn from many different domains simultaneously.

As Artificial General Intelligence continues developing, the ability to store and retrieve knowledge efficiently will become one of its defining characteristics. Intelligence is not measured by how much information a system possesses but by how effectively it accesses the knowledge needed to solve problems, make decisions, and adapt to changing circumstances. Human civilization has advanced because each generation preserved knowledge while developing better methods for retrieving and expanding it. Future AGI systems will continue this tradition by organizing human knowledge into increasingly sophisticated architectures that support lifelong learning, intelligent reasoning, and responsible decision-making.

The study of knowledge storage and retrieval reminds us that intelligence depends not only on learning new information but also on remembering where that information resides and knowing precisely when to use it. Every conversation, scientific discovery, educational lesson, engineering breakthrough, and personal experience contributes to humanity's growing knowledge. By building storage and retrieval systems capable of organizing and accessing this expanding foundation of understanding, Artificial General Intelligence moves one step closer to becoming a lifelong learner capable of supporting human progress for generations to come.

Learn AI. Understand AI. Shape the Future.

— Susie Hala
IntelliGloss Press

Chapter 7 Summary

Knowledge Storage and Retrieval

Knowledge is only valuable if it can be stored efficiently and retrieved when it is needed. Human intelligence depends on remembering previous experiences, locating relevant information, and applying that knowledge to solve problems. Artificial General Intelligence (AGI) faces the same challenge. Future intelligent systems must organize enormous amounts of knowledge while retrieving the most useful information quickly, accurately, and within the appropriate context.

One of the primary tools for organizing digital knowledge is the **database**. Databases store information in structured formats that allow computers to retrieve records efficiently. Schools, hospitals, businesses, banks, governments, and research organizations all rely on databases to organize large amounts of information. However, traditional databases are limited when representing the complex relationships that exist among ideas, making more advanced storage methods necessary for AGI.

Modern AI increasingly uses **vector storage** to organize knowledge based on meaning rather than exact words. Information is converted into mathematical representations called vectors, allowing intelligent systems to recognize similar concepts even when different vocabulary is used. This approach improves semantic search, recommendation systems, language understanding, and information retrieval because AI searches for meaning instead of simple keyword matches.

Retrieval systems allow intelligent machines to locate relevant information from enormous knowledge collections. Instead of relying only on information learned during training, retrieval systems search databases, knowledge graphs, documents, and other knowledge sources to support more accurate reasoning. Semantic search further improves retrieval by identifying concepts with similar meanings rather than searching for identical words.

Context management is another essential component of intelligent retrieval. Human understanding depends heavily on context because words and ideas often have multiple meanings. Future AGI systems must remember previous conversations, understand ongoing situations, and retrieve knowledge that fits the current task rather than providing unrelated information.

Efficient recall strategies help intelligent systems retrieve important knowledge without searching through everything they know. Like the human brain, future AGI will likely organize information into interconnected networks that automatically activate related concepts during reasoning. Retrieval-augmented intelligence further enhances AI by combining learned knowledge with current external information, improving accuracy and allowing intelligent systems to remain up to date.

Knowledge storage and retrieval work together to support learning, reasoning, planning, and decision-making. As AGI develops, these systems will become increasingly sophisticated, allowing intelligent machines to organize, retrieve, update, and apply knowledge in ways that more closely resemble human intelligence.

Reflection

Every day you retrieve knowledge without realizing it. You remember your family's names, solve math problems using concepts learned years ago, recognize familiar faces, understand conversations, and apply previous experiences when making decisions. Your brain constantly searches its own knowledge system, retrieving exactly the information needed for each situation.

Artificial intelligence must learn to do something very similar. Simply storing billions of facts does not create intelligence. Intelligent systems must know where information is stored, recognize when it is relevant, retrieve it efficiently, and apply it correctly. This ability will become one of the defining characteristics of Artificial General Intelligence.

As technology advances, knowledge storage and retrieval will influence nearly every field, including education, healthcare, transportation, finance, engineering, and scientific research. Understanding how these systems work helps us appreciate both the remarkable abilities of the human brain and the exciting possibilities of future AI.

As you continue learning, remember that education is not about memorizing the greatest number of facts. It is about organizing knowledge, building meaningful connections, and developing the ability to retrieve and apply what you know whenever new challenges arise.

Student Worksheet

Name: ____

Date: ____

Part A – Vocabulary

Define each term in your own words.

1. Database

____

2. Vector Storage

____

3. Retrieval System

____

4. Semantic Search

____

5. Context Management

____

6. Efficient Recall

____

7. Retrieval-Augmented Intelligence

____

____

Part B – Short Answer

1. Why is knowledge retrieval just as important as knowledge storage?

___

___

2. Explain how vector storage differs from traditional databases.

___

___

3. Why is semantic search often more effective than keyword search?

___

___

4. What role does context play in intelligent retrieval?

___

___

5. How can retrieval systems improve the accuracy of future AGI?

___

___

___

Part C – Matching

Letter	Term	Number
A	Database	___ Organizes information using structured records
B	Vector Storage	___ Represents meaning mathematically
C	Retrieval System	___ Finds relevant information
D	Semantic Search	___ Searches by meaning
E	Context Management	___ Uses surrounding information to interpret meaning

Part D – Critical Thinking

Imagine you are designing an AGI assistant for a large university.

Describe how it would use:

Databases

Vector Storage

Retrieval Systems

Context Management

Efficient Recall

How would these systems improve learning for students?

Part E – Real-World Application

Think about how you prepare for an important test.

Describe how you use:

- Memory

- Retrieval

- Context

- Recall

How could AI perform these same tasks differently?

Chapter 7 Quiz

Multiple Choice

1. Why is knowledge retrieval important?

A. It helps intelligent systems find and use the right information.

B. It deletes old information.

C. It slows down computers.

D. It replaces memory.

2. Traditional databases organize information using...

A. Rows and structured records

B. Brain cells

C. Paintings

D. Handwritten notes

3. Vector storage represents information based on...

A. File size

B. Meaning and semantic similarity

C. Alphabetical order

D. Memory location

4. Semantic search improves retrieval by...

A. Searching only for identical words

B. Searching for similar meanings and concepts

C. Ignoring relationships

D. Eliminating databases

5. Context management allows AI to...

A. Forget previous conversations

B. Understand information based on surrounding details

C. Store less information

D. Stop learning

True or False

6. Knowledge storage alone is enough to create intelligence.

True / False

7. Vector storage helps AI recognize similar ideas expressed with different words.

True / False

8. Human intelligence constantly retrieves relevant knowledge from memory.

True / False

9. Future AGI will likely combine storage, retrieval, reasoning, and learning into unified systems.

True / False

10. Retrieval-augmented intelligence can improve the accuracy of AI responses.

True / False

Answer Key

Vocabulary

Answers will vary but should demonstrate accurate understanding.

Worksheet

Part B

1. Because knowledge must be available at the right time to solve problems and make decisions.
2. Traditional databases store structured records, while vector storage organizes information by meaning using mathematical representations.
3. Semantic search retrieves information based on concepts rather than identical keywords.
4. Context helps determine the correct meaning of words and ideas within conversations or situations.
5. Retrieval systems locate relevant information, reduce errors, incorporate current knowledge, and improve decision-making.

Part C – Matching

A → Organizes information using structured records

B → Represents meaning mathematically

C → Finds relevant information

D → Searches by meaning

E → Uses surrounding information to interpret meaning

Part D

Answers will vary but should demonstrate understanding of knowledge organization and retrieval.

Part E

Answers will vary based on each student's learning experiences.

Quiz Answers

1. **A**
2. **A**
3. **B**
4. **B**
5. **B**
6. **False**
7. **True**
8. **True**
9. **True**
10. **True**

Key Vocabulary

- Database
- Vector Storage
- Retrieval System
- Semantic Search
- Context
- Context Management
- Efficient Recall
- Knowledge Storage
- Knowledge Retrieval
- Retrieval-Augmented Intelligence
- Semantic Similarity
- Artificial General Intelligence (AGI)
- Knowledge Architecture
- Lifelong Learning

- Intelligent Reasoning

Chapter Takeaway

Intelligence depends not only on acquiring knowledge but also on organizing, retrieving, and applying that knowledge at the right moment. Future Artificial General Intelligence will rely on advanced storage and retrieval systems that understand meaning, manage context, and continuously learn from new experiences, allowing machines to think more efficiently and work more effectively alongside humans.

Learn AI. Understand AI. Shape the Future.

— Susie Hala
IntelliGloss Press

Chapter 8

Learning New Knowledge

Part 1

Learning is the process that transforms information into intelligence. Every person begins life knowing very little about the world, yet over time acquires language, mathematics, science, social skills, and countless other forms of knowledge through continuous learning. A newborn cannot recognize letters, solve equations, or understand history, but through observation, experience, education, and practice, the human brain gradually builds an extraordinary understanding of the world. This lifelong ability to acquire new knowledge is one of the defining characteristics of human intelligence. Artificial General Intelligence (AGI) must possess a similar capability. Instead of relying only on information provided during its initial training, AGI must continually expand its knowledge, adapt to new situations, revise previous understanding, and improve throughout its operational lifetime. Learning therefore becomes one of the most essential building blocks of intelligent behavior because an intelligent system that cannot learn eventually becomes outdated in a constantly changing world.

Human learning occurs in many different ways. Children learn by observing parents and teachers, practicing new skills, asking questions, making mistakes, and exploring unfamiliar environments. Students attend school to study subjects that generations of scholars have developed over centuries. Professionals continue learning throughout their careers as technology, scientific discoveries, and workplace practices evolve. Even older adults continue acquiring new knowledge through reading, travel, hobbies, and everyday experiences. Human intelligence is never completely finished because every new experience has the potential to strengthen, modify, or expand existing understanding. Researchers developing AGI believe that future intelligent systems must demonstrate this same lifelong curiosity and adaptability if they are to function successfully alongside humans.

One of the most common methods used by both humans and artificial intelligence is **supervised learning**. In supervised learning, an intelligent system learns by studying examples that already contain correct answers. Imagine a teacher introducing students to multiplication. The teacher explains the rules, demonstrates several examples, and provides practice problems along with the correct solutions. As students compare their answers with the correct answers, they gradually recognize patterns and improve their understanding. Artificial intelligence follows a remarkably similar process. During supervised learning, developers provide enormous collections of labeled examples. A computer vision system may receive millions of photographs already labeled as dogs, cats, birds, airplanes, bicycles, or trees. By analyzing these labeled examples repeatedly, the AI gradually learns to recognize similar objects in new images it has never seen before.

Supervised learning has become one of the most successful approaches in modern artificial intelligence because it provides clear feedback. Every correct answer helps strengthen useful patterns, while every mistake allows the learning system to make adjustments. This feedback process resembles the way students improve through homework assignments, quizzes, classroom discussions, and teacher guidance. Over time, both humans and AI become more accurate because repeated practice gradually reduces errors. Many familiar AI technologies—including handwriting recognition, speech recognition, medical image analysis, language translation, and facial recognition—depend heavily on supervised learning because large collections of labeled training examples allow computers to achieve impressive performance across many specialized tasks.

Although supervised learning is extremely powerful, much of the world's information does not come with correct answers already attached. Human beings frequently encounter completely unfamiliar situations where no teacher provides immediate guidance. Imagine visiting a country whose language you have never studied. You begin noticing patterns in conversations, road signs, menus, and daily interactions long before anyone formally explains the language. Children also learn many aspects of the world simply by observing how objects behave, how people communicate, and how different events unfold naturally. Artificial intelligence addresses these situations through **unsupervised learning**, a process in which intelligent systems search for patterns within data without receiving predefined answers.

Unsupervised learning allows AI to discover hidden structures that humans may not immediately recognize. Consider a large collection of books stored in a digital library without labels identifying their subjects. An unsupervised learning system might automatically group books about astronomy, biology, history, engineering, economics, and literature according to similarities found within their contents. Likewise, scientists analyzing genetic information may use unsupervised learning to identify previously unknown relationships among genes associated with particular diseases. Businesses use these techniques to understand customer behavior, while astronomers analyze enormous collections of telescope observations searching for unusual cosmic phenomena. Rather than being told exactly what to find, unsupervised learning explores data independently, discovering meaningful patterns that support future understanding.

Human curiosity demonstrates a similar process. Children naturally sort toys into groups, recognize similarities among animals, identify repeating mathematical patterns, and classify objects according to color, shape, or function without formal instruction. The brain continuously searches for order within the surrounding environment because recognizing patterns makes future learning more efficient. Scientists believe this natural pattern-seeking behavior plays a major role in human intelligence and provides valuable guidance for developing AGI systems capable of discovering knowledge independently rather than relying solely on human instruction.

Another important learning method is **reinforcement learning**, which teaches intelligent systems through rewards and consequences rather than direct instruction. Imagine teaching a puppy to sit. Each time the puppy performs the correct behavior, it receives praise or a treat. Incorrect behavior receives little or no reward. Over time, the puppy gradually learns which actions produce positive outcomes. Human learning often follows similar principles. Students receive grades recognizing successful work. Athletes improve by adjusting techniques based on performance. Video game players develop better strategies after experiencing both victories and defeats. Every action generates feedback that influences future decisions.

Artificial intelligence uses reinforcement learning to solve many complex problems where correct answers cannot simply be memorized. Autonomous robots learn how to walk more efficiently by gradually improving their movements after thousands of attempts. Computer programs master strategy games by playing millions of matches against themselves, learning which decisions increase the likelihood of success. Self-driving vehicles improve navigation by evaluating safe driving behaviors under countless simulated conditions. Rather than following fixed instructions, reinforcement learning allows intelligent systems to experiment, evaluate outcomes, and continuously improve performance through experience.

One of the greatest strengths of reinforcement learning is its ability to prepare intelligent systems for unfamiliar situations. Instead of memorizing one correct solution, the system learns general strategies that remain useful even when circumstances change. Imagine teaching a rescue robot to navigate disaster zones. Every emergency presents different obstacles, damaged buildings, weather conditions, and hazards. Reinforcement learning encourages the robot to develop flexible problem-solving strategies rather than relying upon one fixed route or procedure. Scientists believe this adaptability will become increasingly important as AGI systems begin operating within complex real-world environments that cannot be completely predicted in advance.

Despite their differences, supervised learning, unsupervised learning, and reinforcement learning share a common goal: helping intelligent systems improve through experience. Human intelligence naturally combines all three approaches throughout daily life. Teachers provide supervised instruction in classrooms. Observation supports unsupervised discovery. Successes and mistakes reinforce future behavior. Rather than depending upon one learning method alone, the brain integrates multiple forms of learning into a unified cognitive system capable of adapting to an ever-changing world.

Future Artificial General Intelligence will almost certainly follow this same principle. Instead of specializing in only one learning strategy, AGI will likely combine supervised learning, unsupervised learning, reinforcement learning, memory systems, reasoning, perception, and knowledge representation into integrated architectures that support continuous growth. In the next part of this chapter, you will explore **self-directed learning**, **continuous learning**, **lifelong learning systems**, and how future AGI may become increasingly capable of educating itself through experience, curiosity, and autonomous discovery.

(End of Part 1 — Part 2 will continue with Self-Directed Learning, Continuous Learning, Lifelong Learning Systems, Autonomous Knowledge Growth, and a powerful chapter conclusion.)

Chapter 8

Learning New Knowledge

Part 2

As intelligent systems become more advanced, learning must extend far beyond responding to examples or rewards. Human beings do not wait for someone else to provide every lesson they will ever need. Instead, they actively seek new information, ask questions, read books, conduct experiments, observe the world, and improve their understanding throughout their lives. This ability to guide one's own education is known as **self-directed learning**, and it represents one of the most important characteristics of human intelligence. Scientists believe that Artificial General Intelligence (AGI) must eventually develop similar capabilities. Rather than depending entirely on programmers or human instructors, future AGI systems should be able to identify gaps in their knowledge, search for reliable information, evaluate evidence, and expand their understanding through independent learning. This shift from passive learning to active learning marks one of the greatest differences between today's specialized AI systems and the intelligent machines envisioned for the future.

Self-directed learning begins with **curiosity**. Curiosity motivates people to ask questions, investigate unfamiliar ideas, and search for deeper understanding. Young children naturally demonstrate curiosity by constantly asking "Why?" They want to know why the sky is blue, why birds fly, why seasons change, and why plants grow. These questions are not signs of incomplete intelligence; they are evidence of an intelligent mind seeking to expand its understanding. Throughout history, curiosity has driven many of humanity's greatest discoveries. Scientists questioned why planets move through space. Physicians investigated the causes of disease. Engineers wondered how humans might fly. Computer scientists asked whether machines could one day think intelligently. Each breakthrough began with curiosity followed by careful investigation. Future AGI systems may require similar mechanisms that encourage exploration, allowing intelligent machines to recognize unanswered questions and seek new knowledge rather than waiting for external instruction.

An important characteristic of self-directed learning is the ability to recognize **knowledge gaps**. Human beings constantly encounter situations where they realize they do not fully understand something. A student studying chemistry may discover unfamiliar scientific terms. A physician may encounter a rare disease never previously treated. An engineer may face a design challenge requiring knowledge from another discipline. Instead of stopping, intelligent learners recognize these gaps and actively search for reliable information. They consult textbooks, research articles, experienced colleagues, teachers, and trusted experts to strengthen their understanding. Future AGI systems will likely require similar self-assessment capabilities that allow them to identify missing knowledge, evaluate uncertainty, and initiate learning activities that improve future performance.

Closely related to self-directed learning is **continuous learning**. Continuous learning refers to the ongoing process of acquiring new knowledge throughout an intelligent system's lifetime. Human learning never truly ends because the world itself is constantly changing. Scientific discoveries replace outdated theories. New technologies transform industries. Medical research improves treatments. Languages evolve. Environmental conditions shift. Social and cultural developments reshape societies. Successful individuals continue learning throughout their lives because remaining informed allows them to adapt to changing circumstances. Artificial General Intelligence must demonstrate the same adaptability if it is to remain useful in a world where knowledge expands every day.

Modern artificial intelligence often experiences a limitation because many systems learn primarily during an initial training phase. After training is complete, their knowledge remains largely fixed unless engineers perform additional updates or retraining. This approach differs significantly from human intelligence, which learns continuously through everyday experiences. Imagine graduating from school and never learning anything new for the rest of your life. As technology, medicine, science, and society changed, your knowledge would gradually become outdated. Researchers therefore seek to develop AGI architectures capable of continuous learning so intelligent machines remain current without requiring complete retraining every time new information becomes available.

Continuous learning also helps intelligent systems adapt to unfamiliar environments. Imagine an autonomous agricultural robot working on farms across different regions of the world. One farm may grow wheat, another oranges, another rice, and another grapes. Soil conditions, weather patterns, insects, irrigation systems, and harvesting methods vary significantly from one location to another. A robot capable of continuous learning would gradually improve its performance by adapting to each environment rather than relying entirely on knowledge acquired before deployment. Similar continuous learning capabilities could improve autonomous vehicles, medical assistants, educational tutors, manufacturing robots, environmental monitoring systems, and scientific research platforms.

As learning continues throughout life, intelligent systems begin developing what researchers call **lifelong learning**. Lifelong learning extends beyond simply adding new information. It involves integrating new knowledge with existing understanding while preserving valuable previous learning. Human beings constantly revise their mental models as they gain experience. A child first learns that the Earth appears flat when standing on the ground. Later, education reveals that Earth is actually a sphere. Scientific understanding continues expanding as students learn about gravity, planetary motion, geology, and climate science. Each new lesson builds upon previous knowledge while refining earlier understanding. Lifelong learning therefore represents continuous growth rather than isolated episodes of education.

One of the greatest challenges facing artificial intelligence involves preserving old knowledge while acquiring new information. Researchers refer to this problem as **catastrophic forgetting**, where learning new tasks unintentionally erases previously learned knowledge. Human brains generally avoid this problem because they integrate new learning into existing memory systems rather than replacing everything learned before. Scientists developing AGI study biological learning carefully because they hope to create memory architectures that support continuous expansion without destroying earlier knowledge. Solving this challenge will allow future intelligent systems to accumulate decades of experience while remaining flexible enough to learn every day.

Learning also becomes more powerful through **reflection**. Humans frequently pause to evaluate previous experiences, identify mistakes, and improve future decisions. Athletes review recordings of competitions to strengthen performance. Scientists analyze unsuccessful experiments before designing new ones. Teachers reflect on classroom lessons to improve future instruction. Business leaders evaluate completed projects before launching new initiatives. Reflection transforms experience into deeper understanding because it encourages intelligent learners to recognize both strengths and weaknesses. Future AGI systems may include similar self-reflection mechanisms that evaluate completed tasks, identify errors, measure performance, and automatically refine future strategies without direct human supervision.

Another important aspect of lifelong learning involves **knowledge transfer**. Human intelligence excels because knowledge learned in one area often becomes useful in another. A student who understands mathematical patterns may later apply similar reasoning while studying music, engineering, or economics. An experienced physician may use problem-solving skills developed in medicine when managing healthcare organizations. Engineers often borrow ideas from biology to design more efficient machines, a practice known as biomimicry. Future AGI systems must develop similar transfer learning capabilities so they can apply previous knowledge creatively across different domains rather than treating every problem as entirely unrelated.

Scientists also believe future AGI will increasingly combine learning with **reasoning**. Learning gathers information, while reasoning explains how that information should be applied. Imagine observing that dark clouds often appear before rain. Learning recognizes this repeated pattern. Reasoning goes further by explaining how weather systems produce clouds and precipitation. Understanding why events occur allows knowledge to transfer more effectively to new situations. Future AGI systems will likely integrate learning and reasoning continuously, allowing new experiences to strengthen both memory and logical understanding at the same time.

The future of intelligent machines may also include **autonomous knowledge discovery**. Rather than simply learning information created by humans, AGI systems may eventually generate entirely new knowledge by conducting experiments, testing hypotheses, analyzing enormous datasets, and identifying relationships previously unknown to science. Astronomers already use AI to identify unusual patterns within telescope observations. Medical researchers use AI to discover potential drug candidates. Climate scientists analyze environmental data using machine learning to improve predictive models. As AGI becomes increasingly capable, intelligent systems may contribute directly to scientific discovery by expanding humanity's collective understanding of the natural world.

Learning must always remain guided by ethical principles. Acquiring knowledge without considering responsibility can produce harmful outcomes. Human education teaches not only mathematics, science, language, and history but also honesty, fairness, empathy, cooperation, and respect for others. Future AGI systems must likewise learn within ethical frameworks that encourage responsible decision-making, transparency, privacy protection, and respect for human values. Intelligence becomes truly beneficial only when knowledge is applied wisely and responsibly. For this reason, researchers increasingly emphasize aligning future AGI learning systems with ethical principles that prioritize human well-being.

As Artificial General Intelligence continues developing, learning will remain its greatest source of growth. Every observation, conversation, experiment, challenge, and success will contribute to expanding knowledge systems that become increasingly sophisticated over time. Unlike today's narrow AI systems, future AGI will likely learn continuously, identify its own educational needs, reflect on previous experiences, transfer knowledge across different domains, and collaborate with humans to solve problems that neither could solve alone. Learning will no longer be a temporary training phase but a lifelong process that allows intelligent systems to evolve alongside the changing world.

The story of intelligence is ultimately the story of learning. Every scientific discovery, technological innovation, artistic achievement, and educational milestone began because someone was willing to ask questions, seek knowledge, and continue learning. Human civilization has progressed because each generation built upon the discoveries of those who came before. Artificial General Intelligence follows the same path. The more effectively intelligent machines learn, adapt, and expand their understanding, the more capable they become of supporting education, healthcare, science, engineering, environmental stewardship, and countless other fields that improve human life. Learning transforms information into knowledge, knowledge into understanding, and understanding into wisdom. It is the engine that drives intelligence forward, for both humans and the intelligent machines of the future.

Learn AI. Understand AI. Shape the Future.

— Susie Hala
IntelliGloss Press

Chapter 8 Summary

Learning New Knowledge

Learning is one of the most important characteristics of intelligence because it allows both humans and intelligent machines to grow, adapt, and improve over time. Instead of relying only on existing knowledge, intelligent systems must continually acquire new information, recognize patterns, solve problems, and adjust to changing environments. Artificial General Intelligence (AGI) will depend on lifelong learning to remain effective in a world where knowledge is constantly expanding.

Artificial intelligence uses several major learning methods. **Supervised learning** teaches AI through labeled examples with known correct answers. Much like students learning from teachers, AI improves by comparing its predictions with correct solutions and reducing errors through repeated practice. Supervised learning powers many modern AI applications, including image recognition, speech recognition, language translation, and medical diagnosis.

Unsupervised learning allows AI to discover patterns without being given correct answers. Instead of following instructions, the system explores data independently, grouping similar information and identifying hidden relationships. This approach is valuable for scientific research, customer analysis, data organization, and discovering previously unknown patterns within large datasets.

Reinforcement learning teaches intelligent systems through rewards and consequences. Like humans and animals learning through experience, AI experiments with different actions and gradually learns which decisions produce the best outcomes. Reinforcement learning is widely used in robotics, autonomous vehicles, game-playing systems, and complex decision-making environments where direct instruction is not always possible.

Future AGI will require **self-directed learning**, allowing intelligent systems to recognize gaps in their own knowledge and independently search for reliable information. Curiosity, exploration, questioning, and investigation will become essential characteristics of intelligent machines that continue learning throughout their operational lives.

Continuous learning enables intelligent systems to update their knowledge as the world changes. Instead of remaining fixed after initial training, AGI will likely learn from new experiences, scientific discoveries, conversations, and observations while preserving valuable previous knowledge. Researchers continue working to solve challenges such as catastrophic forgetting so AI can expand its understanding without losing what it has already learned.

Learning also involves reflection, knowledge transfer, reasoning, and ethical decision-making. Future AGI will likely combine multiple learning methods into unified cognitive systems capable of lifelong growth. Just as human civilization has advanced through continuous learning across generations, AGI will depend upon ongoing education, adaptation, and responsible knowledge acquisition to support humanity in solving increasingly complex global challenges.

Reflection

Every skill you possess today began with learning. Whether you learned to read, ride a bicycle, solve equations, play music, speak another language, or use technology, your abilities developed gradually through observation, practice, mistakes, and experience. Learning never truly ends because every day presents opportunities to discover something new.

Artificial General Intelligence will require a similar lifelong learning process. Instead of memorizing information once and remaining unchanged, future intelligent systems must continuously update their understanding, recognize new patterns, ask meaningful questions, and adapt to changing environments. These capabilities will allow AGI to remain useful in education, healthcare, science, engineering, and many other fields where knowledge continues to evolve.

One of the most inspiring aspects of human intelligence is curiosity. Curiosity drives exploration, scientific discovery, creativity, and innovation. As researchers design future AGI systems, they hope to create machines capable of learning responsibly while remaining guided by ethical principles that benefit humanity.

Remember that education is not about reaching a point where learning stops. It is about developing the skills and curiosity that allow you to continue growing throughout your entire life.

Student Worksheet

Name: ______________________________

Date: ______________________________

Part A – Vocabulary

Define each term using your own words.

1. Supervised Learning

____

2. Unsupervised Learning

____

3. Reinforcement Learning

____

4. Self-Directed Learning

5. Continuous Learning

6. Lifelong Learning

7. Curiosity

Part B – Short Answer

1. Why is learning considered one of the foundations of intelligence?

2. Explain the difference between supervised and unsupervised learning.

3. How does reinforcement learning resemble the way humans learn?

4. Why is continuous learning important for future AGI?

5. How can curiosity improve both human learning and artificial intelligence?

Part C – Matching

Letter	Learning Method	Number
A	Supervised Learning	___ Learns from rewards and consequences
B	Unsupervised Learning	___ Learns from labeled examples
C	Reinforcement Learning	___ Discovers hidden patterns independently
D	Self-Directed Learning	___ Identifies knowledge gaps independently
E	Continuous Learning	___ Learns throughout its lifetime

Part D – Critical Thinking

Imagine you are designing an AGI assistant for a middle school science classroom.

Explain how the assistant would use:

Supervised Learning

___

Unsupervised Learning

___

Reinforcement Learning

___

Continuous Learning

___

Self-Directed Learning

___

How would these learning methods improve science education?

___

___

___

Part E – Personal Reflection

Think about one difficult subject you have learned.

Describe how each of the following helped you improve:

- Practice

- Mistakes

- Teacher Feedback

- Curiosity

- Repetition

How is this similar to the way AI learns?

Chapter 8 Quiz

Multiple Choice

1. Supervised learning teaches AI by using...

A. Random guessing

B. Labeled examples with correct answers

C. Luck

D. Hardware upgrades

2. Unsupervised learning allows AI to...

A. Discover patterns without labeled answers

B. Memorize only facts

C. Stop learning

D. Delete information

3. Reinforcement learning improves performance through...

A. Rewards and consequences

B. Alphabetical order

C. Random memory

D. Typing speed

4. Self-directed learning allows an intelligent system to...

A. Wait for instructions forever

B. Identify knowledge gaps and learn independently

C. Stop asking questions

D. Ignore new information

5. Lifelong learning means...

A. Learning only during training

B. Continuously acquiring and updating knowledge throughout life

C. Memorizing one textbook

D. Never changing

True or False

6. Human intelligence continues learning throughout life.

True / False

7. Future AGI will likely combine several different learning methods.

True / False

8. Curiosity plays no role in intelligent learning.

True / False

9. Catastrophic forgetting is a challenge researchers hope to solve.

True / False

10. Ethical principles are important when designing learning systems for AGI.

True / False

Answer Key

Vocabulary

Answers will vary but should demonstrate an accurate understanding of each learning method.

Worksheet

Part B

1. Learning allows intelligence to grow, adapt, solve problems, and improve over time.

2. Supervised learning uses labeled examples with correct answers, while unsupervised learning discovers patterns without labels.
3. Reinforcement learning improves through rewards, consequences, practice, and experience.
4. Continuous learning allows AGI to remain current as knowledge changes and expands.
5. Curiosity motivates exploration, questioning, discovery, and independent learning.

Part C – Matching

A → Learns from labeled examples

B → Discovers hidden patterns independently

C → Learns from rewards and consequences

D → Identifies knowledge gaps independently

E → Learns throughout its lifetime

Part D

Answers will vary but should demonstrate understanding of multiple learning methods working together.

Part E

Answers will vary based on each student's personal experiences.

Quiz Answers

1. **B**
2. **A**
3. **A**
4. **B**
5. **B**
6. **True**
7. **True**
8. **False**

9. **True**
10. **True**

Key Vocabulary

- Learning
- Supervised Learning
- Unsupervised Learning
- Reinforcement Learning
- Self-Directed Learning
- Continuous Learning
- Lifelong Learning
- Curiosity
- Knowledge Gap
- Reflection
- Knowledge Transfer
- Artificial General Intelligence (AGI)
- Catastrophic Forgetting
- Autonomous Learning
- Cognitive Growth

Chapter Takeaway

Learning is the engine that drives intelligence. Through observation, practice, curiosity, experience, reflection, and continuous improvement, both humans and future Artificial General Intelligence systems expand their understanding of the world. The ability to learn throughout life transforms information into knowledge, knowledge into understanding, and understanding into intelligent action.

Learn AI. Understand AI. Shape the Future.

— Susie Hala
IntelliGloss Press

Chapter 9

Reasoning with Knowledge

Part 1

Knowledge alone does not create intelligence. A library may contain millions of books filled with valuable information, yet the books themselves cannot solve problems, make decisions, or explain how different ideas connect with one another. Intelligence emerges when knowledge is organized, interpreted, and applied to answer questions, evaluate evidence, and make informed decisions. This process is known as **reasoning**, and it is one of the defining characteristics of both human intelligence and the future vision of Artificial General Intelligence (AGI). Throughout everyday life, people constantly reason about situations without realizing it. They decide which route is safest while driving to school, determine whether a scientific explanation makes sense, evaluate information found online, and choose the best solution to a difficult problem. These decisions require much more than memory because they involve connecting existing knowledge to new situations. Future AGI systems must develop similar reasoning abilities if they are to function as trustworthy partners in education, healthcare, engineering, scientific research, and countless other fields.

Human reasoning begins with observation but extends far beyond simply collecting facts. Imagine a student walking outside and noticing that dark clouds have gathered overhead, strong winds have begun blowing, and the temperature has suddenly dropped. None of these observations alone prove that rain is coming. However, by connecting these pieces of information with previous experience, the student concludes that a storm is probably approaching. This conclusion represents reasoning because the brain combines multiple observations with stored knowledge to predict a future event. Scientists developing AGI seek to build intelligent systems capable of making similar connections rather than simply reporting isolated facts. True intelligence requires understanding how pieces of knowledge fit together to explain the world.

One of the oldest and most reliable forms of reasoning is **deductive reasoning**. Deductive reasoning begins with general principles that are known to be true and applies them to reach logically certain conclusions. If the starting information is correct and the reasoning process follows valid logic, the conclusion must also be correct. For example, consider the following statements:

- All mammals breathe air.
- Dolphins are mammals.
- Therefore, dolphins breathe air.

This conclusion is logically guaranteed because it follows directly from the two original statements. Human beings use deductive reasoning every day, often without realizing it. Teachers apply school rules to classroom situations. Engineers apply mathematical formulas while designing bridges. Physicians use established medical knowledge to diagnose diseases.

Judges apply laws to legal cases. Deductive reasoning provides confidence because conclusions follow logically from reliable principles rather than guesswork.

Artificial intelligence also uses deductive reasoning extensively, especially in systems designed for rule-based decision-making. Early expert systems relied heavily on deductive logic by storing thousands of carefully written rules that guided decision-making. A medical expert system might conclude that a patient requires additional testing because specific symptoms satisfy known diagnostic criteria. Financial software may determine whether a loan application meets established approval requirements. Industrial control systems apply safety rules before operating complex machinery. Although modern AI increasingly relies on machine learning, deductive reasoning remains essential whenever decisions require logical consistency and predictable outcomes.

While deductive reasoning begins with general rules, **inductive reasoning** works in the opposite direction. Inductive reasoning examines specific observations and attempts to identify broader patterns or general principles. Imagine observing that the Sun has risen every morning throughout your lifetime. From these repeated observations, you conclude that the Sun will probably rise again tomorrow. Although this conclusion cannot be guaranteed with absolute certainty, it represents a highly reasonable prediction based on consistent evidence. Scientists rely heavily on inductive reasoning because scientific theories emerge by observing repeated patterns in nature rather than beginning with absolute certainty.

The development of modern science illustrates the importance of inductive reasoning. Early astronomers carefully observed the movement of stars and planets over many years before developing mathematical models describing planetary motion. Biologists studied countless species before developing theories explaining evolution and genetics. Climate scientists analyze decades of weather data before identifying long-term environmental trends. Artificial intelligence uses similar approaches by analyzing enormous datasets to discover patterns that support predictions, recommendations, and decision-making. Machine learning algorithms, in many ways, are sophisticated forms of inductive reasoning because they identify statistical relationships across millions or billions of examples.

Despite its usefulness, inductive reasoning also has limitations. Patterns observed in the past do not always guarantee future outcomes. A student who receives high grades on several quizzes cannot automatically assume every future examination will produce identical results without continued preparation. Stock market trends may change unexpectedly. Weather conditions may behave differently under unusual circumstances. Intelligent systems must therefore recognize that inductive conclusions often involve probabilities rather than certainty. Future AGI systems will need to evaluate confidence levels, consider uncertainty, and remain willing to revise conclusions as new evidence becomes available.

Another fascinating form of reasoning is **abductive reasoning**, often described as reasoning toward the most likely explanation. Unlike deduction, which guarantees conclusions, or induction, which identifies patterns, abductive reasoning attempts to explain incomplete information. Imagine arriving at school and noticing that the sidewalks are wet, students are carrying umbrellas, and puddles have formed near the entrance. Although you did not personally witness rainfall, you naturally conclude that it probably rained earlier. Other explanations are possible—perhaps sprinklers were running—but rainfall appears to be the most reasonable explanation based on available evidence. Humans perform abductive reasoning constantly because real-world situations rarely provide complete information.

Medical diagnosis offers an excellent example of abductive reasoning. Physicians rarely observe diseases directly. Instead, they examine symptoms, laboratory results, medical history, imaging studies, and physical examinations before determining the most likely diagnosis. Detectives solve crimes using similar reasoning by combining evidence to identify the most plausible explanation for observed events. Scientists generate hypotheses explaining experimental results before conducting additional investigations. Future AGI systems operating in healthcare, scientific research, emergency response, and engineering will likely depend heavily on abductive reasoning because many important decisions must be made despite incomplete or uncertain information.

All three forms of reasoning—deductive, inductive, and abductive—work together within human intelligence. Consider a physician evaluating a patient with chest pain. Deductive reasoning applies established medical knowledge to interpret symptoms. Inductive reasoning compares the patient's condition with patterns observed in thousands of previous cases. Abductive reasoning identifies the most likely explanation while considering alternative possibilities. Rather than relying upon one reasoning method alone, the physician integrates multiple approaches into a comprehensive decision-making process. Researchers believe future AGI systems will require similar integration, combining logical certainty, statistical learning, and evidence-based explanation within unified reasoning architectures.

Reasoning also depends upon the quality of the knowledge being used. Incorrect information often produces incorrect conclusions, even when reasoning itself follows perfect logic. This principle explains why scientists continually verify evidence, educators teach critical thinking, and engineers carefully test designs before implementation. Future AGI systems must likewise evaluate the reliability of information, recognize uncertainty, detect contradictions, and revise conclusions whenever stronger evidence becomes available. Intelligence is strengthened not only by better reasoning but also by better knowledge.

As artificial intelligence becomes increasingly capable, reasoning will become one of its most valuable abilities. Knowledge provides the foundation, but reasoning transforms knowledge into understanding by explaining relationships, predicting outcomes, solving unfamiliar problems, and supporting responsible decision-making. In the next part of this chapter, you will explore **logical inference**, **knowledge-driven decision-making**, **complex problem solving**, and how future AGI systems may integrate reasoning with memory, learning, and world models to achieve increasingly human-like intelligence.

(End of Part 1 — Part 2 will continue with Logical Inference, Problem Solving, Knowledge-Driven Decisions, Integrated Reasoning Architectures, and a powerful chapter conclusion.)

Chapter 9

Reasoning with Knowledge

Part 2

Reasoning becomes truly powerful when intelligent systems move beyond recognizing patterns and begin drawing new conclusions from existing knowledge. This process is known as **logical inference**. Logical inference is the ability to use known facts, relationships, and evidence to discover information that has not been stated directly. Human beings perform logical inference constantly throughout daily life. Imagine walking into a classroom and noticing backpacks hanging on chairs, notebooks lying open on desks, and a teacher writing on the whiteboard. Even before anyone speaks, you naturally conclude that a class is in session. No one explicitly tells you this fact. Instead, your brain combines multiple observations with previous knowledge to infer the most reasonable conclusion. This remarkable ability allows humans to understand situations quickly and efficiently, and it represents one of the essential capabilities that future Artificial General Intelligence (AGI) must possess.

Logical inference depends heavily on relationships among concepts. Consider the following information:

- Every bird has feathers.
- Penguins are birds.
- Penguins live in Antarctica.

From these facts, an intelligent system can infer that penguins have feathers, even if that exact statement never appeared in its knowledge base. This ability to generate new knowledge from existing knowledge greatly expands intelligence because it reduces the need to memorize every possible fact separately. Human learning becomes more efficient because people understand principles rather than memorizing isolated details. Scientists designing AGI seek to create reasoning systems capable of making similar inferences across millions or even billions of interconnected concepts. Instead of simply storing information, future AGI systems will actively expand their own understanding by discovering logical relationships hidden within existing knowledge.

Inference also allows intelligent systems to answer questions involving incomplete information. Imagine a weather forecasting system receiving reports of rapidly falling air pressure, increasing humidity, strong winds, and dark storm clouds approaching a coastal city. None of these observations alone prove that severe weather will occur. However, by combining meteorological knowledge with historical weather patterns, the system can infer that dangerous conditions are becoming increasingly likely. Emergency managers may then receive early warnings that help protect lives and property. Similar inference systems already assist meteorologists, physicians, engineers, financial analysts, and scientists by transforming large collections of information into practical recommendations for decision-making.

One of the greatest demonstrations of reasoning occurs during **problem solving**. Every day, people encounter situations they have never experienced before. A student may face a difficult mathematics problem unlike any previously assigned. An engineer may design a bridge across terrain presenting unique environmental challenges. A physician may treat a patient with an extremely rare disease. In each case, success depends not on memorizing one correct answer but on applying existing knowledge creatively to unfamiliar situations. Human intelligence excels because it combines reasoning, memory, observation, and experience to generate new solutions rather than relying solely on previous examples. Artificial General Intelligence must demonstrate similar flexibility if it is to solve problems beyond those encountered during initial training.

Effective problem solving usually follows several logical steps. First, intelligent learners identify the problem clearly. Second, they gather relevant information and evaluate available evidence. Third, they generate possible solutions. Fourth, they compare advantages and disadvantages of each option. Finally, they select the most appropriate solution while remaining prepared to revise their approach if new information becomes available. Although these steps often occur quickly and automatically, they illustrate how reasoning transforms knowledge into intelligent action. Future AGI systems will likely perform similar processes while solving scientific, medical, engineering, educational, and environmental challenges requiring careful analysis rather than simple memorization.

Reasoning also supports **knowledge-driven decision-making**. Every important decision depends upon combining available information with logical thinking. Consider a physician deciding how to treat a patient. Medical knowledge provides information about diseases, medications, laboratory results, and treatment guidelines. Reasoning evaluates how these pieces of information apply to one specific patient whose age, medical history, allergies, lifestyle, and current condition may differ from previous cases. The physician must weigh benefits, risks, uncertainties, and possible outcomes before selecting the best treatment plan. Similar reasoning occurs when pilots respond to emergencies, engineers evaluate structural safety, teachers adapt instruction for different students, or government leaders make public policy decisions. Knowledge provides possibilities, while reasoning determines which possibility best fits the current situation.

Artificial intelligence increasingly supports knowledge-driven decisions across many professions. Financial institutions analyze market conditions before recommending investments. Hospitals use clinical decision-support systems that compare patient information with medical research. Manufacturers optimize production schedules by evaluating supply chains, equipment availability, and customer demand. Agricultural AI systems recommend irrigation schedules based on weather forecasts, soil conditions, and crop growth. Although these systems already assist human decision-makers, future AGI may perform much more sophisticated reasoning by integrating knowledge from multiple disciplines simultaneously. An AGI assisting disaster response, for example, could combine meteorology, transportation, medicine, engineering, communications, and public safety knowledge into one coordinated reasoning process.

Complex reasoning also requires managing **uncertainty**. Human beings rarely possess complete information before making decisions. Physicians may await laboratory results. Scientists often work with incomplete experimental evidence. Business leaders must predict future economic conditions without knowing exactly what will happen. Parents make decisions based on the best available information while recognizing that unexpected events may occur. Intelligent reasoning therefore involves evaluating probabilities rather than demanding absolute certainty in every situation. Future AGI systems must likewise estimate confidence levels, compare competing explanations, and revise conclusions whenever stronger evidence becomes available. This flexibility allows intelligence to remain reliable even when knowledge is incomplete.

Researchers developing AGI often describe reasoning as the bridge connecting **memory**, **learning**, and **action**. Memory stores previous experiences and accumulated knowledge. Learning expands that knowledge through new observations and discoveries. Reasoning determines how knowledge should be applied to current situations. Without memory, reasoning lacks information. Without learning, reasoning becomes outdated. Without reasoning, stored knowledge remains unused. These three capabilities work together continuously, forming the foundation of intelligent behavior. Future AGI systems will require tightly integrated cognitive architectures where memory, learning, perception, planning, and reasoning operate cooperatively rather than independently.

Reasoning becomes even more valuable when intelligent systems collaborate with humans. Imagine a team of medical researchers investigating a newly emerging infectious disease. Human scientists contribute creativity, ethical judgment, clinical experience, and biological expertise. An AGI system contributes rapid analysis of enormous medical databases, scientific literature, genomic information, and epidemiological models. Together, humans and AGI reason through the available evidence, generate hypotheses, evaluate competing explanations, and design new experiments. Neither humans nor machines solve the problem alone. Instead, reasoning becomes a collaborative process in which each partner contributes complementary strengths. Many researchers believe this form of human-AI collaboration represents one of the most promising applications of future AGI.

Reasoning also supports **innovation**. Throughout history, major scientific breakthroughs have occurred because people combined existing knowledge in entirely new ways. The invention of the airplane required understanding physics, engineering, materials science, and observations of birds. Modern smartphones combine telecommunications, computer science, mathematics, electronics, and design. Renewable energy technologies integrate knowledge from chemistry, environmental science, engineering, and economics. Innovation rarely emerges from isolated facts. Instead, it results from reasoning across multiple domains to discover previously unseen connections. Future AGI systems may accelerate innovation by identifying relationships among enormous collections of knowledge that exceed the capacity of individual human researchers to analyze.

Ethical reasoning will become increasingly important as AGI systems assume greater responsibilities. Intelligent machines operating in healthcare, education, transportation, law, finance, and public services will often encounter situations involving competing priorities. For example, an autonomous vehicle may need to balance passenger safety with the safety of pedestrians. A healthcare system may need to prioritize limited medical resources during emergencies. Educational AI tutors must support student learning while protecting privacy and encouraging independent thinking rather than simply providing answers. Solving these challenges requires more than technical reasoning. It also requires ethical reasoning grounded in fairness, transparency, accountability, human dignity, and respect for societal values. Researchers therefore emphasize that future AGI should integrate ethical reasoning into every major decision-making process.

Another important aspect of reasoning involves recognizing when conclusions should change. Human intelligence remains effective because it is willing to revise beliefs when stronger evidence becomes available. Scientists routinely update theories following new discoveries. Physicians modify treatment plans after receiving laboratory results. Engineers redesign systems when testing reveals weaknesses. Students improve understanding after receiving feedback from teachers. This willingness to reconsider previous conclusions reflects intellectual humility and scientific thinking. Future AGI systems must demonstrate similar adaptability by continuously evaluating new evidence rather than treating every conclusion as permanently correct.

Ultimately, reasoning transforms knowledge into understanding. Knowledge tells us **what** is known. Reasoning helps explain **why** it is true, **how** ideas are connected, and **when** that knowledge should be applied. It enables intelligent systems to solve unfamiliar problems, evaluate evidence, make responsible decisions, generate creative ideas, and collaborate effectively with people. As Artificial General Intelligence continues evolving, reasoning will become one of its defining abilities because it allows information to become meaningful action rather than remaining isolated facts stored within memory.

The future of AGI depends not only on collecting larger amounts of information but on developing increasingly sophisticated reasoning systems capable of understanding the world with flexibility, responsibility, and wisdom. Every scientific discovery, educational lesson, engineering achievement, and technological innovation demonstrates that intelligence grows strongest when knowledge and reasoning work together. By learning to reason with knowledge, future AGI systems may become trusted partners that help humanity solve some of its greatest challenges while expanding our collective understanding of the world.

Learn AI. Understand AI. Shape the Future.

— Susie Hala
IntelliGloss Press

Chapter 9 Summary

Reasoning with Knowledge

Reasoning is the process of using knowledge to understand situations, solve problems, make decisions, and draw logical conclusions. While knowledge provides facts and information, reasoning transforms that knowledge into meaningful understanding. Human intelligence depends on reasoning every day, from making simple choices to solving complex scientific and engineering problems. Artificial General Intelligence (AGI) will require advanced reasoning abilities if it is to operate effectively in the real world.

Three major forms of reasoning are especially important in both human thinking and artificial intelligence. **Deductive reasoning** begins with general principles and applies them to specific situations to reach logically certain conclusions. When the starting information is correct, the conclusion is guaranteed to be correct. This type of reasoning is widely used in mathematics, engineering, law, medicine, and rule-based AI systems.

Inductive reasoning works in the opposite direction. It begins by observing specific examples and then identifies broader patterns or general principles. Scientists use inductive reasoning to develop theories by studying repeated observations over time. Machine learning also relies heavily on inductive reasoning because AI systems discover patterns within large datasets to make predictions and recommendations.

Abductive reasoning searches for the most likely explanation when information is incomplete. Physicians diagnosing illnesses, detectives solving crimes, and scientists developing hypotheses all use abductive reasoning by evaluating available evidence and selecting the explanation that best fits the observed facts.

Reasoning also depends on **logical inference**, which allows intelligent systems to discover new knowledge from information already stored in memory. By connecting existing facts, AI can answer questions, solve unfamiliar problems, and make informed decisions without requiring every possible answer to be stored separately.

Effective reasoning supports **problem solving** by identifying challenges, gathering evidence, evaluating possible solutions, and selecting the most appropriate course of action. Knowledge-driven decision-making combines memory, learning, reasoning, and experience to solve real-world problems in healthcare, education, finance, engineering, scientific research, and many other fields.

Future AGI will require integrated reasoning systems that combine deduction, induction, abduction, memory, learning, context, and ethical decision-making. These reasoning abilities will allow intelligent systems to adapt to changing environments, evaluate uncertainty, revise conclusions when new evidence appears, and collaborate effectively with humans.

Reasoning transforms knowledge into intelligent action. It enables both humans and future AGI systems to understand the world, make responsible decisions, and continually expand their understanding through experience and learning.

Reflection

Every decision you make involves reasoning. Whether you choose the fastest route home, solve a difficult math problem, decide what information to trust online, or explain why an event happened, your brain connects previous knowledge with current observations to reach a conclusion.

Reasoning is one of humanity's greatest strengths because it allows us to go beyond memorizing facts. Instead of simply remembering information, we explain it, apply it, question it, and use it to solve new problems. Scientists, doctors, engineers, teachers, and researchers all depend on reasoning every day.

Future Artificial General Intelligence will require similar abilities. Rather than simply storing enormous amounts of information, AGI must understand relationships, evaluate evidence, recognize uncertainty, solve unfamiliar challenges, and make responsible decisions that align with human values.

As you continue learning, remember that true intelligence is not measured by how much information you memorize. It is measured by how well you use your knowledge to think critically, solve problems, make ethical decisions, and continue learning throughout your life.

Student Worksheet

Name: ____________________________________

Date: _____________________________________

Part A – Vocabulary

Define each term using your own words.

1. Reasoning

___

2. Deductive Reasoning

___

3. Inductive Reasoning

___

4. Abductive Reasoning

___

5. Logical Inference

---

6. Problem Solving

---

7. Knowledge-Driven Decision-Making

Part B – Short Answer

1. Why is reasoning considered one of the foundations of intelligence?

---

2. Explain the difference between deductive and inductive reasoning.

---

3. Give one real-world example of abductive reasoning.

---

4. How does logical inference help AI discover new knowledge?

---

5. Why must future AGI manage uncertainty when making decisions?

Part C – Matching

Letter	Reasoning Type	Number
A	Deductive Reasoning ___	Finds the most likely explanation

Letter	Reasoning Type		Number
B	Inductive Reasoning	___	Applies general rules to specific situations
C	Abductive Reasoning	___	Discovers patterns from observations
D	Logical Inference	___	Generates new conclusions from existing knowledge
E	Problem Solving	___	Uses reasoning to overcome challenges

Part D – Critical Thinking

Imagine you are developing an AGI assistant for emergency responders after a major hurricane.

Explain how the system would use:

Deductive Reasoning

___

Inductive Reasoning

___

Abductive Reasoning

___

Logical Inference

___

How would these reasoning methods help save lives?

___

___

___

Part E – Personal Reflection

Think about a difficult decision you have made at school, home, or in sports.

Describe:

What information did you already know?

___

How did you reason through the problem?

What decision did you make?

Looking back, would you change your reasoning? Why or why not?

Chapter 9 Quiz

Multiple Choice

1. Reasoning is the process of...

A. Memorizing information only

B. Using knowledge to solve problems and make decisions

C. Deleting old memories

D. Organizing computer files

2. Deductive reasoning begins with...

A. Specific observations

B. General principles or rules

C. Random guessing

D. Personal opinions

3. Inductive reasoning is used to...

A. Discover patterns from observations

B. Memorize facts

C. Eliminate uncertainty

D. Replace knowledge

4. Abductive reasoning attempts to...

A. Ignore evidence

B. Find the most likely explanation

C. Memorize textbooks

D. Organize databases

5. Logical inference allows intelligent systems to...

A. Delete information

B. Draw new conclusions from existing knowledge

C. Stop learning

D. Avoid reasoning

True or False

6. Knowledge alone is enough to create intelligence.

True / False

7. Scientists frequently use inductive reasoning when developing theories.

True / False

8. Future AGI will likely combine several forms of reasoning.

True / False

9. Ethical reasoning will become important as AGI systems make more decisions.

True / False

10. Reasoning helps transform knowledge into intelligent action.

True / False

Answer Key

Vocabulary

Answers will vary but should accurately explain each reasoning concept.

Worksheet

Part B

1. Reasoning allows knowledge to be applied, evaluated, and used to solve problems and make decisions.
2. Deductive reasoning starts with general rules and reaches specific conclusions, while inductive reasoning starts with observations and develops broader patterns or theories.
3. Possible answers include:

- A doctor diagnosing an illness.
- A detective solving a crime.
- A mechanic identifying why a car will not start.
- A scientist developing a hypothesis.

4. Logical inference combines existing facts to produce new conclusions that were not explicitly stored.
5. Because real-world situations often contain incomplete information, requiring intelligent systems to evaluate probabilities and revise conclusions when new evidence appears.

Part C – Matching

A → Applies general rules to specific situations

B → Discovers patterns from observations

C → Finds the most likely explanation

D → Generates new conclusions from existing knowledge

E → Uses reasoning to overcome challenges

Part D

Answers will vary but should demonstrate understanding of multiple reasoning methods working together during emergency response.

Part E

Answers will vary based on each student's personal experiences.

Quiz Answers

1. **B**
2. **B**
3. **A**
4. **B**
5. **B**
6. **False**
7. **True**
8. **True**
9. **True**
10. **True**

Key Vocabulary

- Reasoning
- Deductive Reasoning

- Inductive Reasoning
- Abductive Reasoning
- Logical Inference
- Evidence
- Pattern Recognition
- Problem Solving
- Knowledge-Driven Decision-Making
- Critical Thinking
- Uncertainty
- Artificial General Intelligence (AGI)
- Ethical Reasoning
- Cognitive Architecture
- Intelligent Decision-Making

Chapter Takeaway

Knowledge provides information, but reasoning transforms that information into understanding. Through deduction, induction, abduction, logical inference, and problem solving, both humans and future Artificial General Intelligence systems can evaluate evidence, make informed decisions, solve unfamiliar challenges, and continuously expand their understanding of the world.

Learn AI. Understand AI. Shape the Future.

— Susie Hala
IntelliGloss Press

Chapter 10

World Models and Understanding Reality

Part 1

One of the greatest strengths of human intelligence is the ability to understand the world without constantly experiencing every possible situation firsthand. Before crossing a busy street, people naturally predict how traffic will move. Before planting crops, farmers anticipate changing seasons and weather patterns. Engineers imagine how a bridge will respond to heavy traffic before construction begins. Physicians predict how a patient's condition may change after beginning a new treatment. These examples demonstrate a remarkable ability to mentally simulate reality before taking action. Humans accomplish this by building **world models**—internal representations of how the world works. These mental models allow people to predict future events, recognize cause-and-effect relationships, solve unfamiliar problems, and make informed decisions. Artificial General Intelligence (AGI) will require similar capabilities if intelligent machines are to move beyond simply reacting to information and instead begin understanding the world in ways that resemble human thinking.

A **world model** is an internal representation that organizes knowledge about objects, people, environments, events, and the relationships among them. Rather than storing isolated facts, a world model explains how different parts of reality interact with one another. Imagine learning how to ride a bicycle. At first, balancing, steering, braking, and pedaling all seem like separate skills. With practice, the brain gradually combines these experiences into a unified understanding of how bicycles behave. Eventually, riders no longer think consciously about every movement because their internal world model predicts how the bicycle will respond under different conditions. This ability allows people to avoid obstacles, maintain balance, and safely navigate unfamiliar roads. Scientists believe future AGI systems must develop comparable world models so they can predict outcomes before acting rather than relying solely on trial and error.

Human world models begin forming almost immediately after birth. Infants gradually learn that objects continue existing even when temporarily hidden from view, a concept known as object permanence. They discover that pushing objects causes movement, that voices belong to people, and that actions often produce predictable consequences. As children grow, their world models become increasingly sophisticated. They learn that gravity causes objects to fall, that fire produces heat, that water flows downhill, and that living things require food and water to survive. Education expands these models even further by introducing scientific principles, mathematical relationships, historical events, and social systems. Every new experience contributes additional knowledge, allowing the brain to construct increasingly accurate representations of reality.

These internal models help humans make predictions continuously throughout daily life. Imagine throwing a ball to a friend. Long before the ball leaves your hand, your brain estimates its speed, direction, distance, and likely path through the air. These calculations occur almost instantly because your world model incorporates previous experiences involving gravity, motion, distance, and physical coordination. Similarly, experienced drivers anticipate how other vehicles may behave, pedestrians predict when traffic lights will change, and athletes estimate where a moving ball will land before it reaches them. Human intelligence depends heavily on prediction because anticipating future events allows people to prepare for challenges before they occur.

Artificial intelligence researchers increasingly recognize that prediction may be one of the most important characteristics separating narrow AI from future AGI. Many current AI systems perform exceptionally well within specific tasks such as image recognition, language translation, or playing games. However, they often struggle when required to imagine unfamiliar situations or predict complex chains of events beyond their training data. Future AGI systems will likely require world models that allow them to mentally simulate possible outcomes before taking action. Rather than reacting only after events occur, they will anticipate consequences, evaluate alternatives, and choose strategies with greater intelligence and flexibility.

One of the most valuable features of world models is their ability to explain **cause and effect**. Human beings naturally understand that actions often produce consequences. Turning on a light switch causes a room to become brighter. Pressing the brakes slows a moving vehicle. Watering a plant regularly helps it grow. These relationships allow people to predict how their decisions influence future events. Cause-and-effect reasoning extends far beyond simple physical interactions. Economists study how changes in interest rates influence business activity. Environmental scientists investigate how pollution affects ecosystems. Physicians examine how medications influence biological systems. Understanding these relationships allows humans to solve problems by identifying which actions are most likely to produce desired outcomes.

Artificial intelligence must also learn cause-and-effect relationships if it is to operate safely and responsibly. Consider an autonomous delivery robot navigating a crowded sidewalk. The robot must understand that increasing speed near pedestrians raises the risk of collisions, that wet pavement reduces traction, and that construction barriers require alternative routes. Simply memorizing previous situations is insufficient because every environment presents unique combinations of conditions. World models allow intelligent systems to predict how different actions may influence future events before making decisions. This predictive capability becomes increasingly important as AGI begins operating within homes, hospitals, schools, factories, transportation systems, and scientific laboratories.

Scientists often compare world models to **mental simulations**. Before acting, humans frequently imagine possible outcomes within their minds. A chess player mentally evaluates several possible moves before selecting one. A teacher plans how students may respond to different instructional approaches. A scientist predicts the results of an experiment before conducting it. Architects visualize buildings before construction begins. These simulations allow people to evaluate alternatives without physically performing every possible action. Future AGI systems may perform similar internal simulations by using world models to test different strategies, estimate risks, compare possible outcomes, and select the most promising solutions before interacting with the real world.

World models also improve learning efficiency. Imagine a child touching a hot stove once and immediately learning to avoid repeating the mistake. The child does not need to touch every hot object repeatedly because the brain generalizes from one experience to many similar situations. The world model expands, allowing previous learning to transfer to unfamiliar environments. Researchers hope future AGI systems will demonstrate similar generalization. Instead of requiring millions of repeated training examples, intelligent machines may eventually learn from relatively few experiences because their world models allow them to predict how similar situations are likely to behave.

Modern AI has already begun taking important steps toward building world models. Autonomous vehicles create digital representations of roads, traffic, pedestrians, and surrounding objects while continuously predicting how each element may move during the next few seconds. Robotics systems develop models describing the weight, shape, and movement of objects they manipulate. Scientific AI systems simulate weather, climate, biological processes, and chemical reactions to predict future outcomes. Although these systems remain specialized, they illustrate how world models allow intelligent machines to reason beyond immediate observations by representing the underlying structure of reality.

As researchers continue developing Artificial General Intelligence, world models are expected to become increasingly comprehensive. Rather than representing only one task or environment, future AGI may develop unified models integrating physical laws, social interactions, language, scientific knowledge, human behavior, and countless other aspects of reality into one coherent understanding. Such models would allow intelligent systems to reason across multiple domains, adapt to unfamiliar situations, and solve problems with flexibility approaching that of human intelligence. In the next part of this chapter, you will explore **predictive modeling**, **cognitive mapping**, **AGI world models**, and how future intelligent systems may build increasingly accurate representations of the world through continuous learning and experience.

(End of Part 1 — Part 2 will continue with Predictive Modeling, Cognitive Mapping, AGI World Models, Continuous Model Updating, and a powerful chapter conclusion.)

Chapter 10

World Models and Understanding Reality

Part 2

A world model becomes increasingly valuable when it can do more than describe the present—it must also **predict the future**. One of the defining characteristics of intelligence is the ability to anticipate what is likely to happen before it actually occurs. Humans make predictions continuously, often without realizing it. A basketball player predicts where the ball will travel after leaving another player's hands. A pilot anticipates changes in wind direction before adjusting the aircraft's controls. A doctor estimates how a patient's condition may improve after beginning a new medication. A teacher predicts which students may need additional help before an important examination. These predictions are possible because the human brain constantly compares current situations with previous experiences, recognizes patterns, and mentally simulates likely outcomes. Artificial General Intelligence (AGI) must develop similar predictive abilities if it is to make safe, intelligent, and responsible decisions in complex environments.

This process is known as **predictive modeling**. Predictive models use existing knowledge, observations, and learned relationships to estimate what is most likely to happen next. Unlike simple memorization, predictive modeling requires intelligent systems to understand how events influence one another over time. Consider weather forecasting. Meteorologists do not simply compare today's weather with yesterday's conditions. Instead, they analyze atmospheric pressure, wind patterns, humidity, temperature, satellite imagery, ocean conditions, and historical climate data to predict future weather. Artificial intelligence assists meteorologists by processing enormous quantities of environmental data and generating forecasts that help communities prepare for storms, droughts, floods, and other natural events. The prediction is valuable because it allows people to act before the event occurs rather than reacting afterward.

Predictive modeling is equally important in healthcare. Physicians often estimate how diseases may progress based on medical history, laboratory results, imaging studies, and clinical research. An intelligent medical system may predict which patients are at higher risk for heart disease, diabetes, or certain types of cancer by analyzing thousands of health indicators. These predictions allow doctors to recommend preventive care before serious illnesses develop. Rather than replacing physicians, predictive AI supports clinical decision-making by identifying patterns that may be difficult for humans to detect when reviewing large amounts of information. Future AGI systems may become even more effective by integrating genetics, environmental factors, lifestyle habits, and continuously updated medical research into comprehensive predictive models that support personalized healthcare.

Prediction also plays a critical role in transportation. Autonomous vehicles constantly build world models that estimate how nearby cars, bicycles, pedestrians, animals, and traffic signals are likely to behave during the next few seconds. The vehicle must anticipate that a child standing near a parked car might suddenly enter the street, that another driver may change lanes unexpectedly, or that heavy rain may increase stopping distances. Safe driving depends not only on recognizing objects but also on predicting future behavior. Scientists believe that increasingly sophisticated world models will allow future AGI-powered transportation systems to navigate complex environments more safely by continuously evaluating possible outcomes before selecting the most appropriate action.

Closely related to predictive modeling is the concept of **cognitive mapping**. A cognitive map is an internal representation that helps an intelligent system understand how different locations, objects, ideas, or events relate to one another. Humans naturally build cognitive maps throughout their lives. When you first enter a new school, you may feel uncertain about where classrooms, offices, restrooms, and exits are located. After several weeks, however, your brain develops an internal map that allows you to move confidently from one location to another without constantly checking signs. Cognitive maps are not limited to physical spaces. People also develop mental maps of ideas, relationships, timelines, scientific concepts, and social interactions. These internal maps help organize knowledge and guide reasoning across many different situations.

Artificial intelligence researchers increasingly use cognitive mapping to improve navigation, planning, and reasoning. Robots operating inside warehouses build maps showing storage locations, delivery routes, obstacles, charging stations, and work areas. Planetary exploration robots create maps of unfamiliar terrain while investigating the surfaces of Mars or the Moon. Intelligent software systems organize knowledge into conceptual maps showing relationships among scientific theories, historical events, mathematical principles, or biological systems. Rather than storing isolated facts, cognitive maps allow AI to understand how information fits together within larger structures, making reasoning more flexible and efficient.

One of the most exciting goals in AGI research is the development of **unified world models**. Today's narrow AI systems usually specialize in one task or one environment. An AI that plays chess cannot automatically drive a car, diagnose diseases, or teach history. Human intelligence, however, combines knowledge from many different areas into one integrated understanding of reality. A student studying environmental science may apply mathematics to analyze climate data, use geography to understand ecosystems, rely on chemistry to explain pollution, and apply economics to evaluate environmental policies. Human intelligence naturally integrates knowledge across multiple disciplines because the brain maintains one continuously expanding world model rather than many isolated systems. Future AGI seeks to achieve a similar form of integrated understanding.

Unified world models may allow intelligent systems to transfer knowledge across entirely different situations. Imagine an AGI learning how water flows through rivers. That same understanding of flow may later help it analyze traffic patterns, electricity moving through circuits, the spread of diseases, or information flowing through communication networks. Although these systems appear very different, they share common underlying principles involving movement, connections, and interactions. Humans frequently recognize such analogies because their world models connect ideas across many domains. Future AGI systems may demonstrate similar flexibility by applying previously learned knowledge creatively to unfamiliar challenges.

World models must also remain **dynamic**. Reality changes continuously, and intelligent systems must update their understanding as new information becomes available. Scientific knowledge evolves as researchers make new discoveries. Medical treatments improve through clinical research. Technologies become more advanced. Environmental conditions change over time. Human intelligence remains effective because people revise their mental models whenever stronger evidence appears. Students may replace misconceptions after studying science. Engineers improve designs following new testing results. Historians revise interpretations after discovering additional historical documents. Future AGI systems must likewise update their world models continuously rather than treating knowledge as permanently fixed. Continuous learning ensures that predictions become increasingly accurate as experience grows.

An important challenge for world models involves distinguishing between **correlation and causation**. Two events occurring together do not necessarily mean that one caused the other. For example, ice cream sales and swimming activity both increase during summer months, but purchasing ice cream does not cause people to swim. Instead, warm weather influences both activities. Human reasoning often evaluates these relationships carefully before drawing conclusions. Future AGI systems must demonstrate the same caution by examining evidence before assuming cause-and-effect relationships. This ability will improve scientific reasoning, medical diagnosis, economic forecasting, and many other forms of intelligent decision-making.

Researchers also believe that world models will strengthen **human-AI collaboration**. Imagine engineers designing a new earthquake-resistant building. Human architects contribute creativity, experience, aesthetics, and knowledge of community needs. An AGI system contributes world models capable of simulating structural behavior during thousands of different earthquake scenarios. Together, humans and AGI evaluate possible designs, predict structural performance, identify weaknesses, and optimize safety before construction begins. Similar collaborations may occur in medicine, education, agriculture, environmental conservation, transportation, and scientific research. Rather than replacing human expertise, AGI world models will enhance decision-making by providing additional insight into complex systems.

As AGI systems become increasingly capable, world models may eventually support **imagination**. Human imagination allows people to mentally explore situations that have never occurred, invent new technologies, compose music, write novels, design spacecraft, and develop scientific theories. Imagination depends upon combining existing knowledge in creative ways while predicting how new ideas might function. Future AGI systems equipped with advanced world models may similarly generate innovative solutions by mentally simulating possibilities before testing them in the real world. Such capabilities could accelerate scientific discovery, engineering design, medical research, and many other areas where creativity and prediction work together.

Despite these exciting possibilities, world models must always operate within strong ethical boundaries. Predictions influence decisions that affect people's lives. An inaccurate medical prediction could delay treatment. A flawed financial forecast might influence investments. An incorrect autonomous vehicle prediction could create dangerous situations. Future AGI systems must therefore evaluate uncertainty carefully, explain the reasoning behind predictions, remain transparent about confidence levels, and allow human oversight whenever decisions involve significant consequences. Responsible prediction requires not only technical accuracy but also accountability, fairness, and respect for human values.

The future of Artificial General Intelligence depends heavily on building increasingly accurate world models. Intelligence is not simply the ability to store facts or retrieve information. It is the ability to understand how the world works, anticipate change, recognize relationships, explain cause and effect, and make informed decisions based on that understanding. World models provide the foundation that allows intelligent systems to move beyond reacting to events and begin thinking ahead, much as humans do every day.

As you continue studying AGI, remember that every experience you have contributes to your own world model. Every science experiment, historical lesson, mathematical concept, conversation, and personal experience expands your understanding of reality. Future AGI systems will learn in similar ways by continuously building richer and more accurate models of the world. The stronger these models become, the better intelligent systems will be able to reason, solve problems, collaborate with people, and help address the complex challenges facing our rapidly changing world.

Learn AI. Understand AI. Shape the Future.

— Susie Hala
IntelliGloss Press

Chapter 10 Summary

World Models and Understanding Reality

World models are internal representations that help intelligent systems understand how the world works. Instead of simply storing facts, a world model organizes knowledge about objects, people, environments, events, and the relationships among them. Humans naturally develop world models throughout life by observing, learning, practicing, and gaining experience. These mental models allow people to predict future events, understand cause-and-effect relationships, solve problems, and make informed decisions. Artificial General Intelligence (AGI) will require similar world models to interact safely and intelligently with the real world.

Human world models begin developing in early childhood as people learn that actions produce predictable consequences. Education, personal experiences, scientific knowledge, and everyday observations continually strengthen these models throughout life. As knowledge grows, people become better at understanding how different parts of the world interact and influence one another.

One of the most important functions of a world model is **predictive modeling**. Prediction allows intelligent systems to estimate what is likely to happen before events occur. Weather forecasting, healthcare, transportation, engineering, finance, and scientific research all depend on predictive models to support planning and decision-making. Instead of reacting after events occur, intelligent systems use prediction to prepare for future situations.

Another important component is the **cognitive map**, which helps organize knowledge about physical locations, ideas, and relationships. Humans develop cognitive maps when learning new environments or organizing concepts within memory. Artificial intelligence uses similar mapping systems for navigation, robotics, scientific research, and knowledge organization.

Future AGI will likely develop **unified world models** that integrate knowledge from many different fields rather than specializing in only one task. These comprehensive models will allow intelligent systems to transfer knowledge across multiple domains, recognize deeper relationships, and solve unfamiliar problems more effectively.

World models must also remain dynamic. As new discoveries are made, intelligent systems must update their understanding instead of relying on outdated information. Continuous learning allows AGI to improve its predictions, revise previous conclusions, and adapt to changing environments.

Scientists also emphasize the importance of distinguishing between **correlation and causation**. Intelligent systems must evaluate evidence carefully before assuming that one event directly causes another. This careful reasoning improves scientific understanding and supports responsible decision-making.

World models represent one of the most important foundations of Artificial General Intelligence because they allow intelligent systems to understand reality, simulate future possibilities, make predictions, and solve complex problems through integrated knowledge rather than isolated facts.

Reflection

Every decision you make depends on a world model that has been developing since you were born. You understand that gravity causes objects to fall, that traffic lights organize traffic, that studying improves learning, and that actions often produce consequences. You rarely think about these ideas because your brain automatically uses them to predict what will happen next.

Artificial General Intelligence must build similar world models if it is to work safely alongside humans. Instead of memorizing isolated facts, AGI must understand how the world functions as an interconnected system. It must recognize patterns, predict outcomes, explain cause and effect, and continuously update its understanding as new information becomes available.

One of the greatest strengths of human intelligence is the ability to imagine future possibilities before acting. Engineers design buildings before construction begins. Scientists test ideas before conducting experiments. Doctors consider several treatment options before making medical decisions. These abilities are possible because humans mentally simulate different outcomes using their world models.

As you continue learning, remember that every new lesson strengthens your own understanding of reality. Your education is continuously expanding the world model that will help guide your decisions throughout your life.

Student Worksheet

Name: ______________________________

Date: ______________________________

Part A – Vocabulary

Define each term using your own words.

1. World Model

____

2. Predictive Modeling

____

3. Cognitive Map

____

4. Cause and Effect

---

5. Correlation

---

6. Causation

---

7. Unified World Model

Part B – Short Answer

1. Why are world models important for intelligence?

---

2. Explain how predictive modeling helps both humans and AI.

---

3. What is the purpose of a cognitive map?

---

4. Why must future AGI continuously update its world model?

---

5. Why is it important to distinguish between correlation and causation?

Part C – Matching

Letter	Concept	Number
A	World Model	___ Internal understanding of reality
B	Predictive Modeling	___ Estimates future outcomes
C	Cognitive Map	___ Organizes locations and relationships
D	Correlation	___ Two events occur together
E	Causation	___ One event directly produces another

Part D – Critical Thinking

Imagine you are developing an AGI assistant to help firefighters respond to large wildfires.

Explain how the system would use:

World Models

____

Predictive Modeling

____

Cognitive Maps

____

Cause-and-Effect Reasoning

____

How could these abilities improve emergency response?

____
____
____

Part E – Real-World Application

Choose one of the following:

- Driving a car
- Playing a sport
- Cooking a meal
- Riding a bicycle

- Performing a science experiment

Describe how your brain uses a world model to predict what will happen next.

____

____

How might an AGI perform the same task?

____

____

____

Chapter 10 Quiz

Multiple Choice

1. A world model is...

A. A map of countries

B. An internal representation of how the world works

C. A computer screen

D. A database only

2. Predictive modeling helps intelligent systems...

A. Forget previous information

B. Estimate future outcomes

C. Stop learning

D. Delete memories

3. A cognitive map helps organize...

A. Music files

B. Physical locations and conceptual relationships

C. Passwords

D. Computer hardware

4. Future AGI will likely require unified world models because they...

A. Limit learning

B. Integrate knowledge across many different domains

C. Store fewer facts

D. Eliminate reasoning

5. Which statement is true?

A. Correlation always proves causation.

B. Two events occurring together automatically mean one caused the other.

C. Intelligent systems must carefully evaluate evidence before identifying cause and effect.

D. Prediction is unnecessary for intelligence.

True or False

6. Human world models continue developing throughout life.

True / False

7. Prediction allows intelligent systems to prepare for future events.

True / False

8. World models only help robots navigate buildings.

True / False

9. Future AGI will likely update its world models continuously.

True / False

10. Understanding reality requires more than memorizing isolated facts.

True / False

Answer Key

Vocabulary

Answers will vary but should demonstrate accurate understanding.

Worksheet

Part B

1. World models organize knowledge, support reasoning, prediction, planning, and decision-making.
2. Predictive modeling estimates future events using previous knowledge, observations, and patterns.
3. Cognitive maps organize relationships among locations, objects, ideas, and concepts.
4. Because the world changes continuously, requiring AGI to learn from new information and improve predictions.
5. Correlation means events occur together, while causation means one event directly produces another. Confusing the two can lead to incorrect conclusions.

Part C – Matching

A → Internal understanding of reality

B → Estimates future outcomes

C → Organizes locations and relationships

D → Two events occur together

E → One event directly produces another

Part D

Answers will vary but should demonstrate understanding of prediction, mapping, reasoning, and planning.

Part E

Answers will vary depending on the student's selected activity.

Quiz Answers

1. **B**
2. **B**
3. **B**
4. **B**
5. **C**
6. **True**
7. **True**
8. **False**
9. **True**
10. **True**

Key Vocabulary

- World Model
- Predictive Modeling
- Cognitive Map
- Internal Representation
- Cause and Effect
- Correlation
- Causation
- Simulation
- Planning
- Prediction

- Artificial General Intelligence (AGI)
- Knowledge Integration
- Reality Modeling
- Continuous Learning
- Intelligent Decision-Making

Chapter Takeaway

World models allow intelligence to understand reality rather than simply memorize information. By organizing knowledge into meaningful representations, predicting future events, recognizing cause-and-effect relationships, and continuously updating understanding through experience, both humans and future Artificial General Intelligence systems can make wiser decisions, solve complex problems, and better prepare for an ever-changing world.

Learn AI. Understand AI. Shape the Future.

Susie Hala

Chapter 11

Knowledge Transfer Across Domains

Part 1

One of the greatest strengths of human intelligence is the ability to use knowledge learned in one situation to solve problems in another. A student who understands fractions can later apply similar mathematical thinking while studying algebra. A musician who learns patterns in rhythm may recognize similar patterns in computer programming. A scientist studying ecosystems may discover ideas that improve engineering designs by observing how nature solves complex problems. Human intelligence rarely keeps knowledge separated into isolated subjects. Instead, the brain continuously connects information from different experiences, allowing learning in one area to strengthen understanding in many others. This remarkable ability is known as **knowledge transfer**, and it represents one of the defining characteristics that future Artificial General Intelligence (AGI) must develop if it is to approach the flexibility of human thought.

Imagine learning to ride a bicycle. At first glance, balancing on two wheels may seem unrelated to skiing, skateboarding, or riding a motorcycle. Yet many of the underlying skills—balance, coordination, spatial awareness, and body control—transfer from one activity to another. Someone who has mastered riding a bicycle often learns similar activities much more quickly than someone beginning without previous experience. The brain recognizes common principles across different situations and applies existing knowledge instead of starting from the beginning each time. This ability allows humans to learn efficiently because previous experiences become building blocks for future learning rather than remaining isolated memories.

Modern artificial intelligence often struggles with this type of flexibility. Today's narrow AI systems are usually designed to perform one specific task extremely well. A chess-playing AI may defeat world champions yet know nothing about biology or economics. An image-recognition system may accurately identify thousands of plant species but remain completely unable to solve mathematical equations. A language translation model may convert sentences between languages while lacking any understanding of engineering design. Each system specializes within one domain, and transferring knowledge between unrelated fields remains difficult. Artificial General Intelligence seeks to overcome this limitation by developing learning systems capable of applying knowledge broadly across many different disciplines, much like human intelligence.

One of the most important concepts supporting knowledge transfer is **generalization**. Generalization occurs when intelligent systems recognize principles that remain useful beyond the specific examples from which they were originally learned. Consider a child learning the concept of gravity. After dropping a toy several times, the child eventually understands that objects generally fall toward the ground when released. Later, this understanding helps explain why apples fall from trees, why rain reaches the ground, why basketballs bounce, and why satellites must remain in orbit. The child has generalized one scientific principle across many different situations. Instead of memorizing thousands of separate examples, the brain develops a broader understanding that applies to countless future experiences.

Generalization is one of the greatest challenges in artificial intelligence. Machine learning systems often perform exceptionally well on problems closely resembling their training data but may struggle when faced with unfamiliar situations. Imagine teaching an AI to recognize dogs using millions of photographs taken during sunny daytime conditions. If the same AI later encounters dogs during heavy snowfall, underwater rescue operations, or thermal imaging, its performance may decline because the new situations differ significantly from its original training examples. Human beings, however, easily recognize dogs under many different conditions because they understand broader concepts rather than memorizing specific images. Researchers developing AGI seek to create systems capable of this kind of flexible generalization across vastly different environments.

Closely related to generalization is **transfer learning**, a technique that allows previously acquired knowledge to accelerate learning in new tasks. Human beings constantly use transfer learning throughout education. Students who understand multiplication often learn division more easily because both subjects share underlying mathematical relationships. Learning one Romance language such as Spanish may make learning Italian or Portuguese easier because of similar vocabulary and grammar. An experienced pianist may adapt more quickly to playing the organ because many musical principles remain the same despite differences between the instruments. Transfer learning saves time and improves efficiency because previously learned knowledge becomes immediately useful when approaching new challenges.

Artificial intelligence increasingly uses transfer learning to reduce the enormous amount of training traditionally required for machine learning. Instead of building every AI system from the beginning, researchers often begin with models that have already learned general features from vast collections of data. For example, an AI trained to recognize millions of everyday objects may later adapt much more quickly to recognizing medical images because it already understands fundamental visual patterns such as edges, shapes, textures, and spatial relationships. Similarly, language models trained on diverse collections of text can later specialize in law, medicine, education, or scientific research with relatively modest additional training. Transfer learning allows AI systems to build upon previous knowledge rather than starting from zero every time a new task appears.

One reason transfer learning works so effectively is that many fields share common underlying principles. Mathematics supports physics, engineering, economics, and computer science. Pattern recognition contributes to music, language, biology, and astronomy. Logical reasoning benefits law, medicine, philosophy, and software development. Communication skills improve leadership, education, business, and scientific collaboration. Human intelligence naturally recognizes these shared structures, allowing knowledge from one discipline to strengthen performance in many others. Scientists believe AGI must eventually identify these deeper principles automatically, enabling intelligent systems to transfer knowledge across domains that may initially appear unrelated.

Transfer learning also plays an important role in scientific discovery. Throughout history, researchers have borrowed ideas from one field to solve problems in another. Engineers have studied bird flight while developing aircraft. Medical researchers have examined shark skin to design bacteria-resistant hospital surfaces. Computer scientists have modeled artificial neural networks after the human brain. Economists have applied biological models to understand complex markets. These examples demonstrate that innovation often emerges when knowledge crosses disciplinary boundaries. Rather than remaining confined within one field, ideas become increasingly powerful as they interact with concepts from many different domains.

As researchers move closer to Artificial General Intelligence, the ability to generalize and transfer knowledge across different situations will become increasingly important. Instead of viewing mathematics, biology, engineering, language, history, and economics as isolated subjects, AGI will likely organize knowledge into interconnected systems where ideas reinforce one another continuously. Such flexibility will allow intelligent systems to solve unfamiliar problems, adapt rapidly to changing environments, and collaborate effectively with people across many professions. In the next part of this chapter, you will explore **analogical reasoning**, **cross-domain thinking**, **adaptive intelligence**, and how knowledge transfer may become one of the defining characteristics that distinguishes Artificial General Intelligence from today's narrow AI systems.

(End of Part 1 — Part 2 will continue with Analogical Reasoning, Cross-Domain Thinking, Adaptive Intelligence, Foundations of AGI Flexibility, and a powerful chapter conclusion.)

Chapter 11

Knowledge Transfer Across Domains

Part 2

Knowledge transfer becomes even more powerful when intelligent systems recognize that two situations appearing completely different may actually share the same underlying principles. This ability is called **analogical reasoning**, and it is one of the most advanced forms of human thinking. Analogical reasoning allows people to compare unfamiliar problems with previous experiences and apply existing knowledge to new situations. For example, a teacher may explain the human circulatory system by comparing it to a city's transportation network. Roads become blood vessels, vehicles become blood cells, and traffic flow resembles the movement of oxygen and nutrients throughout the body. Although the two systems are physically different, they share similar patterns of movement, organization, and distribution. Human intelligence excels because it recognizes these deeper similarities rather than focusing only on surface differences. Scientists believe future Artificial General Intelligence (AGI) must develop this same ability if it is to reason creatively and solve unfamiliar problems.

Analogical reasoning has played an important role throughout the history of science. Many groundbreaking discoveries began when researchers recognized similarities between different fields of study. The development of the modern airplane was inspired by careful observations of birds in flight. Early computer scientists borrowed ideas from the structure of the human brain when designing artificial neural networks. Medical researchers study the immune systems of animals to develop new treatments for human diseases. Engineers examine spider webs when designing lightweight yet incredibly strong materials. These examples illustrate that innovation often occurs when knowledge from one discipline is successfully transferred to another. Rather than inventing solutions from nothing, intelligent thinkers frequently adapt ideas that already exist elsewhere in nature or human knowledge.

Artificial intelligence researchers increasingly study analogical reasoning because it allows learning to become far more efficient. Instead of solving every new problem from the beginning, future AGI systems may search their knowledge bases for situations that share similar structures, relationships, or patterns. Imagine an AGI helping engineers design a more efficient public transportation system. Rather than examining transportation data alone, the system might recognize similarities between transportation networks, blood circulation, communication networks, and even the movement of nutrients through plant roots. Each of these systems distributes resources through connected pathways while balancing efficiency, reliability, and resilience. By transferring knowledge across these different domains, AGI may generate innovative solutions that human experts might never have considered.

Closely related to analogical reasoning is **cross-domain thinking**. Cross-domain thinking refers to the ability to combine knowledge from multiple fields simultaneously when solving complex problems. Human civilization increasingly depends upon this type of thinking because many of today's challenges cannot be solved by one discipline alone. Climate change involves environmental science, engineering, economics, political science, agriculture, chemistry, and international cooperation. Modern healthcare combines medicine, biology, genetics, computer science, psychology, ethics, and public health. Space exploration depends upon physics, mathematics, engineering, robotics, materials science, communications, and artificial intelligence. Human experts work together because each discipline contributes valuable knowledge toward understanding larger systems. Future AGI must also integrate information across many domains instead of limiting itself to one specialized field.

Education itself demonstrates the importance of cross-domain thinking. Students often study mathematics, science, language arts, history, technology, and the arts as separate subjects. However, these disciplines continuously interact in the real world. Architects use mathematics to calculate structural strength while applying artistic design principles to create beautiful buildings. Journalists rely on history, language, ethics, technology, and critical thinking to report accurate information. Environmental scientists combine chemistry, biology, geography, mathematics, and computer modeling when studying ecosystems. One of the goals of education is helping students recognize these connections so they develop flexible thinking rather than viewing each subject as completely independent. AGI systems will likely require similar educational architectures that encourage connections across all areas of knowledge.

Cross-domain thinking also strengthens **creativity**. Creative ideas often emerge when concepts from different disciplines combine in unexpected ways. The invention of the smartphone required advances in telecommunications, computer science, materials engineering, software development, user interface design, and manufacturing. Modern renewable energy technologies combine environmental science, chemistry, engineering, economics, and public policy. Artificial intelligence itself emerged through the combination of mathematics, psychology, neuroscience, philosophy, linguistics, and computer science. Creativity therefore depends not only on possessing knowledge but also on transferring that knowledge across different domains to generate entirely new possibilities. Future AGI systems capable of cross-domain reasoning may become valuable partners in scientific discovery and technological innovation.

Another essential characteristic of knowledge transfer is **adaptive intelligence**. Adaptation means adjusting successfully when circumstances change. Human beings continually adapt to new schools, new jobs, new technologies, changing weather, unexpected emergencies, and evolving scientific knowledge. Adaptation becomes possible because previous learning provides a foundation for understanding unfamiliar situations. Imagine moving to another country where people speak a different language. Although many customs may be unfamiliar, previous experiences with communication, relationships, education, transportation, and problem-solving help you adjust more quickly. The brain does not begin learning from zero because existing knowledge transfers into the new environment.

Future AGI systems must demonstrate similar adaptability. Today's narrow AI often struggles when operating outside carefully controlled environments. An image-recognition system trained in bright lighting may perform poorly under foggy conditions. A warehouse robot may require extensive reprogramming before working inside a hospital. A language model trained primarily in one domain may struggle with highly specialized scientific terminology. Artificial General Intelligence aims to overcome these limitations by developing adaptive learning systems that automatically transfer existing knowledge to unfamiliar situations while continuing to learn from new experiences. This flexibility will become essential as intelligent machines operate in constantly changing real-world environments.

Adaptive intelligence also requires recognizing when previous knowledge should **not** be transferred. Not every similarity represents a useful analogy. A physician treating a viral infection should not automatically prescribe antibiotics effective against bacterial diseases because the biological causes differ. Engineers designing spacecraft cannot simply apply every principle used in automobile manufacturing because space presents entirely different physical conditions. Intelligent reasoning therefore involves carefully evaluating both similarities and differences before transferring knowledge from one domain to another. Future AGI systems must develop this balanced judgment to avoid making incorrect assumptions based on superficial similarities.

Researchers believe that successful knowledge transfer depends heavily on **abstraction**. Abstraction means identifying the deeper principles underlying specific examples. Consider the concept of balance. Balance appears in riding bicycles, walking, engineering bridges, managing financial budgets, maintaining healthy ecosystems, and even resolving disagreements between people. Although these situations differ greatly, they all involve maintaining stability among interacting forces. Human intelligence recognizes these abstract principles and applies them across many different domains. Future AGI systems may likewise organize knowledge according to fundamental concepts rather than isolated facts, making transfer learning more flexible and efficient.

One of the ultimate goals of AGI research is creating systems capable of **general-purpose intelligence**. General-purpose intelligence means solving unfamiliar problems by combining knowledge from many different fields rather than relying upon narrow specialization. Imagine an AGI assisting with a mission to establish a human settlement on Mars. Success would require understanding astronomy, engineering, medicine, biology, agriculture, psychology, communications, environmental science, robotics, economics, and countless other disciplines simultaneously. No narrow AI system designed for only one subject could accomplish such a task alone. General-purpose intelligence emerges because knowledge transfers freely across domains, allowing integrated reasoning about highly complex challenges.

Knowledge transfer also strengthens collaboration between humans and intelligent machines. Human experts contribute creativity, ethical judgment, practical experience, cultural understanding, and emotional intelligence. AGI systems contribute rapid analysis of enormous knowledge collections spanning many scientific and technical fields. Together, humans and AGI may identify connections across disciplines that neither could discover independently. Scientists may accelerate medical research by combining biology with artificial intelligence. Engineers may improve renewable energy by integrating environmental science, materials engineering, and advanced simulations. Educators may personalize learning by combining cognitive science, psychology, and educational technology. Knowledge transfer therefore becomes a bridge connecting human expertise with machine intelligence.

As Artificial General Intelligence continues evolving, knowledge transfer across domains will become one of its defining capabilities. Intelligence is not measured by the number of facts stored within memory but by the ability to recognize patterns, identify deeper principles, and apply previous learning to entirely new situations. Human civilization has advanced because ideas have continually crossed boundaries between cultures, professions, and scientific disciplines. Future AGI systems will continue this tradition by connecting knowledge across increasingly diverse fields, accelerating discovery while supporting responsible decision-making.

Every lesson you learn today becomes more valuable when it connects with knowledge you acquire tomorrow. Mathematics strengthens science. Science supports engineering. History improves citizenship. Language enhances communication. Art encourages creativity. Technology expands opportunity. Human intelligence grows strongest when knowledge flows freely across these disciplines rather than remaining isolated. Artificial General Intelligence seeks to achieve the same flexibility by building learning systems capable of transferring understanding wherever it is needed. In doing so, AGI moves closer to one of the greatest strengths of the human mind: the ability to use yesterday's knowledge to solve tomorrow's problems.

Learn AI. Understand AI. Shape the Future.

— Susie Hala
IntelliGloss Press

Chapter 11 Summary

Knowledge Transfer Across Domains

Knowledge becomes far more valuable when it can be applied beyond the situation in which it was originally learned. Humans naturally transfer knowledge from one subject, experience, or skill to another, allowing them to solve unfamiliar problems more efficiently. This ability is known as **knowledge transfer**, and it is one of the defining characteristics that separates human intelligence from today's narrow artificial intelligence systems. Artificial General Intelligence (AGI) will require this same flexibility to operate successfully across many different fields instead of being limited to one specialized task.

One important aspect of knowledge transfer is **generalization**. Generalization allows intelligent systems to recognize broad principles that apply across many different situations rather than memorizing individual examples. Humans constantly generalize by applying previously learned concepts to new experiences. Scientists, engineers, physicians, and educators all depend on generalization when solving unfamiliar problems. Future AGI must develop similar abilities to adapt successfully to changing environments.

Another key concept is **transfer learning**. Transfer learning allows previously acquired knowledge to speed up learning in new tasks. Students use transfer learning whenever they apply mathematics to science, reading skills to history, or logical thinking to computer programming.

Modern AI also uses transfer learning by adapting previously trained models to new applications, reducing the amount of data and training required for each new task.

Analogical reasoning strengthens knowledge transfer by identifying similarities between different systems. Humans often understand unfamiliar concepts by comparing them with familiar experiences. Engineers study birds when designing aircraft, while medical researchers examine nature to develop new technologies. Analogical reasoning encourages creativity by allowing ideas from one discipline to inspire solutions in another.

Cross-domain thinking integrates knowledge from multiple fields to solve complex problems. Many modern challenges—including healthcare, climate change, engineering, and space exploration—require cooperation among many disciplines. Future AGI systems must combine knowledge from science, mathematics, engineering, medicine, economics, communication, and many other fields to generate effective solutions.

Adaptive intelligence allows both humans and intelligent machines to adjust successfully when circumstances change. Instead of relying only on memorized information, adaptive systems use previous knowledge to understand unfamiliar situations while continuing to learn through new experiences. This flexibility will become one of the most important characteristics of AGI.

Knowledge transfer also depends upon **abstraction**, which identifies deeper principles that connect different situations. Recognizing these common principles allows intelligence to apply learning across many domains rather than treating every new problem as completely unrelated.

The future of AGI depends on its ability to transfer knowledge freely across disciplines. By connecting ideas, recognizing patterns, adapting to new environments, and integrating information from multiple fields, AGI will become more flexible, creative, and capable of solving complex real-world challenges alongside humans.

Reflection

Think about everything you have learned throughout your life. Reading has helped you understand science, history, and mathematics. Communication skills help you build friendships, work in teams, and solve problems. Logical thinking improves everything from computer programming to everyday decision-making. Learning is powerful because knowledge rarely stays within one subject—it continually connects with other ideas.

Artificial General Intelligence must learn in much the same way. Instead of mastering only one task, future AGI must recognize similarities across many different fields, transfer previous learning to new situations, and continue adapting as knowledge grows. This ability will allow intelligent systems to become more flexible, creative, and helpful in solving problems that no single discipline can solve alone.

Some of history's greatest discoveries occurred because people connected ideas from different fields. Scientists, inventors, engineers, artists, and educators often succeed by recognizing patterns that others overlook. Knowledge transfer encourages innovation because it allows existing ideas to become the foundation for entirely new discoveries.

As you continue your education, remember that every subject you study strengthens many others. Learning is not a collection of separate classes—it is one continuously growing network of connected knowledge that prepares you to understand and solve the challenges of the future.

Student Worksheet

Name: ______________________________

Date: ______________________________

Part A – Vocabulary

Define each term using your own words.

1. Knowledge Transfer

____

2. Generalization

____

3. Transfer Learning

____

4. Analogical Reasoning

____

5. Cross-Domain Thinking

____

6. Adaptive Intelligence

____

7. Abstraction

Part B – Short Answer

1. Why is knowledge transfer important for intelligence?

2. Explain the difference between generalization and transfer learning.

3. How does analogical reasoning help solve unfamiliar problems?

4. Why is cross-domain thinking important for solving today's global challenges?

5. Why will adaptive intelligence be important for future AGI?

Part C – Matching

Letter	Concept	Number
A	Generalization	___ Applies previous learning to new tasks
B	Transfer Learning	___ Recognizes broad principles across situations
C	Analogical Reasoning	___ Compares similar systems
D	Cross-Domain Thinking	___ Combines multiple fields of knowledge
E	Adaptive Intelligence	___ Adjusts successfully to changing environments

Part D – Critical Thinking

Imagine you are developing an AGI system to help scientists discover new medicines.

Explain how the system would use:

Generalization

____

Transfer Learning

____

Analogical Reasoning

____

Cross-Domain Thinking

____

Adaptive Intelligence

____

How would combining these abilities improve scientific research?

____

____

____

Part E – Real-World Application

Choose one skill you have learned.

Examples:

- Riding a bicycle
- Playing a musical instrument
- Learning another language
- Playing a sport
- Computer programming

Describe how learning this skill helped you learn something else.

____

____

How is this similar to transfer learning in AGI?

Chapter 11 Quiz

Multiple Choice

1. Knowledge transfer allows intelligence to...

A. Forget previous learning

B. Apply previous knowledge to new situations

C. Memorize isolated facts

D. Eliminate reasoning

2. Generalization means...

A. Memorizing every example separately

B. Recognizing broad principles that apply across many situations

C. Ignoring previous knowledge

D. Learning only one subject

3. Transfer learning allows AI to...

A. Start from the beginning every time

B. Build upon previously learned knowledge

C. Delete existing knowledge

D. Avoid learning

4. Analogical reasoning helps intelligence by...

A. Comparing similar underlying ideas across different situations

B. Memorizing vocabulary

C. Organizing databases

D. Eliminating uncertainty

5. Cross-domain thinking combines...

A. Only mathematics

B. Only science

C. Knowledge from multiple disciplines

D. One subject at a time

True or False

6. Today's narrow AI generally specializes in one task.

True / False

7. Future AGI will likely transfer knowledge across many different domains.

True / False

8. Adaptive intelligence allows systems to adjust to changing environments.

True / False

9. Abstraction helps identify deeper principles shared by different situations.

True / False

10. Knowledge transfer encourages creativity and innovation.

True / False

Answer Key

Vocabulary

Answers will vary but should demonstrate accurate understanding of each concept.

Worksheet

Part B

1. Knowledge transfer allows previous learning to improve understanding and problem-solving in new situations.
2. Generalization identifies broad principles from examples, while transfer learning applies previously learned knowledge to accelerate new learning.
3. Analogical reasoning compares familiar situations with unfamiliar ones to identify useful similarities.
4. Many real-world problems require knowledge from several disciplines working together.
5. Adaptive intelligence allows AGI to continue learning and perform successfully as environments and information change.

Part C – Matching

A → Recognizes broad principles across situations

B → Applies previous learning to new tasks

C → Compares similar systems

D → Combines multiple fields of knowledge

E → Adjusts successfully to changing environments

Part D

Answers will vary but should demonstrate understanding of knowledge transfer, interdisciplinary learning, and adaptive intelligence.

Part E

Answers will vary based on each student's personal experiences.

Quiz Answers

1. **B**
2. **B**
3. **B**
4. **A**
5. **C**
6. **True**
7. **True**
8. **True**
9. **True**
10. **True**

Key Vocabulary

- Knowledge Transfer
- Generalization
- Transfer Learning
- Analogical Reasoning
- Cross-Domain Thinking
- Adaptive Intelligence
- Abstraction
- Cognitive Flexibility
- Pattern Recognition
- Interdisciplinary Learning
- Artificial General Intelligence (AGI)
- Innovation
- Problem Solving
- Knowledge Integration

- General-Purpose Intelligence

Chapter Takeaway

Knowledge becomes truly powerful when it moves beyond the boundaries of a single subject. By recognizing patterns, transferring learning, building analogies, integrating ideas from multiple disciplines, and adapting to new situations, both humans and future Artificial General Intelligence systems can solve increasingly complex problems, drive innovation, and expand understanding across every field of knowledge.

Learn AI. Understand AI. Shape the Future.

— Susie Hala
IntelliGloss Press

Chapter 12

Knowledge Sharing Among Intelligent Agents

Part 1

Human civilization has advanced because people have learned to share knowledge. Every scientific discovery, mathematical formula, engineering breakthrough, medical treatment, and historical lesson has become more valuable because it was communicated to others rather than remaining known by only one individual. A teacher passes knowledge to students. Scientists publish research so others can continue building upon their discoveries. Physicians share successful treatments with medical communities around the world. Engineers document new technologies so future generations can improve them further. Human progress depends not only on learning but also on the ability to exchange knowledge efficiently. Artificial General Intelligence (AGI) will require similar capabilities. Instead of operating as isolated intelligent systems, future AGI agents will likely collaborate, exchange information, coordinate decisions, and solve complex problems together. Knowledge sharing among intelligent agents therefore represents one of the most important foundations of future AI ecosystems.

Imagine attempting to build an entire modern city using only one person's knowledge. One individual would need to master architecture, engineering, medicine, law, education, agriculture, economics, transportation, communications, environmental science, and hundreds of other disciplines. Such a task would be nearly impossible because no single human possesses complete knowledge of every field. Human societies overcome this limitation through collaboration.

Specialists contribute expertise within their own disciplines while communicating effectively with others. Together they accomplish far more than any individual working alone. Future AGI systems will likely function in much the same way, with specialized intelligent agents cooperating to solve problems that exceed the capabilities of any single AI model.

Researchers describe these cooperative systems as **multi-agent systems**. A multi-agent system consists of multiple intelligent agents that work together toward common goals while sharing information, coordinating actions, and dividing responsibilities. Each agent may possess specialized knowledge or perform particular tasks, but all contribute to solving larger problems through communication and collaboration. Consider a hospital of the future. One intelligent agent monitors patient vital signs. Another analyzes laboratory results. A third reviews medical imaging. A fourth schedules operating rooms. A fifth manages medication inventories. Individually, each agent performs valuable work. Together, however, they create a coordinated healthcare system capable of supporting physicians, nurses, and patients with greater efficiency and accuracy than isolated systems could achieve independently.

Multi-agent systems already exist in limited forms within today's technology. Air traffic control coordinates information among airports, aircraft, weather systems, and navigation networks. Smart electrical grids balance energy production and consumption across thousands of power stations and communities. Financial institutions monitor millions of transactions using specialized systems responsible for fraud detection, risk assessment, customer service, and regulatory compliance. Although these systems remain relatively specialized, they demonstrate the advantages of distributing responsibilities among cooperating intelligent components rather than concentrating every function within one centralized system.

A major advantage of multi-agent systems is **distributed knowledge**. Distributed knowledge means that important information is spread across multiple intelligent agents instead of being stored entirely within one system. Human societies naturally operate this way. Teachers possess educational expertise. Physicians understand medicine. Engineers specialize in technology. Farmers understand agriculture. Lawyers interpret legal systems. No individual knows everything, yet society functions effectively because people communicate, collaborate, and share knowledge whenever needed. Future AGI ecosystems may organize knowledge similarly, allowing specialized agents to contribute expertise while benefiting from information supplied by others.

Distributed knowledge also improves reliability. Imagine an autonomous spacecraft traveling toward Mars. Instead of relying on one computer to perform every task, separate intelligent agents manage navigation, communications, power systems, scientific instruments, environmental monitoring, and emergency procedures. If one subsystem encounters difficulties, the remaining agents continue functioning while assisting with recovery. This distributed architecture increases resilience because no single point of failure controls the entire mission. Scientists increasingly design complex AI systems using similar principles to improve reliability, safety, and fault tolerance.

Knowledge sharing also supports **collaborative intelligence**, where multiple intelligent systems combine their expertise to achieve outcomes impossible for any one system acting alone. Human collaboration demonstrates this principle every day. A team of physicians treating a complicated patient may include surgeons, radiologists, cardiologists, pharmacists, nurses, nutritionists, and rehabilitation specialists. Each professional contributes unique expertise while communicating continuously with the rest of the medical team. The patient benefits because decisions reflect the combined knowledge of many experts rather than the perspective of only one individual. Future AGI systems may support similar forms of collaborative intelligence by integrating knowledge across many specialized domains.

Collaborative intelligence becomes especially valuable when solving global challenges. Climate change, pandemic response, food security, disaster relief, cybersecurity, and space exploration all involve enormous complexity extending across many scientific disciplines. Imagine responding to a powerful hurricane approaching a coastal city. One intelligent agent analyzes weather forecasts. Another predicts flooding. A third evaluates transportation networks. Another manages emergency communications. Medical agents estimate hospital capacity, while infrastructure agents monitor power grids and water systems. By sharing knowledge continuously, these agents create a coordinated response that allows emergency managers to make faster and more informed decisions. Collaboration transforms individual expertise into collective intelligence capable of addressing challenges far beyond the capacity of isolated systems.

Effective collaboration depends upon **communication**. Human teams succeed because members exchange ideas, ask questions, explain reasoning, and coordinate activities toward shared objectives. Artificial intelligence faces similar communication challenges. Future AGI agents must develop standardized methods for sharing information accurately while avoiding misunderstandings, conflicting instructions, or duplicated effort. Scientists refer to these methods as **communication protocols**. Communication protocols define how intelligent systems exchange messages, verify information, resolve disagreements, and maintain consistent understanding across large networks of cooperating agents.

Communication among intelligent agents requires more than simply transmitting data. The receiving agent must interpret the information correctly, understand its context, evaluate its reliability, and determine how it relates to ongoing tasks. Imagine one emergency response agent reporting that "water levels are rising rapidly." Another agent responsible for transportation must understand whether the flooding affects roads, bridges, hospitals, evacuation routes, or electrical infrastructure. Context transforms isolated messages into meaningful knowledge that supports coordinated decision-making. Future AGI systems will likely combine natural language understanding, knowledge graphs, semantic reasoning, and shared world models to communicate with one another as effectively as human experts working together.

As intelligent systems become increasingly sophisticated, knowledge sharing will allow learning to spread rapidly across entire networks. Imagine one educational AGI discovering a more effective method for teaching fractions. Instead of waiting years for textbooks to be revised, that knowledge could immediately become available to educational agents supporting students around the world. Similarly, medical discoveries, engineering innovations, environmental research, and scientific breakthroughs may spread almost instantly among collaborating AGI systems, accelerating human progress while maintaining consistent standards of accuracy and quality.

Knowledge sharing among intelligent agents represents one of the most exciting frontiers of Artificial General Intelligence. Rather than building one enormous AI responsible for every task, researchers increasingly envision ecosystems of specialized agents cooperating through shared knowledge, communication, and coordinated reasoning. In the next part of this chapter, you will explore **collective problem solving**, **shared understanding**, **coordinated decision-making**, and how networks of intelligent agents may become one of the defining characteristics of future AGI systems.

(End of Part 1 — Part 2 will continue with Collective Problem Solving, Shared Understanding, Communication Protocols, Coordinated Intelligence, and a powerful chapter conclusion.)

Chapter 12

Knowledge Sharing Among Intelligent Agents

Part 2

Knowledge sharing becomes truly powerful when individual intelligent agents begin solving problems **collectively** rather than independently. Human civilization provides countless examples of this principle. No single scientist developed modern medicine alone. No individual engineer built the entire Internet. No single researcher discovered every principle behind space exploration. Instead, generations of people contributed ideas, tested theories, corrected mistakes, shared discoveries, and improved one another's work. The result is a constantly expanding body of collective knowledge that belongs to humanity as a whole rather than to any one individual. Artificial General Intelligence (AGI) may eventually function in much the same way. Instead of relying upon one massive intelligence responsible for every task, future AGI ecosystems may consist of many specialized agents working together, each contributing knowledge that strengthens the capabilities of the entire system.

This process is known as **collective problem solving**. Collective problem solving occurs when multiple intelligent agents combine their expertise to solve challenges that would be difficult or impossible for one agent alone. Imagine an international mission to respond to a powerful earthquake. One AI agent analyzes satellite imagery to identify damaged buildings. Another evaluates road conditions and transportation routes. A third predicts aftershocks using geological models. Medical agents estimate hospital capacity and identify areas needing emergency supplies. Communication agents coordinate rescue teams, while logistics agents manage food, water, fuel, and shelter distribution. Individually, each agent performs an important task. Collectively, they create a comprehensive response that allows emergency managers to make faster, more accurate, and more informed decisions. Collaboration transforms specialized knowledge into coordinated intelligence capable of addressing highly complex real-world situations.

Collective problem solving also increases the quality of decisions. Human teams often produce better results because individuals contribute different perspectives and expertise. A physician may recognize medical concerns that an engineer would overlook, while an engineer may identify technical issues that a physician has never encountered. Teachers, psychologists, computer scientists, economists, and environmental researchers all contribute unique viewpoints that improve the overall quality of solutions. Future AGI systems may benefit from similar diversity by allowing specialized agents to examine the same problem from multiple perspectives before reaching a shared conclusion. This approach reduces the likelihood of important information being overlooked and encourages more balanced decision-making.

Successful collaboration requires more than exchanging information; it also requires developing **shared understanding**. Shared understanding means that multiple intelligent agents interpret information in compatible ways so they can coordinate their actions effectively. Imagine a team of firefighters responding to a rapidly spreading wildfire. If one team describes locations using street names while another uses geographic coordinates and a third uses local landmarks, confusion could delay rescue operations. Human teams overcome this problem by agreeing upon common maps, terminology, communication procedures, and operational plans. Artificial intelligence must solve similar challenges by developing standardized knowledge representations that allow different intelligent agents to understand information consistently, even when they were developed by different organizations or specialize in different tasks.

Shared understanding depends heavily on **communication protocols**. Communication protocols establish the rules governing how intelligent systems exchange information. These rules define message formats, verification procedures, priorities, timing, and methods for resolving conflicting information. Human communication follows similar principles. Pilots and air traffic controllers use standardized aviation terminology to prevent misunderstandings. Emergency responders follow established communication procedures during disasters. Scientists use common measurement systems so research can be reproduced accurately around the world. Future AGI systems will require equally reliable communication protocols to ensure that information moves safely, accurately, and efficiently across networks of intelligent agents.

Communication protocols become especially important when intelligent agents disagree. Consider a self-driving emergency vehicle approaching an intersection. One navigation agent recommends the fastest route to the hospital. A traffic-monitoring agent reports heavy congestion ahead. A weather agent warns of flooding on nearby roads. A safety agent identifies pedestrians entering the crosswalk. Each agent contributes valuable information, but their recommendations may conflict. The overall intelligence of the system depends on its ability to compare evidence, prioritize safety, evaluate risks, and reach a coordinated decision that reflects the combined knowledge of every participating agent. Researchers continue developing methods that allow intelligent systems to negotiate, cooperate, and resolve disagreements while maintaining consistent and reliable decision-making.

Another important feature of collaborative intelligence is **distributed decision-making**. Instead of sending every decision to one central computer, future AGI systems may allow specialized agents to make local decisions while sharing important information with the broader network. Human organizations operate similarly. Teachers make classroom decisions while principals manage schools, district administrators coordinate educational policy, and government agencies establish national educational standards. Each level contributes to larger goals while maintaining appropriate local authority. Distributed decision-making allows organizations to respond more quickly because many problems can be solved locally without waiting for centralized approval. Future AGI networks may adopt similar architectures to improve speed, flexibility, and resilience.

Distributed decision-making also improves **scalability**. As intelligent systems expand to support entire cities, nations, or even planetary exploration missions, no single computer can efficiently manage every detail simultaneously. Instead, many specialized agents divide responsibilities while sharing essential information. Smart cities may include intelligent transportation agents, energy management agents, water distribution agents, environmental monitoring agents, healthcare agents, educational agents, and emergency response agents. Together, these systems coordinate public services while allowing each specialized network to respond rapidly to local conditions. This scalable architecture enables intelligent systems to grow without overwhelming any single component.

Knowledge sharing also accelerates **learning**. Imagine an agricultural AI system discovering a new method for reducing water consumption while maintaining healthy crops during drought conditions. Rather than benefiting only one farm, that knowledge could immediately be shared with agricultural agents supporting farms across many regions. Similar sharing could occur in medicine when one hospital develops a more effective treatment protocol, in education when new instructional strategies improve student learning, or in engineering when safer construction techniques are developed. Networks of collaborating AGI systems may therefore learn collectively, allowing discoveries made anywhere within the network to strengthen the intelligence of the entire ecosystem.

Scientists believe future AGI systems may also develop **collective memory**. Human civilization possesses collective memory through books, libraries, universities, museums, scientific journals, digital archives, and educational institutions that preserve knowledge across generations. Individual people eventually retire or pass away, but humanity continues learning because knowledge is preserved and shared. Future AGI ecosystems may create similar collective memory systems where experiences, discoveries, successful solutions, and lessons learned become permanently available to all participating intelligent agents. This continuously expanding shared memory could allow future AI systems to improve far more rapidly than isolated models trained independently.

Despite its many advantages, collaborative intelligence also introduces important responsibilities. Information shared among intelligent agents must remain accurate, secure, and trustworthy. Incorrect information spreading throughout a network could influence many decisions simultaneously. Cybersecurity therefore becomes essential. Future AGI systems must verify information before accepting it, protect sensitive personal data, identify unreliable sources, and prevent unauthorized access to shared knowledge. Privacy protections, authentication methods, encryption, and continuous monitoring will all play critical roles in maintaining trustworthy knowledge-sharing ecosystems.

Ethics becomes equally important when intelligent agents collaborate. Networks of AGI systems operating in healthcare, education, transportation, finance, or government must make decisions that respect human rights, fairness, transparency, accountability, and individual privacy. Shared intelligence should never reduce human oversight when important decisions affect people's lives. Instead, collaborative AGI should support human experts by providing better information, broader analysis, and more coordinated recommendations while allowing people to remain responsible for final decisions. This partnership between humans and intelligent agents reflects one of the central goals of responsible AGI development.

Many researchers envision the future of AGI not as one supercomputer controlling everything, but as an **ecosystem of cooperating intelligences**. Much like ecosystems in nature, where different organisms perform specialized roles while depending upon one another for survival, future AGI networks may consist of countless specialized agents sharing knowledge continuously. Some agents may focus on education, others on healthcare, scientific research, transportation, manufacturing, environmental protection, or space exploration. Through communication, cooperation, and shared understanding, these intelligent agents could collectively solve problems far beyond the capabilities of any individual system.

The future of intelligence is therefore not only about making machines smarter—it is about making them better collaborators. Human civilization has advanced because people learned to share knowledge across cultures, generations, and scientific disciplines. Artificial General Intelligence follows the same path. By enabling intelligent agents to communicate effectively, develop shared understanding, solve problems collectively, and learn continuously from one another, AGI may become one of humanity's greatest collaborative partners. Together, humans and networks of intelligent agents may build a future where knowledge grows faster, solutions become more effective, and global challenges are addressed through cooperation rather than isolation.

Learn AI. Understand AI. Shape the Future.

— Susie Hala
IntelliGloss Press

Chapter 12 Summary

Knowledge Sharing Among Intelligent Agents

Knowledge becomes far more valuable when it is shared. Human civilization has advanced because people communicate discoveries, teach one another, publish research, and work together to solve problems. Future Artificial General Intelligence (AGI) will likely depend on similar forms of collaboration. Instead of functioning as isolated systems, intelligent agents will exchange information, coordinate decisions, and combine their expertise to solve challenges that no single agent could solve alone.

A **multi-agent system** consists of multiple intelligent agents working together toward common goals. Each agent may specialize in a different task, such as navigation, healthcare, communication, education, or scientific research. By cooperating and sharing information, these specialized agents create more powerful and flexible intelligent systems than a single agent working independently.

Knowledge sharing relies on **distributed knowledge**, where information is stored across many intelligent agents rather than within one central system. This approach improves efficiency, reliability, and resilience because each agent contributes specialized expertise while benefiting from knowledge provided by others. Distributed systems also reduce the risk of a single point of failure affecting the entire network.

Collaborative intelligence occurs when multiple intelligent agents combine their knowledge and reasoning abilities to solve complex problems. Future AGI systems may support emergency response, scientific research, healthcare, education, transportation, environmental protection, and many other fields by coordinating the expertise of numerous specialized agents working together.

Successful collaboration requires **communication protocols**, which establish standardized methods for exchanging information. Communication protocols ensure that intelligent agents interpret messages consistently, verify information accurately, resolve disagreements, and coordinate their actions efficiently. Shared understanding allows different agents to interpret information using the same meanings and context, reducing confusion and improving decision-making.

Future AGI systems may also use **distributed decision-making**, allowing specialized agents to solve local problems while sharing important information with larger networks. This approach improves scalability because intelligent systems can expand without depending entirely on one centralized controller.

Knowledge sharing also supports **collective learning** and **collective memory**. When one intelligent agent discovers a better solution, that knowledge can be shared across the entire network, allowing all participating agents to improve. Just as libraries and universities preserve human knowledge across generations, future AGI may maintain continuously expanding knowledge systems that benefit every intelligent agent within the network.

Ethics, cybersecurity, privacy, and human oversight remain essential. Shared intelligence must protect sensitive information, verify the accuracy of knowledge, prevent unauthorized access, and ensure that AI systems continue supporting human decision-makers responsibly.

The future of AGI is likely to involve networks of intelligent agents that collaborate continuously. By sharing knowledge, coordinating expertise, and learning together, these systems may help humanity solve increasingly complex challenges while improving education, healthcare, science, engineering, and many other fields.

Reflection

Think about the biggest projects you have completed in school. Chances are you worked with classmates, teachers, family members, or friends. Each person contributed different skills and ideas that helped achieve a better result than anyone could have produced alone. Collaboration allows knowledge to grow because people learn from one another.

Artificial General Intelligence will likely operate in much the same way. Instead of depending on one enormous AI system to solve every problem, future AGI may consist of many intelligent agents that specialize in different areas while sharing information continuously. This cooperative approach allows each agent to contribute its strengths while benefiting from the knowledge of others.

One of the greatest strengths of human civilization is our ability to preserve and share knowledge across generations. Every scientific discovery, technological innovation, and educational advancement becomes the starting point for future learning. AGI systems may one day accelerate this process by sharing new knowledge almost instantly across networks of intelligent agents.

As you continue learning, remember that education is not only about increasing your own knowledge. It is also about sharing what you learn with others so that everyone can grow together.

Student Worksheet

Name: ____

Date: ____

Part A – Vocabulary

Define each term using your own words.

1. Multi-Agent System

---

2. Distributed Knowledge

3. Collaborative Intelligence

4. Communication Protocol

5. Shared Understanding

6. Distributed Decision-Making

7. Collective Memory

Part B – Short Answer

1. Why is knowledge sharing important for both humans and AGI?

2. Explain the difference between a single AI system and a multi-agent system.

3. Why are communication protocols important for intelligent agents?

4. How does collective problem solving improve decision-making?

5. Why must future AGI protect privacy and cybersecurity while sharing knowledge?

Part C – Matching

Letter	Concept	Number
A	Multi-Agent System	___ Many intelligent agents working together
B	Distributed Knowledge	___ Knowledge shared across multiple agents
C	Collaborative Intelligence	___ Combines expertise to solve complex problems
D	Communication Protocol	___ Standardized method of exchanging information
E	Collective Memory	___ Shared knowledge preserved for future learning

Part D – Critical Thinking

Imagine your city is preparing for a major hurricane.

Describe how different AGI agents would work together:

Weather Agent

Transportation Agent

Hospital Agent

Emergency Communication Agent

Infrastructure Agent

How would sharing knowledge improve public safety?

Part E – Real-World Application

Think about a group project you completed at school.

Describe:

What was each person's responsibility?

How did everyone communicate?

What happened when information was shared effectively?

How is this similar to a multi-agent AGI system?

Chapter 12 Quiz

Multiple Choice

1. A multi-agent system consists of...

A. One intelligent computer only

B. Multiple intelligent agents working together

C. One database

D. One robot

2. Distributed knowledge means...

A. Information stored across multiple intelligent agents

B. Knowledge stored in one location only

C. No communication

D. Memorization only

3. Collaborative intelligence allows agents to...

A. Ignore one another

B. Combine expertise to solve complex problems

C. Delete information

D. Stop learning

4. Communication protocols help intelligent agents...

A. Exchange information accurately and consistently

B. Forget previous knowledge

C. Replace memory

D. Eliminate reasoning

5. Collective memory refers to...

A. Shared knowledge preserved across intelligent systems

B. Personal memory only

C. Temporary storage

D. Computer hardware

True or False

6. Multi-agent systems often perform better than isolated intelligent systems when solving large, complex problems.

True / False

7. Shared understanding helps intelligent agents interpret information consistently.

True / False

8. Future AGI systems will not need cybersecurity.

True / False

9. Distributed decision-making can improve scalability and flexibility.

True / False

10. Human oversight will continue to be important as AGI systems collaborate.

True / False

Answer Key

Vocabulary

Answers will vary but should demonstrate an accurate understanding of each concept.

Worksheet

Part B

1. Knowledge sharing allows intelligence to grow collectively, improves decision-making, and enables collaboration.

2. A single AI system performs tasks independently, while a multi-agent system consists of multiple specialized agents working together.
3. Communication protocols ensure accurate, reliable, and consistent information exchange.
4. Collective problem solving combines different perspectives and areas of expertise to create stronger solutions.
5. Protecting privacy, preventing cyberattacks, and verifying information help maintain trustworthy AI systems.

Part C – Matching

A → Many intelligent agents working together

B → Knowledge shared across multiple agents

C → Combines expertise to solve complex problems

D → Standardized method of exchanging information

E → Shared knowledge preserved for future learning

Part D

Answers will vary but should demonstrate understanding of collaboration, communication, and coordinated decision-making.

Part E

Answers will vary based on each student's own experiences with teamwork.

Quiz Answers

1. **B**
2. **A**
3. **B**
4. **A**
5. **A**
6. **True**
7. **True**

8. **False**
9. **True**
10. **True**

Key Vocabulary

- Multi-Agent System
- Distributed Knowledge
- Collaborative Intelligence
- Collective Problem Solving
- Communication Protocol
- Shared Understanding
- Distributed Decision-Making
- Collective Memory
- Knowledge Sharing
- Human-AI Collaboration
- Artificial General Intelligence (AGI)
- Cybersecurity
- Privacy
- Intelligent Networks
- Cooperative Intelligence

Chapter Takeaway

The future of Artificial General Intelligence will depend not only on how much individual systems know but also on how effectively they share knowledge. Through collaboration, communication, distributed expertise, and collective learning, networks of intelligent agents will be able to solve complex problems more efficiently, support human decision-making, and expand knowledge for the benefit of society.

Learn AI. Understand AI. Shape the Future.

— Susie Hala
IntelliGloss Press

Chapter 13

Knowledge Updating and Self-Correction

Part 1

One of the greatest strengths of intelligence is not knowing everything—it is recognizing when something needs to change. Throughout history, human knowledge has grown because people have been willing to question old ideas, test new evidence, correct mistakes, and improve their understanding of the world. Early astronomers once believed that Earth was the center of the universe. Later observations showed that Earth revolves around the Sun. Physicians once practiced medical treatments that modern science has proven ineffective or even harmful. Engineers continually improve designs after discovering safer materials and better construction methods. Every scientific breakthrough demonstrates an important lesson: intelligence grows stronger through correction. Artificial General Intelligence (AGI) must possess this same ability. Instead of treating every piece of knowledge as permanently correct, future AGI systems must recognize errors, update their understanding, and continuously improve as new information becomes available.

Human learning depends heavily on **feedback**. Students receive grades that help them understand which concepts they have mastered and which require additional study. Athletes review recordings of competitions to improve their techniques. Musicians listen carefully to performances while identifying areas for improvement. Scientists analyze experimental results to determine whether their hypotheses accurately explain observed evidence. In each case, feedback serves as a guide for learning. Rather than viewing mistakes as failures, intelligent learners use them as opportunities for growth. Future AGI systems will require similar feedback mechanisms that allow them to evaluate their own performance, identify weaknesses, and strengthen future decision-making.

One of the first steps in self-improvement is **detecting errors**. Error detection involves recognizing when knowledge, reasoning, predictions, or actions differ from reality. Imagine solving a mathematics problem and receiving an answer that does not match the correct solution. The difference immediately signals that something went wrong. A physician may notice that a patient's condition is not improving as expected, suggesting that the diagnosis should be reconsidered. A weather forecasting system may compare predicted temperatures with actual observations and identify differences that reveal weaknesses in its forecasting model. Detecting these inconsistencies allows intelligent systems to begin correcting their understanding rather than repeating the same mistakes.

Modern artificial intelligence already uses error detection extensively during training. Machine learning systems compare their predictions with correct answers, calculate the size of the error, and adjust internal parameters to improve future performance. This process repeats millions or even billions of times while the system gradually becomes more accurate. However, many current AI systems stop learning after their initial training is complete. Artificial General

Intelligence will likely continue detecting errors throughout its operational lifetime, allowing learning to occur continuously rather than only during development.

Detecting errors alone is not enough. Intelligence must also determine **why** the error occurred. Consider a self-driving vehicle that unexpectedly brakes while passing beneath a highway bridge because it mistakenly interprets the shadow as a physical obstacle. Engineers studying this behavior would not simply record that an error occurred. They would investigate sensor data, environmental conditions, software decisions, and perception algorithms to identify the underlying cause. Human intelligence naturally follows similar reasoning. When students answer test questions incorrectly, teachers encourage them to understand why the mistake occurred rather than merely memorizing the correct answer. Understanding causes prevents repeated errors and leads to deeper learning.

After identifying an error, intelligent systems must perform **knowledge updating**. Knowledge updating means replacing outdated, incomplete, or incorrect information with improved understanding supported by stronger evidence. Human knowledge constantly evolves through this process. Medical textbooks change as researchers discover better treatments. Scientific theories become more accurate through new experiments. Technology improves as engineers develop more effective designs. Even everyday understanding changes when people gain new experiences that challenge previous assumptions. Rather than weakening intelligence, updating knowledge strengthens it by bringing understanding closer to reality.

Knowledge updating requires careful evaluation of evidence. Imagine reading two articles presenting different explanations for the same scientific phenomenon. An intelligent learner does not simply accept whichever explanation appears first. Instead, the learner compares evidence, evaluates sources, considers expert consensus, and determines which explanation is better supported by reliable information. Future AGI systems must perform similar evaluations before modifying their knowledge bases. Updating knowledge responsibly means distinguishing trustworthy evidence from rumors, misinformation, incomplete data, or unreliable sources.

Researchers often describe this process as **belief revision**. Belief revision refers to changing conclusions when stronger evidence becomes available. Scientists demonstrate belief revision regularly. When new experimental evidence contradicts previous theories, researchers investigate carefully before modifying scientific understanding. This willingness to revise conclusions represents one of the greatest strengths of science because it allows knowledge to improve continuously. Future AGI systems must demonstrate similar intellectual flexibility by avoiding rigid adherence to outdated information while remaining cautious about accepting unsupported claims.

Belief revision becomes especially important in rapidly changing fields such as medicine, cybersecurity, climate science, economics, and artificial intelligence itself. Medical researchers continually discover new diseases, treatments, and biological mechanisms. Cybersecurity experts respond daily to newly emerging digital threats. Climate scientists refine environmental models using updated observations collected worldwide. Artificial intelligence researchers publish thousands of new findings every year. Future AGI systems operating within these environments must update their knowledge continuously while preserving reliable previous learning. This balance between stability and flexibility represents one of the greatest challenges in intelligent system design.

Knowledge updating also depends upon recognizing **uncertainty**. Human intelligence rarely possesses complete certainty about every situation. Physicians sometimes order additional laboratory tests before making diagnoses. Scientists perform repeated experiments before accepting conclusions. Engineers test prototypes extensively before approving final designs. Students ask questions when uncertain rather than pretending to understand concepts they have not yet mastered. Recognizing uncertainty allows intelligent learners to seek additional evidence before making important decisions. Future AGI systems must likewise estimate confidence levels, identify gaps in knowledge, and request additional information whenever existing evidence remains insufficient.

One remarkable characteristic of human intelligence is the ability to reflect upon previous decisions. People often reconsider conversations, review completed projects, analyze unsuccessful experiments, or evaluate personal choices while asking themselves what could have been done differently. This process prepares the mind for better future decisions by transforming experience into learning. Scientists believe future AGI systems will require similar reflective capabilities that allow intelligent machines to review completed tasks, compare expected outcomes with actual results, identify opportunities for improvement, and strengthen future reasoning.

Knowledge updating and self-correction represent essential foundations for lifelong learning. Rather than viewing intelligence as a fixed collection of facts, researchers increasingly understand intelligence as a continuously evolving process of observation, reasoning, correction, and improvement. In the next part of this chapter, you will explore **managing uncertainty**, **dynamic learning architectures**, **self-reflection systems**, and how future AGI may continually refine its own knowledge while remaining aligned with truth, evidence, and human values.

(End of Part 1 — Part 2 will continue with Managing Uncertainty, Self-Reflection Systems, Dynamic Learning Architectures, Continuous Improvement, and a powerful chapter conclusion.)

Chapter 13

Knowledge Updating and Self-Correction

Part 2

As intelligent systems become more advanced, one of their greatest challenges will not be acquiring new knowledge but determining **how confident they should be in what they already know**. Human beings rarely possess complete certainty about every decision they make. Doctors may order additional medical tests before confirming a diagnosis. Scientists often repeat experiments many times before accepting a new discovery. Engineers perform extensive safety testing before approving bridges, airplanes, or spacecraft for public use. Teachers evaluate multiple assignments before determining how well students understand a subject. These examples demonstrate an important principle of intelligence: wise decision-makers recognize uncertainty and seek stronger evidence before reaching important conclusions. Artificial General Intelligence (AGI) must develop this same ability if it is to make safe, reliable, and responsible decisions.

Managing uncertainty is the process of recognizing that some information is incomplete, conflicting, or still evolving. Imagine an emergency physician treating a patient with a high fever, severe fatigue, and difficulty breathing. Several illnesses may produce similar symptoms, making an immediate diagnosis difficult. Instead of assuming one answer is correct, the physician orders laboratory tests, reviews the patient's medical history, and consults additional specialists. Each new piece of evidence increases confidence while reducing uncertainty. Future AGI systems operating in medicine, engineering, education, finance, environmental science, and many other fields must perform similar evaluations by measuring confidence levels, identifying missing information, and requesting additional evidence whenever uncertainty remains high.

Managing uncertainty also protects intelligent systems from making overly confident mistakes. Human history contains many examples where incomplete knowledge led to incorrect conclusions. Scientific theories have changed as better evidence became available. Medical treatments once considered effective were later replaced by safer alternatives. New technologies have transformed industries that previously relied on outdated methods. These examples remind us that knowledge is constantly evolving. Future AGI systems must remain open to new evidence rather than assuming their current understanding is permanently complete. Intellectual flexibility allows intelligence to improve continuously while reducing the risk of repeating previous mistakes.

One of the most important tools supporting continuous improvement is **self-reflection**. Human beings naturally review their own thinking. A student may realize after an examination that more preparation was needed. An athlete studies recordings of competitions to improve performance. A scientist carefully examines unsuccessful experiments to understand why results differed from expectations. Business leaders analyze completed projects before planning future initiatives. Reflection transforms experience into wisdom because it encourages learners to examine both successes and failures. Future AGI systems may include similar self-reflection mechanisms that evaluate completed tasks, compare predictions with actual outcomes, identify weaknesses, and automatically improve future reasoning strategies.

Self-reflection differs from simply correcting errors because it examines the entire thinking process rather than only the final result. Imagine two students receiving the same incorrect answer on a mathematics problem. One student misunderstood the formula, while the other made a simple arithmetic mistake after applying the correct method. Although both answers were incorrect, the underlying causes differ significantly. Effective learning requires identifying not only **what** was wrong but also **why** it happened. Researchers believe future AGI systems will benefit from similar reflective analysis by examining how conclusions were reached, where reasoning became unreliable, and how future decisions can become more accurate.

Closely connected to self-reflection are **dynamic learning architectures**. Unlike traditional software that follows fixed instructions, dynamic learning architectures continuously update themselves as new experiences occur. Human intelligence naturally functions this way throughout life. Children gradually develop language skills. Students expand scientific understanding through education. Professionals continue learning as technology evolves within their careers. Even older adults acquire new knowledge through travel, reading, hobbies, and personal experiences. Intelligence remains dynamic because learning never truly ends. Future AGI systems must likewise update their internal knowledge structures continuously instead of remaining fixed after initial training.

Dynamic learning architectures allow intelligent systems to integrate new information without losing valuable previous knowledge. Researchers continue studying methods that prevent catastrophic forgetting, where learning new information unintentionally erases earlier understanding. Human memory generally avoids this problem by connecting new experiences with existing knowledge rather than replacing everything previously learned. Scientists developing AGI hope to design similar architectures that preserve important knowledge while continuously expanding understanding throughout the system's operational lifetime. Such architectures will allow intelligent machines to accumulate years or even decades of experience while remaining flexible enough to learn every day.

Another important aspect of self-correction involves **evaluating information sources**. Not all information deserves equal trust. Human intelligence learns to distinguish between reliable evidence and unsupported claims. Scientists rely on carefully designed experiments, peer-reviewed research, and reproducible results. Journalists verify information using multiple trustworthy sources before publishing important stories. Teachers encourage students to evaluate websites critically rather than believing everything they read online. Future AGI systems must develop similar source evaluation capabilities by considering evidence quality, source credibility, consistency with established knowledge, and the possibility of misinformation before updating their knowledge bases.

Knowledge updating also requires balancing **stability and flexibility**. If intelligent systems changed their beliefs every time new information appeared, they would become unstable and inconsistent. On the other hand, refusing to update knowledge despite overwhelming evidence would prevent learning altogether. Human intelligence solves this challenge by gradually adjusting beliefs according to the strength and reliability of available evidence. Scientific theories remain stable because they are supported by extensive research, yet scientists remain willing to revise them if convincing new evidence appears. Future AGI systems must maintain this same balance by preserving reliable knowledge while remaining open to continuous improvement.

Scientists often describe this ongoing process as **continuous improvement**. Continuous improvement means that intelligence becomes progressively more accurate, efficient, and reliable through repeated cycles of observation, evaluation, correction, learning, and application. Manufacturing companies improve product quality through continuous monitoring and refinement. Athletes strengthen performance through regular practice and coaching. Physicians improve patient care by incorporating new medical research. Software developers release updates that correct problems while introducing improved features. Artificial General Intelligence will likely follow similar improvement cycles, allowing intelligent systems to become increasingly capable as experience accumulates over time.

Self-correction also supports **responsible artificial intelligence**. Imagine an educational AGI tutor discovering that some students consistently misunderstand a particular lesson. Instead of continuing the same teaching approach, the system reflects on learning outcomes, identifies weaknesses in its explanations, and develops improved instructional strategies. Similarly, a medical AGI reviewing patient outcomes may recognize opportunities to improve diagnostic recommendations. An autonomous transportation system may analyze traffic incidents to strengthen future safety decisions. These examples illustrate how self-correction transforms mistakes into opportunities for continuous improvement while reducing future risks.

Future AGI systems may also collaborate during self-correction. Multiple intelligent agents could compare conclusions, identify disagreements, evaluate supporting evidence, and collectively determine which explanation best reflects reality. This collaborative self-correction resembles scientific research, where independent investigators review one another's work, replicate experiments, and strengthen conclusions through collective evaluation. By combining distributed knowledge with continuous self-improvement, AGI ecosystems may become increasingly reliable while avoiding many of the limitations associated with isolated learning systems.

Ethics remains central throughout every stage of knowledge updating. Intelligent systems should never modify important knowledge without careful evaluation of evidence, transparency, and appropriate human oversight when significant decisions affect people's lives. Updating medical knowledge, educational recommendations, legal guidance, or public policy requires careful consideration because incorrect changes may have serious consequences. Responsible AGI therefore combines technical learning with ethical reasoning, accountability, fairness, and respect for human values. Intelligence becomes truly trustworthy only when it improves responsibly.

Ultimately, self-correction represents one of the defining characteristics of genuine intelligence. Intelligent systems are not distinguished by never making mistakes. Rather, they are distinguished by recognizing mistakes, understanding why they occurred, learning from experience, and becoming better prepared for future challenges. Human civilization has advanced through countless cycles of observation, experimentation, correction, and discovery. Artificial General Intelligence seeks to continue this tradition by creating systems that learn continuously, revise their understanding when evidence changes, and improve responsibly throughout their operational lives.

Every lesson you learn, every mistake you correct, and every new experience you gain contributes to your own lifelong growth. The same principle will guide future AGI. Knowledge is never truly finished. It evolves through curiosity, evidence, reflection, and continuous improvement. By embracing self-correction rather than fearing mistakes, both humans and intelligent machines become wiser, more capable, and better prepared to solve the challenges of tomorrow.

Learn AI. Understand AI. Shape the Future.

— Susie Hala
IntelliGloss Press

Chapter 13 Summary

Knowledge Updating and Self-Correction

Intelligence is not measured by never making mistakes. Instead, true intelligence is demonstrated by recognizing mistakes, understanding why they happened, correcting them, and improving future decisions. Human knowledge has advanced throughout history because scientists, engineers, physicians, educators, and researchers have continually revised their understanding as new evidence became available. Artificial General Intelligence (AGI) must possess these same abilities if it is to remain accurate, trustworthy, and capable of lifelong learning.

One of the first steps in improvement is **error detection**. Intelligent systems must recognize when predictions, decisions, or knowledge differ from reality. Detecting errors allows both humans and AI to identify weaknesses and begin improving their understanding rather than repeating the same mistakes.

After identifying an error, intelligent systems must perform **knowledge updating**, replacing outdated or incorrect information with stronger evidence. Responsible knowledge updating requires evaluating reliable sources, comparing evidence, and distinguishing accurate information from misinformation or unsupported claims.

An important part of this process is **belief revision**, which allows intelligent systems to modify conclusions when better evidence becomes available. Science depends upon belief revision because researchers continuously refine theories through observation, experimentation, and discovery. Future AGI must demonstrate similar flexibility while maintaining stable and reliable knowledge.

Managing **uncertainty** is another essential capability. Intelligent systems should recognize when information is incomplete or confidence is low. Instead of making overly confident decisions, AGI should gather additional evidence, consult other sources, and communicate uncertainty honestly. This ability improves decision-making in healthcare, education, engineering, finance, emergency response, and many other fields.

Self-reflection allows intelligent systems to evaluate their own thinking processes. Rather than correcting only final answers, self-reflective systems analyze why mistakes occurred, identify weaknesses in reasoning, and improve future performance. Reflection transforms experience into deeper understanding and supports continuous learning.

Future AGI will likely rely on **dynamic learning architectures**, allowing knowledge systems to update continuously without forgetting valuable previous learning. These architectures support lifelong learning by integrating new information while preserving important existing knowledge.

Responsible knowledge updating also requires evaluating information sources carefully. Intelligent systems must consider evidence quality, credibility, consistency, and reliability before modifying their knowledge. This protects against misinformation and strengthens trust in AI-assisted decision-making.

Continuous improvement combines learning, reflection, correction, and adaptation into an ongoing cycle that strengthens intelligence over time. Rather than treating learning as a one-time event, AGI will likely improve throughout its operational life by continually refining its understanding of the world.

Knowledge updating and self-correction represent essential foundations of Artificial General Intelligence because they allow intelligent systems to remain accurate, adaptable, ethical, and capable of growing alongside humanity.

Reflection

Think about the first time you learned something difficult. You probably made mistakes, received feedback, practiced again, and gradually improved. Those mistakes were not signs of failure—they were an important part of learning. Every scientist, engineer, teacher, physician, athlete, musician, and inventor has improved by recognizing errors and making corrections.

Future Artificial General Intelligence must learn in much the same way. Instead of assuming it is always correct, AGI must evaluate new evidence, revise outdated knowledge, reflect on previous decisions, and continuously improve. This willingness to learn from mistakes will make intelligent systems more reliable, responsible, and helpful to society.

One of the most important lessons from this chapter is that intelligence requires humility. Truly intelligent learners understand that there is always more to discover and that better evidence can improve existing knowledge. This attitude has allowed humanity to advance in science, medicine, engineering, and every other field of learning.

As you continue your education, remember that mistakes are opportunities to grow. Every correction strengthens your understanding and prepares you for even greater learning in the future.

Student Worksheet

Name: ____

Date: ______________________________

Part A – Vocabulary

Define each term using your own words.

1. Error Detection

____

2. Knowledge Updating

____

3. Belief Revision

____

4. Uncertainty

____

5. Self-Reflection

____

6. Dynamic Learning Architecture

____

7. Continuous Improvement

____

____

Part B – Short Answer

1. Why is recognizing mistakes an important part of intelligence?

____

____

2. Explain the difference between error detection and knowledge updating.

3. Why must AGI evaluate information sources before updating knowledge?

4. How does self-reflection improve future decision-making?

5. Why is managing uncertainty important for responsible AI?

Part C – Matching

Letter	Concept	Number
A	Error Detection	___ Recognizes mistakes
B	Knowledge Updating	___ Replaces outdated knowledge
C	Belief Revision	___ Changes conclusions using better evidence
D	Self-Reflection	___ Evaluates previous thinking
E	Continuous Improvement	___ Ongoing cycle of learning and refinement

Part D – Critical Thinking

Imagine you are designing an AGI system to help hospitals improve patient care.

Explain how the system would use:

Error Detection

Knowledge Updating

Self-Reflection

Managing Uncertainty

Continuous Improvement

How would these abilities improve patient safety?

Part E – Personal Reflection

Think about a time you made a mistake while learning something new.

Describe:

What mistake did you make?

How did you discover the mistake?

What did you learn from correcting it?

How is this similar to how future AGI may improve itself?

Chapter 13 Quiz

Multiple Choice

1. Error detection allows intelligent systems to...

A. Ignore mistakes

B. Recognize when something is incorrect

C. Stop learning

D. Memorize information

2. Knowledge updating means...

A. Deleting all previous knowledge

B. Replacing outdated information with better evidence

C. Ignoring new discoveries

D. Memorizing facts repeatedly

3. Belief revision occurs when...

A. Better evidence leads to changing previous conclusions

B. Information never changes

C. Mistakes are ignored

D. Learning stops

4. Self-reflection helps intelligent systems...

A. Evaluate their own reasoning and improve future decisions

B. Forget previous experiences

C. Stop making decisions

D. Remove knowledge

5. Continuous improvement involves...

A. One-time learning only

B. Ongoing learning, correction, and refinement

C. Memorizing information once

D. Avoiding feedback

True or False

6. Future AGI should recognize uncertainty before making important decisions.

True / False

7. Dynamic learning architectures allow knowledge to continue growing over time.

True / False

8. Reliable information sources are important when updating knowledge.

True / False

9. Self-correction is one of the defining characteristics of intelligence.

True / False

10. Mistakes can become valuable learning opportunities.

True / False

Answer Key

Vocabulary

Answers will vary but should demonstrate accurate understanding of each concept.

Worksheet

Part B

1. Recognizing mistakes allows intelligence to improve, learn, and avoid repeating errors.
2. Error detection identifies that something is wrong, while knowledge updating replaces incorrect or outdated information with better evidence.
3. Reliable sources reduce misinformation and improve the accuracy of intelligent systems.
4. Self-reflection examines previous reasoning, identifies weaknesses, and strengthens future decisions.
5. Managing uncertainty encourages intelligent systems to gather additional evidence before making important decisions.

Part C – Matching

A → Recognizes mistakes

B → Replaces outdated knowledge

C → Changes conclusions using better evidence

D → Evaluates previous thinking

E → Ongoing cycle of learning and refinement

Part D

Answers will vary but should demonstrate understanding of feedback, reflection, uncertainty, and continuous improvement.

Part E

Answers will vary based on each student's personal learning experiences.

Quiz Answers

1. **B**
2. **B**
3. **A**
4. **A**
5. **B**
6. **True**
7. **True**
8. **True**
9. **True**
10. **True**

Key Vocabulary

- Error Detection
- Knowledge Updating
- Belief Revision
- Managing Uncertainty
- Self-Reflection
- Dynamic Learning Architecture
- Continuous Improvement
- Feedback
- Evidence
- Confidence Level
- Artificial General Intelligence (AGI)
- Lifelong Learning
- Responsible AI
- Critical Thinking
- Adaptive Intelligence

Chapter Takeaway

The ability to recognize mistakes, evaluate evidence, revise knowledge, and continuously improve is one of the strongest indicators of true intelligence. Through self-correction, reflection, uncertainty management, and lifelong learning, both humans and future Artificial General Intelligence systems become more accurate, adaptable, responsible, and capable of solving increasingly complex challenges.

Learn AI. Understand AI. Shape the Future.

— Susie Hala
IntelliGloss Press

Chapter 14

Knowledge Systems in Agentic AI

Part 1

Artificial intelligence is entering a new stage of development. For many years, most AI systems were designed to complete individual tasks after receiving direct instructions from humans. They could recognize images, translate languages, answer questions, recommend movies, or classify data, but they usually waited for someone to tell them exactly what to do next. Once a task was completed, the interaction often ended. Future Artificial General Intelligence (AGI), however, is expected to operate very differently. Instead of responding to one instruction at a time, intelligent systems will increasingly pursue long-term objectives, organize complex activities, adapt to changing situations, and coordinate multiple decisions over extended periods. These capabilities define **Agentic AI**, a new generation of intelligent systems that use knowledge to plan, reason, remember, and act toward meaningful goals. At the center of every successful agent lies one essential component: a powerful knowledge system.

A **knowledge system** serves as the foundation that allows an intelligent agent to understand its environment, interpret information, evaluate possible actions, and learn from experience. Without organized knowledge, an agent would simply react to incoming information without understanding its meaning or remembering previous experiences. Human beings demonstrate the importance of knowledge systems every day. Imagine preparing for an important school science fair. You begin by gathering information about the topic, reviewing previous experiments, creating a schedule, collecting materials, predicting possible challenges, and adjusting your plans as new information becomes available. Every step depends upon knowledge stored in memory and organized in ways that support decision-making. Future Agentic AI systems must perform similar processes by continuously acquiring, organizing, retrieving, updating, and applying knowledge throughout the entire life of a task.

One of the defining characteristics of Agentic AI is **goal-directed behavior**. Unlike traditional software that simply follows fixed instructions, intelligent agents pursue objectives while adapting their actions as circumstances change. Consider a household service robot asked to prepare a room for visiting guests. Completing this task involves much more than following one command. The robot must recognize the current condition of the room, identify objects that need attention, determine the proper order of activities, locate necessary cleaning supplies, avoid obstacles, respond to unexpected situations, and verify that the goal has been achieved. Throughout this process, knowledge systems guide every decision. The agent retrieves information about cleaning procedures, understands the locations of household objects, remembers previous experiences, evaluates environmental conditions, and adjusts its behavior whenever new information appears.

Goal-directed behavior also requires intelligent agents to distinguish between immediate actions and long-term objectives. Humans naturally perform this type of planning. A student preparing for college understands that earning good grades today contributes to future educational opportunities. Athletes follow daily training schedules because they recognize that small improvements accumulate over time into stronger performance. Farmers plant seeds months before harvesting crops because they understand long-term biological processes. Agentic AI systems must demonstrate similar thinking by connecting present decisions with future outcomes. Knowledge systems provide the information necessary to understand how individual actions contribute to larger goals over time.

Planning represents another essential capability supported by knowledge systems. Planning involves determining the sequence of actions most likely to achieve a desired objective. Imagine organizing a family vacation. Before leaving home, people typically choose destinations, reserve transportation, book hotels, estimate expenses, review weather forecasts, pack appropriate clothing, and prepare emergency contacts. These activities occur before the journey begins because intelligent planning reduces uncertainty and improves the likelihood of success. Future Agentic AI systems will perform similar planning processes while solving scientific problems, managing transportation systems, coordinating healthcare services, supporting manufacturing operations, or assisting emergency response teams.

Planning depends heavily on **world models**, which students explored in the previous chapter. World models allow intelligent agents to mentally simulate possible future events before taking action. Consider an autonomous agricultural robot responsible for watering crops. Instead of simply activating irrigation every morning, the robot consults weather forecasts, soil moisture measurements, plant growth stages, and water availability before determining the best irrigation schedule. If heavy rain is expected, watering may be postponed to conserve water. If temperatures rise unexpectedly, irrigation plans may change to protect crops from heat stress. Rather than reacting blindly, the agent predicts future conditions using knowledge stored within its world model. This ability to anticipate consequences allows Agentic AI to make more intelligent decisions while reducing unnecessary actions.

Knowledge systems also support **execution**, the process of carrying out plans successfully. Even carefully designed plans often require adjustment because real-world environments constantly change. Imagine organizing an outdoor school event when unexpected rain begins shortly before students arrive. Event organizers quickly modify seating arrangements, relocate activities indoors, and communicate changes to participants. The original goal remains the same, but the execution changes in response to new conditions. Future Agentic AI systems must demonstrate similar flexibility. Knowledge systems allow agents to compare current conditions with expected conditions, identify differences, and revise plans without abandoning overall objectives.

Another important responsibility of knowledge systems involves **tracking progress**. Human beings regularly evaluate whether they are moving closer to their goals. Students monitor assignment deadlines. Business managers review project schedules. Physicians evaluate patient recovery following treatment. Scientists compare experimental results with research objectives. These evaluations help determine whether current strategies remain effective or require modification. Future Agentic AI systems will likely monitor their own performance continuously by comparing completed actions with planned objectives, identifying delays or unexpected outcomes, and adjusting future decisions accordingly.

Planning and execution also require understanding **priorities**. Many situations present more possible tasks than can be completed simultaneously. Hospitals prioritize emergency patients requiring immediate care. Emergency responders rescue individuals facing the greatest danger first. Teachers allocate additional time to students needing extra assistance. Intelligent agents must likewise determine which actions deserve immediate attention while postponing less urgent activities. Knowledge systems organize information about urgency, importance, available resources, deadlines, and potential consequences, allowing Agentic AI to allocate effort efficiently while remaining focused on long-term goals.

Throughout every stage of planning and execution, knowledge systems interact continuously with memory, reasoning, learning, prediction, and decision-making. Rather than functioning independently, these cognitive abilities cooperate to guide intelligent behavior. As researchers continue developing Artificial General Intelligence, they increasingly recognize that successful Agentic AI will require tightly integrated knowledge systems capable of supporting every phase of goal-directed activity. In the next part of this chapter, you will explore **agent memory**, **agent reasoning**, **autonomous workflows**, **decision support systems**, and how future knowledge systems may enable intelligent agents to perform increasingly complex responsibilities while remaining aligned with human values.

(End of Part 1 — Part 2 will continue with Agent Memory, Agent Reasoning, Autonomous Workflows, Decision Support Systems, and a powerful chapter conclusion.)

Chapter 14

Knowledge Systems in Agentic AI

Part 2

As intelligent agents become more capable, they must remember far more than simple facts. They must remember **what they are trying to accomplish, what has already been completed, what resources remain available, what problems have been encountered, and what actions should happen next**. This capability is known as **agent memory**, and it represents one of the most important components of Agentic AI. Human beings constantly rely on memory while working toward long-term goals. Imagine building a science project over several weeks. You remember the research you completed, the materials you purchased, the experiments you have already conducted, and the improvements that still need to be made. Without memory, you would begin each day as if the project had never started. Future Artificial General Intelligence

(AGI) systems must avoid this limitation by maintaining organized memories that allow them to continue complex tasks over long periods of time.

Agent memory extends beyond simply storing information. It also organizes knowledge according to purpose. A physician treating a patient remembers medical history, laboratory results, previous medications, allergies, and ongoing treatments because each piece of information contributes to future medical decisions. A construction manager remembers completed inspections, delivery schedules, building codes, and project milestones while coordinating a large construction project. Likewise, an intelligent agent supporting scientific research must remember previous experiments, successful methods, failed approaches, and unanswered questions while continuing its investigation. Effective agent memory allows knowledge to remain available whenever it is needed, transforming isolated information into a continuously evolving understanding of long-term objectives.

Closely connected to memory is **agent reasoning**. Reasoning allows intelligent agents to evaluate situations, compare possible actions, anticipate consequences, and select strategies that best support their goals. Imagine an autonomous search-and-rescue robot entering a partially collapsed building after an earthquake. The robot receives information from cameras, temperature sensors, structural monitors, and communication systems. Rather than reacting to each sensor independently, the robot reasons about how all of this information fits together. It evaluates structural stability, predicts potential hazards, identifies the safest rescue routes, and adjusts its plans as new information becomes available. Agent reasoning transforms knowledge into intelligent action by connecting memory, perception, prediction, and decision-making into one coordinated process.

Agent reasoning becomes especially valuable when unexpected situations occur. Human beings rarely follow plans exactly as originally designed because real-world environments constantly change. Flights may be delayed because of weather. Scientific experiments may produce surprising results. Medical treatments sometimes require adjustment after new laboratory findings appear. Teachers modify lesson plans when students need additional instruction. Future Agentic AI systems must demonstrate similar flexibility. Rather than abandoning a goal when obstacles appear, intelligent agents will reason through the new situation, evaluate alternative strategies, and continue working toward success using updated knowledge. This adaptability distinguishes intelligent behavior from rigid automation.

Another important capability supported by knowledge systems is the development of **autonomous workflows**. A workflow is a sequence of organized steps required to complete a task. Humans use workflows every day, often without noticing them. Baking bread involves gathering ingredients, mixing dough, allowing it to rise, baking it, and cooling it before serving. Launching a spacecraft requires years of planning, manufacturing, testing, fueling, countdown procedures, and mission control operations. Hospitals follow carefully organized workflows when treating patients from admission through diagnosis, treatment, recovery, and discharge. Future Agentic AI systems will increasingly manage complex workflows while coordinating many smaller tasks that contribute toward larger objectives.

Autonomous workflows differ from traditional computer programs because they can adjust themselves as circumstances change. Imagine an intelligent agricultural system responsible for growing crops throughout an entire season. Instead of following one fixed schedule, the system continuously evaluates weather forecasts, soil moisture, plant growth, insect activity, water availability, and equipment performance. If drought conditions develop, irrigation schedules change automatically. If insects threaten crops, monitoring systems increase inspection frequency. If storms are approaching, harvesting plans may be adjusted to reduce losses. Rather than simply executing one prewritten sequence of instructions, the workflow evolves as new information becomes available. Knowledge systems provide the understanding necessary for these adjustments while keeping the overall goal unchanged.

Knowledge systems also strengthen **decision support systems**, which assist humans by organizing information, evaluating alternatives, and presenting evidence-based recommendations. Decision support systems do not replace human judgment. Instead, they provide additional insight that helps people make better-informed choices. Physicians use decision support systems to compare patient information with medical research. Financial analysts evaluate economic trends before making investment recommendations. Environmental scientists use predictive models to assess conservation strategies. School administrators analyze student performance data when planning educational improvements. Future AGI systems will expand these capabilities by integrating information from many disciplines, allowing human decision-makers to consider more evidence than any individual could analyze alone.

Decision support systems become particularly valuable when decisions involve enormous amounts of information. Imagine a team of scientists studying climate change. They may need to examine satellite observations, ocean temperatures, atmospheric chemistry, historical weather records, population growth, energy consumption, and environmental policies simultaneously. No individual researcher can personally analyze every available dataset in real time. An AGI-powered decision support system could organize this information, identify important relationships, simulate possible future outcomes, and present understandable recommendations while leaving final decisions to human experts. In this way, knowledge systems enhance human intelligence rather than replacing it.

Agent memory, reasoning, autonomous workflows, and decision support systems all depend upon one critical capability: **continuous feedback**. Intelligent agents must constantly compare expected outcomes with actual results. Imagine a robotic warehouse system responsible for filling customer orders. If inventory information indicates that an item should be available but the shelf is empty, the system immediately recognizes a discrepancy. It investigates possible explanations, updates inventory records, notifies managers, and adjusts future decisions to prevent additional errors. This continuous feedback loop allows intelligent systems to remain accurate even as conditions change. Future AGI will likely rely on similar feedback processes throughout every stage of planning, execution, and learning.

As knowledge systems become increasingly sophisticated, intelligent agents may also begin **coordinating with other agents** to accomplish larger objectives. Imagine a future smart city. Transportation agents monitor traffic flow. Energy agents balance electricity demand. Environmental agents measure air quality. Emergency response agents coordinate ambulances and fire departments. Educational agents support schools and libraries. Healthcare agents monitor hospital capacity and public health trends. Each agent specializes in one area, yet all communicate continuously through shared knowledge systems. Together they create a coordinated urban intelligence capable of responding rapidly to changing conditions while improving the quality of life for millions of people.

Despite these exciting possibilities, knowledge systems in Agentic AI must always operate within strong ethical boundaries. Intelligent agents may increasingly influence healthcare, education, transportation, finance, public safety, and scientific research. Decisions made by these systems can affect people's lives in significant ways. Therefore, future Agentic AI must remain transparent, accountable, fair, and aligned with human values. Human oversight will continue to play an essential role, especially when decisions involve safety, privacy, legal responsibilities, or ethical questions. Knowledge systems should support human decision-making rather than replacing human responsibility.

Researchers often describe Agentic AI as moving from **reactive intelligence** to **purposeful intelligence**. Reactive systems wait for commands and respond to individual requests. Purposeful systems pursue goals over time by remembering previous actions, reasoning through challenges, adjusting plans, coordinating resources, and learning from experience. This transformation depends entirely on powerful knowledge systems that connect memory, reasoning, learning, prediction, communication, and decision-making into one unified cognitive architecture. Without these knowledge systems, intelligent agents would lack the understanding needed to operate independently in complex environments.

As Artificial General Intelligence continues developing, knowledge systems will become the foundation upon which intelligent agents plan, act, learn, and improve. Every goal an agent pursues, every decision it makes, every obstacle it overcomes, and every lesson it learns depends upon organized knowledge that can be retrieved, updated, shared, and applied effectively. In many ways, knowledge systems function as the cognitive engine that powers Agentic AI, allowing intelligent machines to move beyond simply responding to questions and toward actively helping people solve meaningful problems.

The future of Agentic AI is not simply about building machines that work faster. It is about creating intelligent partners that understand goals, adapt responsibly to changing situations, remember what matters, reason carefully before acting, and continuously improve through experience. By combining powerful knowledge systems with ethical decision-making and human collaboration, future AGI may become one of the most valuable tools humanity has ever created—helping people learn, innovate, solve global challenges, and build a safer, healthier, and more knowledgeable world.

Learn AI. Understand AI. Shape the Future.

— Susie Hala
IntelliGloss Press

Chapter 14 Summary

Knowledge Systems in Agentic AI

Knowledge systems are the foundation that allows Agentic AI to pursue goals, make decisions, solve problems, and adapt to changing environments. Unlike traditional AI systems that simply respond to individual requests, Agentic AI uses organized knowledge to plan long-term activities, monitor progress, adjust strategies, and continue working until goals are achieved. These capabilities move artificial intelligence closer to the flexible and purposeful behavior expected in Artificial General Intelligence (AGI).

One of the defining characteristics of Agentic AI is **goal-directed behavior**. Intelligent agents work toward specific objectives rather than performing isolated tasks. To accomplish these goals, they gather information, organize knowledge, evaluate possible actions, predict outcomes, and continuously monitor their progress. Knowledge systems guide every stage of this process.

Planning is another essential capability supported by knowledge systems. Intelligent agents analyze available information, anticipate future conditions, organize tasks into logical sequences, and prepare for unexpected situations. By using world models and prediction, Agentic AI can evaluate several possible solutions before taking action.

As plans are carried out, knowledge systems support **execution** by helping agents compare expected outcomes with actual results. When environments change or unexpected obstacles appear, intelligent agents can modify their plans while remaining focused on their overall objectives. This flexibility distinguishes Agentic AI from traditional software that follows fixed instructions.

Agent memory allows intelligent systems to remember goals, previous actions, important observations, available resources, and lessons learned throughout long-term tasks. Instead of beginning every task from the start, agents build upon previous experiences and continue learning over time.

Agent reasoning enables intelligent systems to evaluate information, compare alternatives, predict consequences, and select actions that best support their goals. Reasoning transforms stored knowledge into intelligent decision-making by integrating memory, learning, perception, and planning.

Knowledge systems also support **autonomous workflows**, allowing intelligent agents to complete complex sequences of tasks while adjusting automatically as new information becomes available. These workflows are widely applicable in healthcare, agriculture, transportation, manufacturing, education, and scientific research.

Decision support systems assist humans by organizing information, evaluating alternatives, and providing evidence-based recommendations. Rather than replacing human decision-makers, AGI-powered decision support systems strengthen human judgment by analyzing far more information than individuals could evaluate alone.

Future Agentic AI systems will increasingly collaborate with other intelligent agents, sharing knowledge to solve larger and more complex problems. Throughout this process, ethics, transparency, privacy, accountability, and human oversight remain essential to ensure that intelligent systems continue serving society responsibly.

Knowledge systems are the cognitive engine that powers Agentic AI. They allow intelligent agents to remember, reason, plan, adapt, collaborate, and continuously improve while pursuing meaningful goals that benefit humanity.

Reflection

Every important goal you have achieved required planning, memory, reasoning, and persistence. Whether completing a school project, preparing for an athletic competition, learning to play an instrument, or solving a difficult problem, your brain continuously organized knowledge, adjusted plans, and learned from experience.

Agentic AI must perform many of these same functions. Instead of responding to one request at a time, future intelligent agents will pursue long-term goals while adapting to changing situations. They will remember previous work, evaluate new information, revise plans, and continue improving until objectives are achieved.

One important lesson from this chapter is that intelligence is more than answering questions. True intelligence involves setting goals, making responsible decisions, solving unexpected problems, learning from experience, and working together with others. These qualities will help define the future of Artificial General Intelligence.

As technology continues advancing, humans and intelligent agents will likely collaborate more closely than ever before. The strongest future will be one where knowledge systems support human creativity, ethical judgment, and problem-solving while helping build a safer, healthier, and more innovative world.

Student Worksheet

Name: ____

Date: ____

Part A – Vocabulary

Define each term using your own words.

1. Agentic AI

2. Goal-Directed Behavior

3. Agent Memory

4. Agent Reasoning

5. Autonomous Workflow

6. Decision Support System

7. Knowledge System

Part B – Short Answer

1. How does Agentic AI differ from traditional AI systems?

2. Why is agent memory important for completing long-term goals?

3. How does planning improve intelligent decision-making?

4. What is the purpose of a decision support system?

5. Why must Agentic AI remain aligned with human values?

Part C – Matching

Letter	Concept		Number
A	Goal-Directed Behavior	___	Works toward long-term objectives
B	Agent Memory	___	Stores previous experiences and task progress
C	Agent Reasoning	___	Evaluates alternatives and selects actions
D	Autonomous Workflow	___	Completes organized sequences of tasks
E	Decision Support System	___	Assists people with evidence-based recommendations

Part D – Critical Thinking

Imagine you are designing an AGI assistant to help a hospital during a large public health emergency.

Explain how the system would use:

Goal-Directed Behavior

Agent Memory

Agent Reasoning

Autonomous Workflows

Decision Support Systems

How would these capabilities improve patient care and hospital operations?

Part E – Real-World Application

Think about a long-term goal you have worked toward.

Examples:

- Completing a science project
- Preparing for a sports season
- Learning a musical instrument
- Improving your grades
- Building something

Describe:

Your goal

Your plan

How you adjusted when problems occurred

How is this similar to the way Agentic AI works?

Chapter 14 Quiz

Multiple Choice

1. Agentic AI is designed to...

A. Only answer questions

B. Pursue goals through planning, reasoning, and adaptation

C. Store information only

D. Perform one fixed task forever

2. Agent memory allows intelligent systems to...

A. Forget previous work

B. Remember goals, actions, and experiences

C. Stop learning

D. Delete information

3. Agent reasoning helps intelligent systems...

A. Ignore evidence

B. Evaluate alternatives and make informed decisions

C. Memorize data only

D. Eliminate planning

4. Autonomous workflows allow agents to...

A. Complete organized tasks while adapting to change

B. Wait for every instruction

C. Stop when problems occur

D. Avoid decision-making

5. Decision support systems are designed to...

A. Replace human judgment completely

B. Help humans make informed decisions using organized knowledge

C. Eliminate experts

D. Memorize information

True or False

6. Knowledge systems provide the foundation for Agentic AI.

True / False

7. Goal-directed behavior focuses on achieving long-term objectives.

True / False

8. Future Agentic AI will likely collaborate with other intelligent agents.

True / False

9. Ethics and human oversight remain important as Agentic AI becomes more capable.

True / False

10. Planning, memory, reasoning, and learning work together within Agentic AI.

True / False

Answer Key

Vocabulary

Answers will vary but should accurately explain each concept.

Worksheet

Part B

1. Traditional AI usually performs individual tasks after receiving instructions, while Agentic AI pursues long-term goals through planning, reasoning, memory, learning, and adaptation.
2. Agent memory stores previous experiences, completed tasks, available resources, and important information needed to continue long-term work.
3. Planning organizes tasks, predicts future conditions, prepares for challenges, and improves the likelihood of achieving goals.
4. Decision support systems organize information, analyze evidence, compare alternatives, and provide recommendations that strengthen human decision-making.
5. Alignment with human values helps ensure fairness, safety, privacy, accountability, and responsible use of intelligent systems.

Part C – Matching

A → Works toward long-term objectives

B → Stores previous experiences and task progress

C → Evaluates alternatives and selects actions

D → Completes organized sequences of tasks

E → Assists people with evidence-based recommendations

Part D

Answers will vary but should demonstrate understanding of planning, reasoning, memory, workflows, and collaboration.

Part E

Answers will vary based on each student's personal experiences.

Quiz Answers

1. **B**
2. **B**
3. **B**
4. **A**
5. **B**
6. **True**
7. **True**
8. **True**
9. **True**
10. **True**

Key Vocabulary

- Agentic AI
- Knowledge System
- Goal-Directed Behavior
- Planning
- Execution
- Agent Memory
- Agent Reasoning
- Autonomous Workflow
- Decision Support System
- World Model
- Artificial General Intelligence (AGI)
- Human-AI Collaboration
- Ethical AI
- Adaptive Intelligence
- Cognitive Architecture

Chapter Takeaway

Knowledge systems transform artificial intelligence from a tool that simply responds to instructions into an intelligent agent capable of planning, reasoning, remembering, adapting, and pursuing meaningful goals. By combining memory, decision-making,

autonomous workflows, and ethical collaboration with humans, Agentic AI represents an important step toward the development of Artificial General Intelligence that can responsibly solve complex real-world challenges.

Learn AI. Understand AI. Shape the Future.

— Susie Hala
IntelliGloss Press

Chapter 15

Knowledge Systems and Artificial General Intelligence

Part 1

Artificial intelligence has achieved remarkable success during the past several decades. Today's AI systems can recognize faces, translate languages, recommend movies, diagnose certain diseases, write computer code, generate realistic images, and assist scientists in analyzing enormous collections of data. These accomplishments demonstrate tremendous technological progress, yet they also reveal an important limitation. Most modern AI systems remain highly specialized. They perform exceptionally well within carefully defined tasks but often struggle when faced with unfamiliar situations requiring flexible reasoning, broad understanding, and knowledge that spans many different disciplines. Artificial General Intelligence (AGI) seeks to overcome these limitations by creating intelligent systems capable of learning, reasoning, adapting, and solving problems across virtually any domain. Achieving this goal will require knowledge systems far more sophisticated than anything available today.

Throughout this book, you have explored many individual components of knowledge systems. You learned how knowledge differs from raw information, how intelligent systems organize concepts, build memory, retrieve knowledge, learn continuously, reason logically, develop world models, transfer knowledge across domains, collaborate with other intelligent agents, and improve through self-correction. Each of these capabilities contributes an important piece of the puzzle. However, true AGI requires something even more powerful: the integration of all these capabilities into one unified cognitive architecture that functions as a coherent whole rather than as separate independent systems.

Human intelligence provides an excellent example of this integration. Imagine a physician treating a patient arriving at the emergency department with severe chest pain. Within moments, the physician retrieves medical knowledge, recalls previous clinical experience, interprets laboratory results, analyzes medical images, evaluates possible diagnoses, predicts treatment outcomes, communicates with specialists, explains options to the patient, considers ethical responsibilities, and continuously updates decisions as new information becomes available. These cognitive processes occur together almost seamlessly. Memory, reasoning, perception, communication, learning, planning, and decision-making all cooperate within one integrated knowledge system. Future AGI must demonstrate similar coordination if it is to function with human-like flexibility.

Researchers often describe this type of organization as a **unified knowledge architecture**. A unified knowledge architecture connects every major cognitive capability into one continuously interacting system. Instead of maintaining isolated databases for language, vision, planning, memory, or reasoning, AGI integrates knowledge across all domains so that information learned in one area immediately becomes available throughout the entire cognitive system. This interconnected structure allows intelligent systems to recognize relationships that specialized AI might overlook, making reasoning more flexible and adaptive.

Consider how humans learn about water. A child first recognizes water as something to drink. Later, science classes explain the water cycle, chemistry describes molecular structure, geography explores rivers and oceans, biology examines the role of water in living organisms, engineering studies dams and irrigation systems, and environmental science investigates conservation. Although these lessons come from different school subjects, the brain gradually integrates them into one comprehensive understanding of water. Future AGI systems must develop similar unified knowledge architectures that combine information from mathematics, science, medicine, engineering, history, language, economics, art, and many other disciplines into one coherent model of reality.

Another essential requirement for AGI is the development of **general reasoning systems**. Current AI often excels within narrow reasoning tasks but struggles when multiple forms of reasoning must operate together. Human intelligence naturally combines deductive reasoning, inductive reasoning, abductive reasoning, analogical thinking, causal reasoning, ethical reasoning, and creative problem-solving while adapting to new situations. Imagine planning a mission to establish a research station on Mars. Such a challenge requires understanding astronomy, engineering, biology, medicine, psychology, environmental science, communications, robotics, economics, and countless other fields simultaneously. No single reasoning method is sufficient. Future AGI systems must coordinate many forms of reasoning while integrating knowledge from across the entire cognitive architecture.

General reasoning also depends upon **context**. Human beings rarely interpret information in isolation. The meaning of words, actions, images, and events often depends on surrounding circumstances. Imagine hearing someone say, "It's getting cold." During winter, this may simply describe the weather. During a scientific experiment, it may refer to changing laboratory conditions. While camping, it may suggest starting a fire. During a medical procedure, it may indicate concern about a patient's body temperature. Human intelligence automatically interprets these different meanings because knowledge systems combine language with environmental awareness, previous experience, and current goals. Future AGI systems must develop similarly rich contextual understanding to communicate effectively and make appropriate decisions.

AGI also requires **human-like understanding**, which extends beyond memorizing facts or recognizing statistical patterns. Human understanding involves explaining why events occur, predicting future outcomes, recognizing cause-and-effect relationships, evaluating consequences, and transferring knowledge across entirely different situations. Imagine observing leaves falling from trees during autumn. Human understanding connects this observation with seasonal changes, plant biology, climate, energy conservation, and the life cycle of ecosystems. A truly intelligent machine must demonstrate similar depth of understanding rather than simply identifying leaves within photographs. Knowledge systems therefore become much more than storage systems—they become frameworks for interpreting reality itself.

Another important characteristic of AGI knowledge systems is their ability to **integrate perception with reasoning**. Humans continuously combine information from vision, hearing, touch, language, memory, and previous experience while interacting with the world. Imagine walking through a crowded train station. You recognize signs, hear announcements, avoid obstacles, remember your destination, estimate travel time, interpret conversations, and adjust your route when necessary. These activities require multiple cognitive systems working together simultaneously. Future AGI must similarly integrate information from cameras, microphones, sensors, language systems, world models, and reasoning engines into one coordinated understanding of complex environments.

Researchers increasingly believe that AGI knowledge systems must also support **continuous cognitive integration**. Learning should immediately strengthen reasoning. New experiences should update world models. Improved reasoning should refine future planning. Memory should influence decision-making. Ethical principles should guide every action. Rather than functioning independently, every component of intelligence should continuously influence every other component. This integrated architecture allows intelligence to remain flexible, adaptive, and capable of lifelong improvement.

Building such unified systems presents one of the greatest scientific and engineering challenges of the twenty-first century. Researchers must determine how knowledge should be represented, organized, updated, retrieved, reasoned about, and shared while maintaining consistency across enormous collections of interconnected information. Success will require advances in computer science, neuroscience, psychology, mathematics, linguistics, robotics, ethics, and many other fields. Artificial General Intelligence will likely emerge not from one breakthrough alone but from successfully integrating many different cognitive capabilities into one coherent knowledge system.

As you have discovered throughout this book, knowledge is the foundation upon which every intelligent capability depends. Learning, reasoning, planning, prediction, communication, collaboration, and decision-making all require organized knowledge that can be understood, updated, and applied effectively. In the next part of this chapter, you will explore **cognitive integration**, **the path toward AGI**, **responsible intelligence**, and how unified knowledge systems may eventually allow machines to learn, reason, and collaborate with humans in ways that transform education, science, healthcare, and society itself.

(End of Part 1 — Part 2 will continue with Cognitive Integration, Responsible AGI, Unified Intelligence, Human-AI Collaboration, and a powerful chapter conclusion.)

Chapter 15

Knowledge Systems and Artificial General Intelligence

Part 2

As researchers continue developing Artificial General Intelligence (AGI), they increasingly recognize that intelligence cannot be built by improving one ability at a time. A machine that has excellent memory but poor reasoning will make ineffective decisions. A system with advanced reasoning but limited knowledge will struggle to solve unfamiliar problems. An intelligent agent capable of planning but unable to learn from experience will eventually become outdated as the world changes. True AGI requires every major cognitive capability to work together continuously, forming a single, coordinated system. This process is known as **cognitive integration**, and many researchers believe it represents one of the final and most important steps toward achieving general intelligence.

Cognitive integration refers to the seamless cooperation of memory, perception, learning, reasoning, planning, communication, world models, decision-making, and self-correction. Human intelligence demonstrates this integration every moment of every day. Imagine a firefighter responding to a rapidly spreading wildfire. The firefighter observes changing wind conditions, remembers previous training, communicates with teammates, predicts how the fire may spread, reasons about evacuation routes, evaluates risks to nearby communities, and continuously adjusts decisions as new information becomes available. None of these abilities operates independently. Each supports and strengthens the others in real time. Future AGI systems must achieve similar coordination if they are to function safely and effectively in dynamic environments.

One of the greatest advantages of cognitive integration is **flexibility**. Human beings rarely encounter problems that fit neatly into one category. Most real-world challenges require knowledge from several different disciplines. Consider designing a sustainable city of the future. Architects contribute expertise in building design. Civil engineers develop transportation systems. Environmental scientists evaluate natural resources. Economists study financial sustainability. Urban planners organize neighborhoods. Educators consider schools and lifelong learning. Public health experts improve community well-being. Computer scientists develop intelligent infrastructure. Future AGI systems will need knowledge architectures capable of combining all of these perspectives simultaneously rather than solving each problem in isolation. This flexibility allows intelligence to address increasingly complex challenges that extend across multiple domains.

Another defining characteristic of AGI is the ability to **understand relationships** instead of simply storing information. Human intelligence naturally recognizes that events influence one another. A change in climate may affect agriculture, food supplies, public health, migration patterns, and economic stability. A scientific discovery may influence medicine, manufacturing, education, and environmental conservation. Students who understand these relationships develop deeper knowledge than those who simply memorize isolated facts. Future AGI systems must build similar networks of interconnected understanding, allowing one piece of knowledge to strengthen many others throughout the entire cognitive system.

As knowledge systems become more integrated, they also become better at **anticipating consequences**. Every important decision produces a chain of effects that extends far beyond the immediate action. Imagine an AGI helping government leaders prepare for a major drought. Instead of focusing only on water shortages, the system would evaluate agriculture, electricity generation, public health, wildlife conservation, transportation, economic activity, and emergency planning. By integrating knowledge from many different disciplines, AGI could identify long-term consequences that might otherwise remain unnoticed. This ability to evaluate interconnected systems may become one of the greatest strengths of future intelligent machines.

Cognitive integration also supports **lifelong learning**, one of the defining goals of Artificial General Intelligence. Human beings continue learning throughout their lives. Children develop language skills, students master academic subjects, professionals acquire new technical expertise, and older adults continue learning through travel, reading, hobbies, and personal experiences. Every new experience becomes connected to previous knowledge, gradually expanding the brain's understanding of the world. Future AGI systems must function similarly by continuously integrating new information into existing knowledge while preserving valuable previous learning. This ability will allow intelligent systems to remain current as science, technology, and society continue evolving.

Another important requirement for AGI is **responsible intelligence**. Intelligence becomes valuable only when it benefits people while respecting ethical principles, fairness, privacy, safety, and human rights. Throughout history, powerful technologies have improved society when used responsibly but have also created challenges when misused. Artificial General Intelligence will likely become one of the most influential technologies ever developed, making ethical knowledge an essential component of every intelligent system. Future AGI must understand not only what it can do but also what it should do. Knowledge systems therefore must include ethical reasoning alongside scientific, technical, and practical knowledge.

Responsible intelligence also requires **transparency**. Human experts often explain the reasoning behind important decisions. Physicians describe treatment options to patients. Teachers explain how students earned grades. Engineers document safety calculations before constructing bridges. Judges explain legal decisions using established laws. Future AGI systems must likewise provide understandable explanations for their recommendations whenever possible. Transparent reasoning allows people to evaluate conclusions, identify possible mistakes, and maintain trust in intelligent systems. Knowledge that cannot be explained becomes much more difficult to verify and improve.

Human oversight will remain essential throughout the development of AGI. Although intelligent systems may analyze enormous amounts of information, humans continue contributing qualities that extend beyond computational ability. Creativity, compassion, wisdom, cultural understanding, empathy, ethical judgment, and personal responsibility remain deeply human strengths. Future AGI should strengthen these qualities rather than replace them. Imagine physicians working alongside AGI systems that rapidly analyze medical research while doctors provide compassionate patient care. Teachers may use AGI to personalize lessons while continuing to inspire curiosity and character development. Engineers may rely on AGI simulations while making final design decisions that reflect public safety and community values. The future of intelligence is most likely a partnership between human expertise and machine capability.

Another defining feature of AGI will be its ability to operate across **many environments**. Current AI systems often require retraining when conditions change significantly. Future AGI should adapt naturally whether operating in classrooms, hospitals, scientific laboratories, manufacturing facilities, agricultural fields, transportation networks, disaster response centers, or even future space colonies. This adaptability depends upon unified knowledge systems capable of transferring learning across entirely different domains while preserving a consistent understanding of the world.

Scientists also believe that AGI knowledge systems must remain **self-improving** throughout their operational lives. New discoveries, changing environments, and unexpected situations require continuous refinement. AGI should evaluate its own performance, identify weaknesses, revise outdated knowledge, and strengthen future reasoning through ongoing learning. Unlike traditional software that remains largely unchanged after installation, future AGI systems may evolve responsibly over years or even decades while maintaining alignment with human values and ethical principles. Continuous improvement ensures that intelligence remains relevant in a rapidly changing world.

The path toward Artificial General Intelligence is therefore not simply a technological challenge—it is also an educational challenge. Building AGI requires understanding how humans learn, reason, communicate, remember, collaborate, solve problems, and make ethical decisions. It requires contributions from computer science, neuroscience, psychology, education, engineering, mathematics, philosophy, linguistics, medicine, and many other disciplines. AGI represents one of the most interdisciplinary scientific efforts in human history because intelligence itself cannot be understood through only one field of study.

As you reach the end of this chapter, it becomes clear that knowledge systems are much more than collections of information. They form the foundation upon which every intelligent behavior depends. Memory gives knowledge continuity. Learning expands understanding. Reasoning transforms information into solutions. World models explain reality. Planning organizes future actions. Communication shares discoveries. Self-correction improves accuracy. Ethics guides responsible behavior. Together these capabilities create an integrated cognitive architecture capable of supporting Artificial General Intelligence.

The future of AGI will ultimately depend not on how many facts a machine can memorize, but on how effectively it can organize knowledge, connect ideas, adapt to change, collaborate with people, and apply understanding to solve meaningful problems. Knowledge systems provide the framework that makes every one of these abilities possible. They transform isolated pieces of information into intelligent understanding, thoughtful reasoning, and purposeful action. As researchers continue advancing toward AGI, these integrated knowledge systems may become one of humanity's greatest achievements—helping people expand scientific discovery, improve education, strengthen healthcare, protect the environment, explore space, and solve challenges that today seem impossible.

Learn AI. Understand AI. Shape the Future.

— Susie Hala
IntelliGloss Press

Chapter 15 Summary

Knowledge Systems and Artificial General Intelligence

Artificial General Intelligence (AGI) represents the next stage in the evolution of artificial intelligence. Unlike today's narrow AI systems, which specialize in specific tasks, AGI aims to learn, reason, adapt, and solve problems across many different domains. Achieving this goal requires far more than faster computers or larger databases. It requires highly integrated knowledge systems that combine learning, memory, reasoning, planning, perception, communication, and ethical decision-making into one unified cognitive architecture.

Throughout this book, you have explored the many components of knowledge systems. Knowledge begins with collecting and organizing information, but true intelligence depends on how that knowledge is stored, connected, updated, retrieved, and applied. Human intelligence demonstrates these abilities naturally by combining experience, observation, reasoning, memory, and continuous learning to understand the world.

A **unified knowledge architecture** allows every cognitive system to work together. Instead of maintaining separate collections of information, AGI integrates knowledge so that learning in one area strengthens understanding in many others. This integration allows intelligent systems to recognize relationships, transfer knowledge across domains, and solve unfamiliar problems more effectively.

AGI also depends on **general reasoning systems** that combine deductive, inductive, abductive, analogical, and causal reasoning. These reasoning methods help intelligent systems analyze evidence, evaluate alternatives, predict outcomes, explain decisions, and adapt to changing environments.

Another essential characteristic of AGI is **human-like understanding**. Rather than simply memorizing facts, AGI seeks to understand why events occur, how systems interact, and what consequences actions may produce. This deeper understanding supports prediction, planning, creativity, and responsible decision-making.

Cognitive integration allows memory, learning, reasoning, planning, communication, world models, and decision-making to function together as one coordinated system. This integration gives AGI the flexibility to operate successfully across many different environments and disciplines.

Future AGI must also support **lifelong learning**, continuously updating knowledge without forgetting previous learning. Dynamic learning architectures allow intelligent systems to improve through experience while adapting to new discoveries, technologies, and changing conditions.

Ethics remains one of the most important components of AGI. Knowledge systems must include fairness, transparency, accountability, privacy, safety, and respect for human values. Responsible intelligence requires not only technical capability but also careful judgment about how knowledge should be applied.

Human oversight will continue to play an essential role as AGI develops. Intelligent systems are expected to support—not replace—human creativity, wisdom, compassion, and ethical responsibility. By working together, humans and AGI may solve increasingly complex scientific, medical, environmental, educational, and technological challenges.

Knowledge systems form the cognitive foundation of Artificial General Intelligence. They organize information into meaningful understanding, allowing intelligent systems to reason, learn, collaborate, and continuously improve while serving humanity responsibly.

Reflection

Artificial General Intelligence is often described as the future of intelligent machines, but this future depends on something much deeper than technology. It depends on knowledge. Every important human achievement—from discovering electricity to landing on the Moon—began with people learning, asking questions, sharing ideas, correcting mistakes, and building knowledge over many generations.

Future AGI will likely learn in similar ways. Instead of memorizing isolated facts, it will organize knowledge into meaningful relationships, continuously improve through experience, and apply understanding across many different situations. This ability to connect ideas is one of the defining characteristics of intelligence.

Perhaps the most important lesson from this chapter is that intelligence alone is not enough. Knowledge must be guided by ethics, responsibility, transparency, and respect for humanity. The goal of AGI is not to replace human intelligence but to become a trusted partner that helps people solve difficult problems while supporting education, healthcare, scientific discovery, environmental protection, and many other areas of society.

As you continue learning throughout your own life, remember that every new idea becomes part of your personal knowledge system. The more connections you build between subjects, experiences, and people, the stronger your own intelligence becomes.

Student Worksheet

Name: ______________________________

Date: ______________________________

Part A – Vocabulary

Define each term using your own words.

1. Artificial General Intelligence (AGI)

____

2. Unified Knowledge Architecture

____

3. Cognitive Integration

____

4. General Reasoning

____

5. Lifelong Learning

____

6. Responsible Intelligence

____

7. Human-AI Collaboration

____

____

Part B – Short Answer

1. How does AGI differ from today's narrow AI?

___

___

2. Why is a unified knowledge architecture important?

___

___

3. What is cognitive integration?

___

___

4. Why must ethics be included in AGI knowledge systems?

___

___

5. Why will human oversight remain important as AGI develops?

___

___

___

Part C – Matching

Letter	Concept	Number
A	Unified Knowledge Architecture	___ Integrates all cognitive abilities
B	General Reasoning	___ Combines multiple reasoning methods
C	Cognitive Integration	___ Coordinates learning, memory, planning, and reasoning
D	Lifelong Learning	___ Continuously updates knowledge
E	Responsible Intelligence	___ Applies ethics and human values

Part D – Critical Thinking

Imagine you are helping design an AGI system to assist scientists searching for new treatments for rare diseases.

Explain how the system would use:

Unified Knowledge Architecture

____

General Reasoning

____

Cognitive Integration

____

Lifelong Learning

____

Responsible Intelligence

____

How could these abilities improve scientific discovery while protecting patients?

____

____

____

Part E – Personal Reflection

Think about everything you have learned in school.

Describe:

How do different school subjects connect with one another?

____

____

How has learning one subject helped you understand another?

____

____

How is this similar to a unified knowledge system in AGI?

Chapter 15 Quiz

Multiple Choice

1. Artificial General Intelligence is designed to...

A. Perform only one specific task

B. Learn and reason across many different domains

C. Store information only

D. Replace human memory

2. A unified knowledge architecture...

A. Separates every subject completely

B. Integrates knowledge across cognitive systems

C. Eliminates learning

D. Removes reasoning

3. Cognitive integration means...

A. Independent systems never communicate

B. Memory, learning, reasoning, and planning work together

C. Memorizing information

D. Replacing knowledge

4. Responsible intelligence includes...

A. Ignoring ethics

B. Fairness, transparency, accountability, and human values

C. Eliminating human oversight

D. Making every decision automatically

5. Human-AI collaboration is expected to...

A. Replace human experts completely

B. Combine human strengths with intelligent machine capabilities

C. Eliminate education

D. Prevent learning

True or False

6. AGI seeks to solve problems across many different domains.

True / False

7. Lifelong learning allows intelligent systems to continue improving throughout their operational lives.

True / False

8. Ethics is an important part of future AGI systems.

True / False

9. Human oversight will likely remain important as AGI becomes more capable.

True / False

10. Knowledge systems form the foundation of Artificial General Intelligence.

True / False

Answer Key

Vocabulary

Answers will vary but should accurately explain each concept.

Worksheet

Part B

1. Narrow AI specializes in specific tasks, while AGI aims to learn, reason, and adapt across many different fields.
2. A unified knowledge architecture allows all cognitive systems to share information and work together efficiently.
3. Cognitive integration combines memory, learning, reasoning, planning, communication, perception, and decision-making into one coordinated system.
4. Ethics ensures that AGI respects fairness, privacy, safety, transparency, accountability, and human values.
5. Human oversight provides ethical judgment, compassion, responsibility, and final decision-making when important consequences are involved.

Part C – Matching

A → Integrates all cognitive abilities

B → Combines multiple reasoning methods

C → Coordinates learning, memory, planning, and reasoning

D → Continuously updates knowledge

E → Applies ethics and human values

Part D

Answers will vary but should demonstrate understanding of integrated knowledge systems, reasoning, learning, ethics, and scientific collaboration.

Part E

Answers will vary based on each student's educational experiences.

Quiz Answers

1. **B**
2. **B**
3. **B**
4. **B**
5. **B**
6. **True**
7. **True**
8. **True**
9. **True**
10. **True**

Key Vocabulary

- Artificial General Intelligence (AGI)
- Unified Knowledge Architecture
- Cognitive Integration
- General Reasoning
- Human-Like Understanding
- Lifelong Learning
- Responsible Intelligence
- Ethical AI
- Human-AI Collaboration
- Knowledge System
- World Model
- Decision-Making
- Adaptive Intelligence
- Cognitive Architecture

- Interdisciplinary Learning

Chapter Takeaway

Artificial General Intelligence will depend on far more than powerful computers or large amounts of data. Its true strength will come from integrated knowledge systems that unite memory, learning, reasoning, planning, ethics, communication, and continuous improvement into one intelligent cognitive architecture. By combining these capabilities with human oversight and responsible decision-making, AGI has the potential to become one of humanity's greatest partners in advancing education, science, healthcare, technology, and the future of society.

Learn AI. Understand AI. Shape the Future.

— Susie Hala
IntelliGloss Press

Chapter 16

The Future of Machine Knowledge

Part 1

Every generation experiences a technological transformation that changes the way people live, work, communicate, and learn. The invention of the printing press allowed knowledge to spread beyond handwritten manuscripts. The Industrial Revolution transformed manufacturing through machines and engineering. Electricity illuminated cities and powered modern civilization. Computers introduced the digital age, and the Internet connected billions of people around the world almost instantly. Today, humanity stands at the beginning of another extraordinary transformation—the Age of Artificial Intelligence. At the center of this transformation lies one essential resource that has driven every great advancement throughout history: **knowledge**. Artificial General Intelligence (AGI) will not become powerful because it stores enormous amounts of information. It will become powerful because it can organize, understand, expand, and responsibly apply knowledge in ways that help people solve increasingly complex challenges.

Throughout this book, you have explored how knowledge systems serve as the foundation of intelligent behavior. You learned that data becomes information, information becomes knowledge, and knowledge becomes understanding when it is organized into meaningful relationships. You discovered how intelligent systems represent knowledge, build memory, retrieve information efficiently, reason logically, develop world models, transfer learning across different subjects, collaborate through intelligent agents, correct mistakes, and continuously improve through experience. Each chapter has shown that intelligence depends not on isolated facts but on the ability to connect ideas into a coherent understanding of reality. These same principles will guide the future development of AGI.

One of the most exciting possibilities for future AGI is the ability to support **autonomous knowledge creation**. Today, artificial intelligence already assists researchers by analyzing enormous scientific datasets, identifying hidden patterns, and suggesting possible discoveries. In the future, AGI systems may become valuable research partners capable of generating new scientific hypotheses, designing experiments, evaluating evidence, and proposing innovative solutions that human researchers can investigate further. Imagine an AGI helping medical scientists discover treatments for diseases that have resisted decades of research. By integrating genetics, chemistry, biology, physics, medicine, and global clinical data into one unified knowledge system, AGI may identify relationships that would be nearly impossible for individual researchers to recognize alone. Rather than replacing scientists, AGI may greatly accelerate scientific discovery while allowing human experts to verify, evaluate, and apply new knowledge responsibly.

Future knowledge systems may also become **self-expanding knowledge networks**. Human knowledge has traditionally grown through books, universities, libraries, laboratories, and educational institutions that preserve discoveries across generations. Future AGI systems may build upon this tradition by continuously integrating new scientific research, educational resources, engineering innovations, environmental observations, and cultural knowledge into dynamic knowledge networks that expand every day. Unlike static databases that require manual updates, these intelligent knowledge ecosystems may evaluate new information automatically, connect it with existing knowledge, identify inconsistencies, and organize discoveries into increasingly sophisticated representations of reality. This continuous expansion will allow intelligent systems to remain current while supporting lifelong learning for both machines and people.

One of the greatest strengths of future knowledge systems will be their ability to **connect disciplines that have traditionally been studied separately**. Modern education organizes learning into subjects such as mathematics, science, history, language arts, engineering, and the arts. Although these subjects are taught individually, the real world rarely separates them so neatly. Climate change involves environmental science, economics, engineering, agriculture, political science, and public health. Space exploration combines astronomy, robotics, medicine, materials science, communications, psychology, and mathematics. Future AGI systems may help people recognize these interdisciplinary relationships by organizing knowledge into connected networks rather than isolated subjects. Students who understand these connections will be better prepared to solve the complex challenges of tomorrow.

Researchers also envision AGI contributing to **scientific discovery** in entirely new ways. Scientific progress often requires analyzing enormous amounts of information while recognizing subtle patterns that may remain hidden for years. Future AGI systems may assist researchers by examining millions of research papers, laboratory experiments, satellite observations, medical records, and environmental measurements simultaneously. By integrating these diverse sources of knowledge, intelligent systems may generate hypotheses that inspire new discoveries in medicine, renewable energy, agriculture, climate science, materials engineering, and countless other fields. Importantly, these discoveries should always remain subject to careful human verification, scientific testing, and ethical review. Responsible knowledge creation depends upon collaboration between human expertise and intelligent technology.

Another exciting possibility involves the development of **knowledge ecosystems**. A knowledge ecosystem is an interconnected network in which people, intelligent agents, educational institutions, research laboratories, businesses, governments, and communities continuously exchange information, collaborate on solving problems, and build upon one another's discoveries. Human civilization already functions as a knowledge ecosystem through schools, universities, libraries, scientific journals, and digital communication. Future AGI may strengthen these ecosystems by improving how knowledge is organized, shared, translated, verified, and applied across cultures and disciplines. Students may one day collaborate with intelligent tutors that personalize education while connecting classrooms around the world through shared learning experiences.

Education itself will likely experience significant transformation as knowledge systems continue evolving. Instead of every student learning through identical lessons presented at the same pace, future educational systems may adapt instruction according to each learner's strengths, interests, background knowledge, and learning style. Intelligent educational assistants may identify concepts requiring additional practice, recommend personalized activities, answer questions, provide immediate feedback, and encourage curiosity through interactive exploration. Teachers will remain essential because they provide mentorship, encouragement, ethical guidance, creativity, and human connection that technology cannot replace. Future classrooms will likely combine the strengths of both human educators and intelligent learning systems.

As knowledge systems become increasingly sophisticated, they may also help humanity address some of the greatest challenges facing our world. Climate change, emerging diseases, food security, clean energy, water conservation, disaster preparedness, cybersecurity, and space exploration all require coordinated understanding across many scientific disciplines. AGI systems capable of organizing enormous knowledge networks may assist experts by identifying relationships, evaluating possible solutions, predicting outcomes, and supporting evidence-based decision-making. These capabilities have the potential to improve lives while expanding humanity's understanding of the universe.

The future of machine knowledge is not simply about creating smarter computers. It is about building intelligent systems that expand human understanding, strengthen scientific discovery, improve education, encourage collaboration, and help solve problems responsibly. In the next part of this final chapter, you will explore **AGI and society**, **the responsibilities of future innovators**, **human-AI partnerships**, and why your generation may become the first to shape the future of truly intelligent machines.

(End of Part 1 — Part 2 will provide a powerful conclusion to the entire book, bringing together every major idea students have learned while inspiring them to become responsible builders of the AI future.)

Chapter 16

The Future of Machine Knowledge

Part 2

The future of machine knowledge will not be determined by computers alone. It will be shaped by the choices that people make every day. Every generation inherits powerful technologies from those who came before them, but each generation must also decide how those technologies will be used. Electricity can power hospitals or weapons. The Internet can connect people around the world or spread misinformation. Artificial intelligence offers the same challenge. The future of AGI will depend not only on scientific breakthroughs but also on the wisdom, ethics, creativity, and responsibility of the people who build, guide, and use it. As students, educators, parents, researchers, and citizens, we all have a role in shaping the future of machine knowledge.

One of the greatest opportunities presented by AGI is the possibility of creating a true **partnership between human intelligence and machine intelligence**. Throughout history, tools have expanded human abilities rather than replacing them. Telescopes allowed astronomers to observe distant galaxies. Microscopes revealed invisible microorganisms. Calculators accelerated mathematical calculations. Computers enabled people to process information at extraordinary speeds. Artificial General Intelligence may become another powerful tool that extends human capabilities by organizing knowledge, identifying patterns, simulating complex systems, and supporting thoughtful decision-making. Yet the most important ideas, values, and goals will continue to come from people. AGI may become an extraordinary partner, but humanity will remain responsible for deciding how that partnership serves society.

This partnership will require **trust**, and trust must be earned. Future AGI systems will need to demonstrate reliability, transparency, fairness, and accountability. People should understand why important recommendations are made, how conclusions were reached, and what evidence supports those conclusions. If an AGI system assists a physician with diagnosing a disease, the doctor should be able to review the supporting medical evidence. If an educational system recommends changes to a student's learning plan, teachers and parents should understand the reasoning behind those recommendations. Transparent knowledge systems encourage confidence because people can evaluate, question, and verify intelligent decisions rather than accepting them without explanation.

The future of AGI will also depend on protecting **human values**. Intelligence without ethics can produce harmful outcomes. Knowledge without compassion can overlook human needs. Speed without careful judgment can create unnecessary risks. Future knowledge systems must therefore include principles such as honesty, fairness, respect, privacy, safety, accountability, and responsibility. These values cannot simply be added at the end of development; they must become part of the knowledge architecture itself. Every recommendation, prediction, or decision made by an intelligent system should reflect not only technical accuracy but also consideration for the well-being of individuals and communities.

As AGI becomes more capable, **education** will become even more important, not less. Some people wonder whether students will still need to learn mathematics, science, writing, history, or critical thinking if intelligent machines can answer questions instantly. The answer is yes. In fact, education may become even more valuable because people must understand enough to evaluate AI-generated information, ask meaningful questions, recognize misinformation, and make responsible decisions. A person who understands science can determine whether an AI-generated explanation is supported by evidence. A person who understands history can recognize important cultural and historical context. A person who develops strong critical thinking skills will know when to trust technology and when to investigate further. Education prepares people to become thoughtful partners with intelligent machines rather than passive users of technology.

Future careers will also evolve as knowledge systems become increasingly sophisticated. Many jobs will continue changing just as they have throughout previous technological revolutions. New professions will emerge that combine human creativity with advanced AI systems. Students may become AI educators, ethical AI specialists, intelligent robotics engineers, cognitive system designers, AI healthcare coordinators, environmental intelligence analysts, space exploration researchers, or knowledge architects who organize information for future AGI systems. Some careers that do not yet exist will be created by the students reading this book. Preparing for these opportunities requires curiosity, adaptability, lifelong learning, and the willingness to explore new ideas.

Another important responsibility belongs to **global cooperation**. Knowledge has always grown strongest when people from different cultures, backgrounds, and disciplines share ideas. Scientific discoveries often result from international collaboration. Medical breakthroughs emerge when researchers combine expertise from many countries. Environmental protection requires cooperation across national borders because climate, oceans, and ecosystems are shared by everyone. Future AGI development will likewise benefit from global collaboration. Researchers, educators, governments, businesses, and communities will need to work together to establish standards that encourage innovation while protecting privacy, security, fairness, and human rights.

The future of machine knowledge also depends upon **curiosity**. Every important scientific discovery began with someone asking a question that had never been answered before. Why do planets move the way they do? How can diseases be prevented? What causes lightning? How can clean energy be produced? Curiosity drives discovery because it encourages people to seek understanding beyond what is already known. Artificial General Intelligence may help answer many difficult questions, but it will also inspire entirely new questions that future generations will explore. Curiosity will remain one of humanity's greatest strengths because it fuels both education and innovation.

Another essential quality is **adaptability**. The world will continue changing as new technologies, discoveries, and challenges appear. The students of today will likely witness advances that are difficult to imagine today. Some may help develop new medical treatments, design intelligent cities, protect endangered ecosystems, explore distant planets, or invent technologies that transform society in positive ways. Success in this rapidly changing world will depend not on memorizing every fact but on learning how to learn, how to adapt, how to collaborate, and how to continue growing throughout life. These qualities have been central themes throughout this book because they represent the foundation of both human intelligence and future AGI.

Perhaps the most important lesson from this book is that **knowledge is never finished**. Every generation inherits knowledge from those who came before and then expands it through discovery, creativity, and experience. Libraries continue growing. Scientific understanding becomes more accurate. Technologies improve. Educational methods evolve. Artificial General Intelligence will become part of this ongoing journey by helping organize, analyze, and expand humanity's collective knowledge. Yet no machine can replace the uniquely human qualities of imagination, compassion, moral responsibility, cultural understanding, and the desire to build a better future for others.

As you close this book, remember that you are living during one of the most important periods in the history of technology. The decisions made during your lifetime may shape how Artificial General Intelligence develops for generations to come. Whether you become a teacher, engineer, scientist, healthcare professional, artist, entrepreneur, public servant, or parent, your understanding of AI will help guide responsible decisions in an increasingly intelligent world. You do not need to become a computer programmer to contribute. You need curiosity, integrity, critical thinking, compassion, and a commitment to lifelong learning.

The future of machine knowledge is not only about creating intelligent machines—it is about creating a more knowledgeable humanity. The greatest success of AGI will not be measured by how much information machines can process, but by how much they help people learn, discover, solve problems, and improve the human experience. When knowledge is guided by wisdom, strengthened by ethics, and shared through collaboration, it becomes one of the most powerful forces for positive change.

This book began by asking how intelligent machines acquire, organize, store, and apply knowledge. It ends with a much larger question—**How will humanity use knowledge to shape the future?** The answer has not yet been written. It will be written by researchers, educators, families, communities, and students like you who choose to learn, ask questions, think critically, and use knowledge responsibly. The future of Artificial General Intelligence is ultimately connected to the future of human intelligence, because the most important knowledge will always be the knowledge we choose to create, share, and use for the benefit of others.

Congratulations on completing this journey through **Knowledge Systems**. May this be only the beginning of your lifelong exploration of artificial intelligence, science, discovery, and innovation. The future is not something we simply wait for—it is something we build together, one idea, one question, and one discovery at a time.

Final Thoughts

Knowledge is the foundation of intelligence.

Understanding is the foundation of wisdom.

Wisdom is the foundation of responsible action.

As Artificial General Intelligence continues to evolve, may we always remember that technology is most powerful when it serves humanity with integrity, compassion, curiosity, and hope.

Learn AI. Understand AI. Shape the Future.

— Susie Hala
IntelliGloss Press

Chapter 16 Summary

The Future of Machine Knowledge

The future of machine knowledge will be shaped by both technological innovation and human responsibility. Artificial General Intelligence (AGI) has the potential to become one of the most transformative technologies in history, but its success will depend on how people choose to develop, guide, and use it. Knowledge systems will enable intelligent machines to organize information, learn continuously, reason across many disciplines, and support human decision-making in ways that improve education, healthcare, science, engineering, and countless other fields.

Throughout this book, you have learned that knowledge is much more than stored information. Knowledge systems organize ideas, connect concepts, build memory, support reasoning, create world models, transfer learning across different domains, collaborate through intelligent agents, and improve through continuous self-correction. These capabilities form the cognitive foundation upon which future AGI will operate.

One exciting possibility is **autonomous knowledge creation**, where AGI assists researchers by generating scientific hypotheses, analyzing enormous collections of information, identifying hidden patterns, and supporting new discoveries. Rather than replacing scientists, AGI may become a valuable research partner that accelerates innovation while leaving final verification and ethical judgment to human experts.

Future AGI may also develop **self-expanding knowledge networks** that continuously integrate new discoveries into organized knowledge systems. These intelligent networks will help keep information current while connecting ideas across many different disciplines.

Another important development will be the growth of **knowledge ecosystems**. These ecosystems will allow people, intelligent agents, schools, universities, businesses, governments, and research organizations to collaborate by sharing knowledge, solving problems, and expanding human understanding together.

Education will continue playing a central role in the future of AGI. Students must develop critical thinking, creativity, communication, ethics, and lifelong learning skills so they can work effectively alongside intelligent systems. AI may personalize education and provide powerful learning tools, but teachers will remain essential because they inspire curiosity, build character, encourage collaboration, and provide the human relationships that technology cannot replace.

Future careers will increasingly combine human expertise with artificial intelligence. Many new professions will emerge as AGI becomes integrated into healthcare, engineering, education, environmental science, business, robotics, cybersecurity, and space exploration.

The future of AGI also depends upon global cooperation. Researchers, educators, governments, businesses, and communities must work together to establish ethical standards that promote innovation while protecting privacy, fairness, transparency, accountability, and human rights.

Perhaps the greatest lesson of this book is that knowledge never stops growing. Every generation builds upon the discoveries of those who came before. Future AGI will become another powerful tool for expanding humanity's understanding, but people will remain responsible for deciding how that knowledge is used.

The future of machine knowledge is ultimately connected to the future of human knowledge. Together, humans and intelligent machines may build a safer, healthier, more creative, and more knowledgeable world.

Reflection

As you finish this book, think about how much your understanding of artificial intelligence has grown. At the beginning, AI may have seemed like a mysterious technology found only in science fiction movies or computer laboratories. Now you understand that behind every intelligent system lies something much more important than technology alone—knowledge.

Knowledge allows intelligence to learn, reason, solve problems, make decisions, and improve over time. Whether the intelligence belongs to a person or a machine, the quality of that knowledge determines the quality of the decisions that follow.

One of the greatest lessons from this book is that technology should always serve humanity. Artificial General Intelligence has the potential to improve education, medicine, environmental protection, scientific research, engineering, and many other areas of life. However, these benefits can only be achieved when intelligent systems are guided by ethics, transparency, responsibility, and respect for human values.

You are part of the first generation that may witness the development of true Artificial General Intelligence. Some of you may become scientists, engineers, educators, physicians, entrepreneurs, artists, policymakers, or researchers who help shape that future. Others may simply become informed citizens who use AI wisely in everyday life. Every role matters because the future of AI depends on millions of responsible decisions made by ordinary people.

Continue asking questions.

Continue learning.

Continue thinking critically.

Most importantly, continue using knowledge to improve the lives of others.

Student Worksheet

Name: ____

Date: ____

Part A – Vocabulary

Define each term using your own words.

1. Autonomous Knowledge Creation

____

2. Knowledge Ecosystem

____

3. Human-AI Partnership

____

4. Lifelong Learning

---

5. Responsible Innovation

---

6. Ethical Artificial Intelligence

---

7. Future Machine Knowledge

Part B – Short Answer

1. Why will human responsibility remain important as AGI develops?

---

2. How might AGI help scientists make new discoveries?

---

3. Why will teachers continue to be important in an AI-powered future?

---

4. What is a knowledge ecosystem?

---

5. Why is lifelong learning important for both humans and AGI?

Part C – Matching

Letter	Concept	Number
A	Knowledge Ecosystem	___ Network that shares knowledge
B	Human-AI Partnership	___ People and intelligent systems working together
C	Responsible Innovation	___ Developing technology ethically
D	Lifelong Learning	___ Continuous growth through learning
E	Autonomous Knowledge Creation	___ AI helping discover new knowledge

Part D – Critical Thinking

Imagine it is the year **2045**.

You are leading a team using AGI to solve one major global challenge.

Choose one:

- Climate change
- Disease prevention
- Space exploration
- Ocean conservation
- Food security
- Renewable energy
- Disaster response

Explain how AGI would help by using:

Knowledge Systems

Human Expertise

____

Ethical Decision-Making

____

Global Collaboration

____

How could your project improve life around the world?

____

Part E – My Future and AI

Imagine yourself 20 years from now.

1. What career would you like to have?

2. How could AI help you perform your job better?

3. What human qualities will always remain important?

4. How will you make sure AI is used responsibly?

Chapter 16 Quiz

Multiple Choice

1. The future of machine knowledge depends on...

A. Computers only

B. Human responsibility and technological innovation

C. Faster processors only

D. More storage space

2. Autonomous knowledge creation allows AGI to...

A. Ignore research

B. Help generate new scientific discoveries

C. Replace education

D. Eliminate scientists

3. A knowledge ecosystem is...

A. One computer

B. A network of people and intelligent systems sharing knowledge

C. One database

D. A robot factory

4. Teachers will continue to be important because they...

A. Only give homework

B. Provide mentorship, ethics, creativity, and human connection

C. Build computers

D. Replace AI

5. The greatest success of AGI will be measured by...

A. Processing the most information

B. Helping humanity solve problems and improve lives responsibly

C. Owning the largest database

D. Replacing human workers

True or False

6. Knowledge continues growing across generations.

True / False

7. Human values should guide the development of AGI.

True / False

8. Lifelong learning is important for both humans and future AGI systems.

True / False

9. Human-AI collaboration may help solve global challenges.

True / False

10. Students today may help shape the future of Artificial General Intelligence.

True / False

Answer Key

Vocabulary

Answers will vary but should demonstrate a clear understanding of each concept.

Worksheet

Part B

1. Humans provide ethics, accountability, creativity, compassion, and responsibility for how AGI is developed and used.
2. AGI can analyze large amounts of information, recognize hidden patterns, generate hypotheses, and support scientific research.
3. Teachers provide mentorship, encouragement, ethical guidance, creativity, communication, and personal relationships that technology cannot replace.
4. A knowledge ecosystem is a connected network of people, organizations, and intelligent systems that share, improve, and apply knowledge collaboratively.
5. Lifelong learning allows both humans and AGI to continue adapting, improving, and responding to new discoveries and changing conditions.

Part C – Matching

A → Network that shares knowledge

B → People and intelligent systems working together

C → Developing technology ethically

D → Continuous growth through learning

E → AI helping discover new knowledge

Part D

Answers will vary but should demonstrate thoughtful application of knowledge systems, collaboration, ethics, and problem-solving.

Part E

Answers will vary based on each student's career interests and future goals.

Quiz Answers

1. **B**
2. **B**
3. **B**
4. **B**

5. **B**
6. **True**
7. **True**
8. **True**
9. **True**
10. **True**

Key Vocabulary

- Artificial General Intelligence (AGI)
- Machine Knowledge
- Autonomous Knowledge Creation
- Knowledge Ecosystem
- Human-AI Partnership
- Responsible Innovation
- Ethical AI
- Lifelong Learning
- Scientific Discovery
- Critical Thinking
- Global Collaboration
- Human Values
- Continuous Learning
- Future Technologies
- Knowledge Systems

Final Chapter Takeaway

Knowledge is the foundation of intelligence, but wisdom is the foundation of responsible action. The future of Artificial General Intelligence will not be defined only by faster computers or larger amounts of data—it will be defined by how thoughtfully people organize knowledge, apply ethical principles, collaborate across disciplines, and use intelligent technology to improve the lives of others. The students of today are the innovators, leaders, educators, scientists, engineers, and citizens who will help shape that future. By embracing curiosity, lifelong learning, integrity, and compassion, they can ensure that machine knowledge becomes a powerful force for human progress, discovery, and hope.

Learn AI. Understand AI. Shape the Future.

— Susie Hala
IntelliGloss Press

GLOSSARY

Letter A

1. Access Time

The amount of time it takes for an AI system or computer to locate and retrieve data from memory or storage. Access time affects how quickly megabytes of data can be used during AI processing.

2. Activation Data

Intermediate data generated inside an AI model while it is running. Activation data is stored temporarily in memory and often measured in megabytes during model execution.

3. Adaptive Storage

A storage approach that automatically adjusts how data is stored or moved based on usage patterns. In AI systems, adaptive storage helps manage large volumes of megabytes efficiently.

4. Algorithmic Data Size

The total amount of data an algorithm needs to operate effectively. In AI, this size is often measured in megabytes or larger units, depending on model complexity.

5. Allocation (Memory Allocation)

The process of assigning a specific number of megabytes in memory or storage for an AI task, model, or dataset.

6. Analytics Dataset

A structured collection of data used for analysis or AI training. The size of an analytics dataset is commonly measured in megabytes, gigabytes, or more.

7. Annotation Storage

The space required to store labels, tags, or explanations added to AI training data. These annotations contribute additional megabytes to total dataset size.

8. Artificial Neural Network (ANN) Size

The total memory footprint of a neural network, including weights, biases, and parameters. ANN size is often described in megabytes when discussing model efficiency.

9. Asset Compression

The process of reducing the number of megabytes required to store AI-related files such as models, images, or datasets without losing essential information.

10. Available Memory

The amount of free memory, measured in megabytes, that an AI system can still use to load data, run models, or perform computations.

ANI (Artificial Narrow Intelligence)

Artificial Narrow Intelligence refers to AI systems designed to perform **one specific task or a narrow set of tasks** rather than general intelligence. ANI systems rely on data stored and processed in memory and storage measured in **megabytes, gigabytes, or more**. Examples include image recognition, speech-to-text, recommendation systems, and chatbots. ANI does not understand beyond its training scope, but it can process large amounts of data efficiently within its defined function.

Letter B

1. Bandwidth

The amount of data that can be transferred between systems in a given time. In AI systems, bandwidth determines how quickly megabytes of data can move between storage, memory, and processors.

2. Batch Processing

A method where AI systems process large groups of data all at once instead of one item at a time. Batch processing often involves handling many megabytes of data in a single operation.

3. Binary Encoding

The process of representing information using binary values (0s and 1s). All megabytes of AI data are ultimately stored and transmitted using binary encoding. **4. Bit Depth**

The number of bits used to represent a single piece of data, such as a pixel or audio sample. Higher bit depth increases data quality but also increases the number of megabytes required.

5. Bitmap Data

A type of image data where each pixel is stored as a set of bits. Bitmap images can quickly grow in size, consuming large numbers of megabytes in AI vision systems.

6. Buffer Memory

Temporary memory used to hold data while it is being transferred or processed. Buffers store data in chunks measured in megabytes to keep AI systems running smoothly.

7. Bulk Data Storage

Large-scale storage designed to hold massive datasets used for AI training or analysis. Bulk storage capacity is measured in megabytes, gigabytes, or larger units.

8. Byte Stream

A continuous flow of bytes transmitted or processed by a system. AI applications often analyze byte streams that accumulate into megabytes of data.

9. Bytecode

An intermediate form of program code that is easier for machines to execute than human-written code. Bytecode files occupy storage space measured in megabytes.

10. Byzantine Fault Tolerance (BFT)

A system property that allows AI or distributed systems to continue functioning even when some components fail or act unpredictably. Implementing BFT requires additional data handling and storage overhead measured in megabytes.

Letter C

1. Cache Memory

A small, high-speed memory area that stores frequently used data so the processor can access it faster. Cache helps reduce the time needed to move megabytes of data from main memory or storage.

2. Capacity Planning

The process of estimating how much memory and storage an AI system will need. Capacity planning ensures there are enough megabytes available to handle data, models, and future growth.

3. Checkpoint File

A saved snapshot of an AI model during training. Checkpoint files are stored in memory or storage and often consume many megabytes so training can resume without starting over.

4. Chunking

The practice of breaking large datasets into smaller pieces. Chunking helps AI systems process megabytes of data more efficiently by handling them in manageable parts.

5. Cloud Storage

A method of storing data on remote servers accessed through the internet. Cloud storage manages files measured in megabytes and allows AI systems to scale beyond local hardware limits.

6. Compression

The process of reducing the size of data so it uses fewer megabytes. Compression helps AI systems store, transfer, and process data more efficiently.

7. Compute Load

The amount of processing work required to run an AI task. Compute load often increases as the number of megabytes being processed grows.

8. Context Window

The amount of data an AI model can consider at one time. Context windows consume memory measured in megabytes, especially in language and vision models.

9. Corpus

A large collection of text or data used to train AI models. A corpus is usually measured in megabytes or larger units depending on its size.

10. CUDA Memory

Specialized memory used by GPUs to accelerate AI computations. CUDA memory holds model data and intermediate results measured in megabytes during processing.

Letter D

1. Data Allocation

The process of assigning a specific amount of memory or storage for data use. In AI systems, data allocation determines how many megabytes are reserved for datasets, models, or tasks.

2. Data Buffer

A temporary storage area that holds data while it is being transferred or processed. Data buffers manage megabytes of information to keep AI systems running smoothly.

3. Data Compression

A technique used to reduce the size of data so it consumes fewer megabytes. AI systems use data compression to save storage space and speed up data transfer.

4. Data Footprint

The total amount of data an AI system uses, including datasets, models, and temporary files. A data footprint is measured in megabytes, gigabytes, or more.

5. Data Loader

A software component that loads data into memory for AI training or inference. Data loaders handle batches of data measured in megabytes.

6. Data Migration

The process of moving data from one storage system to another. During AI system upgrades, data migration may involve transferring large numbers of megabytes.

7. Data Throughput

The rate at which data is processed or transferred by a system. Higher throughput allows AI systems to move more megabytes efficiently.

8. Dataset Size

The total amount of data in a dataset used for AI training or testing. Dataset size is commonly measured in megabytes or larger units.

9. Deep Learning Model Size

The amount of memory required to store a deep learning model, including its parameters and weights. Model size is often described in megabytes to assess efficiency.

10. Disk Storage

Long-term storage used to save files, datasets, and AI models. Disk storage capacity and usage are measured in megabytes, gigabytes, or terabytes.

Letter E

1. Edge Computing

A computing approach where data is processed closer to where it is generated rather than sent to a central server. Edge computing reduces how many megabytes must be transferred over networks.

2. Embedding Size

The amount of memory required to store vector representations used by AI models. Embedding size is often measured in megabytes and affects model performance and storage needs.

3. Encoded Data

Data that has been converted into a specific format for storage or transmission. Encoded data occupies megabytes depending on the encoding method used.

4. Encoding Scheme

A rule set that defines how data is represented digitally, such as text or images. Different encoding schemes can increase or reduce the number of megabytes required.

5. Encrypted Storage

Storage that protects data by converting it into a secure format. Encryption may slightly increase the number of megabytes used due to added security information.

6. End-to-End Data Pipeline

The full path data takes from collection to processing and storage. Each stage of the pipeline manages data volumes measured in megabytes.

7. Energy Efficiency (AI Systems)

A measure of how much energy an AI system uses to process data. Systems that move and store fewer megabytes are often more energy efficient.

8. Execution Memory

The memory required while a program or AI model is running. Execution memory usage is tracked in megabytes during runtime.

9. External Storage

Storage devices located outside a computer, such as USB drives or external hard drives. External storage capacity is measured in megabytes and larger units.

10. Extracted Features

Important data patterns identified by AI models during processing. Extracted features are stored temporarily or permanently in memory measured in megabytes.

Letter F

1. Feature Map

A structured output produced by AI models, especially in image and signal processing. Feature maps are stored in memory and can consume significant megabytes during computation.

2. Feature Scaling

The process of adjusting data values to a consistent range before training an AI model. Feature scaling affects how efficiently megabytes of data are processed and stored.

3. File Allocation Table (FAT)

A file system structure that tracks where files are stored on a disk. FAT helps manage how megabytes are organized and retrieved from storage.

4. File Compression Format

A standardized way to reduce file size so it uses fewer megabytes. Compression formats help AI systems store and transfer data efficiently.

5. File System Cache

A temporary memory area that stores frequently accessed files. File system caches reduce repeated access to storage and manage megabytes more efficiently.

6. Floating-Point Data

Numerical data that includes decimal values and is commonly used in AI calculations. Floating-point data requires more bits per value, increasing memory usage measured in megabytes.

7. Frame Buffer

A region of memory that stores image or video frames before they are displayed or processed. Frame buffers often consume large numbers of megabytes in AI vision systems.

8. Fragmentation

A condition where data is stored in scattered locations instead of one continuous block. Fragmentation can reduce storage efficiency even when megabytes appear available.

9. Free Memory

The amount of unused memory available for programs or AI tasks. Free memory is measured in megabytes and determines how much additional data can be loaded.

10. Full Dataset Load

The act of loading an entire dataset into memory at once. This approach can require large amounts of megabytes and is common in AI training scenarios.

Letter G

1. Garbage Collection

An automatic memory-management process that frees memory no longer in use. Garbage collection helps reclaim megabytes so AI programs can continue running efficiently.

2. Generalization Data

Data used to test how well an AI model performs on new, unseen inputs. Storing and evaluating generalization data requires additional megabytes beyond training data.

3. Gigabyte (GB)

A larger unit of data measurement equal to 1,024 megabytes (or commonly approximated as 1,000 MB). Gigabytes are used when datasets or models grow beyond megabyte scale.

4. Graph Data Structure

A way of organizing data using nodes and connections. Graph-based AI systems store graph data in memory and storage measured in megabytes.

5. GPU Memory

Specialized memory used by graphics processing units to accelerate AI workloads. GPU memory holds model parameters and data batches measured in megabytes.

6. Gradient Data

Numerical values calculated during AI training to update model parameters. Gradient data is stored temporarily in memory and contributes to overall megabyte usage.

7. Granularity

The level of detail at which data is stored or processed. Finer granularity often increases the number of megabytes required.

8. Greedy Algorithm

An algorithm that makes the best immediate choice at each step. Greedy algorithms may reduce memory usage by limiting how many megabytes of data must be stored at once.

9. Ground Truth Data

Correct, labeled data used to train or evaluate AI systems. Ground truth datasets are stored in files measured in megabytes or larger units.

10. Growth Rate (Data)

The speed at which data size increases over time. In AI systems, a high data growth rate means storage needs measured in megabytes can expand quickly.

Letter H

1. Hard Disk Capacity

The total amount of data a hard disk can store. Capacity is measured in megabytes and larger units.

2. Hardware Acceleration

The use of specialized hardware to speed up AI processing. Acceleration often reduces how long megabytes of data stay in memory.

3. Hash Table

A data structure that stores information for fast lookup. Hash tables occupy memory measured in megabytes in large AI systems.

4. Hierarchical Storage

A storage design that uses multiple layers such as RAM, disk, and cloud. Each layer manages data measured in megabytes.

5. High-Dimensional Data

Data with many features or variables. High-dimensional datasets often require large numbers of megabytes.

6. Host Memory

Main system memory used by the CPU. Host memory stores AI data and models measured in megabytes.

7. Hybrid Storage

A combination of different storage types working together. Hybrid storage systems manage megabytes across multiple devices.

8. Hyperparameter Storage

Memory used to store configuration values for AI models. These settings are saved in files measured in megabytes.

9. Hyperscale Data

Extremely large datasets used by major AI systems. Hyperscale data is tracked from megabytes up to much larger units.

10. Heuristic Data

Information used by AI systems to guide decision-making. Heuristic data contributes to the overall data size in megabytes.

Letter I

1. Image Dataset Size

The total amount of storage required for image data. Size is measured in megabytes or more.

2. Inference Memory

The memory used when an AI model is making predictions. Inference memory usage is tracked in megabytes.

3. Input Buffer

A temporary area where incoming data is stored. Input buffers hold megabytes before processing begins.

4. Intermediate Data

Data produced during processing steps. Intermediate data can significantly increase memory usage in megabytes.

5. Index File

A file that helps locate data quickly. Index files use additional megabytes to improve performance.

6. Information Density

The amount of useful data stored within a given size. Higher density means more information per megabyte.

7. Initialization Data

Data loaded when an AI system starts. Initialization data occupies memory measured in megabytes.

8. In-Memory Processing

Processing data directly in RAM instead of storage. This approach uses large amounts of memory measured in megabytes.

9. Input Feature Size

The amount of data required to represent input features. Feature size affects how many megabytes are needed.

10. Instruction Cache

A small memory area that stores frequently used instructions. Instruction caches manage small but critical megabytes.

Letter J

1. Job Queue

A list of tasks waiting to be processed. Job queues may store task data measured in megabytes.

2. Joint Dataset

A dataset created by combining multiple sources. Joint datasets often increase total size in megabytes.

3. JSON Data Size

The amount of storage required for data stored in JSON format. JSON files can grow quickly in megabytes.

4. Jitter Buffer

A temporary storage area that smooths data flow. Jitter buffers store megabytes during real-time processing.

5. Job Scheduler

A system that decides when tasks run. Schedulers manage memory and data measured in megabytes.

6. Just-in-Time Processing

Processing data only when needed. This approach can reduce how many megabytes are stored at once.

7. Joint Memory Allocation

Memory shared across multiple AI tasks. Joint allocation must carefully manage available megabytes.

8. Java Bytecode Size

The storage size of compiled Java programs. Bytecode files occupy megabytes on disk.

9. Job Metadata

Information describing AI tasks. Metadata adds additional megabytes to total system storage.

10. Junction Storage Point

A logical link between storage locations. Junctions help organize data measured in megabytes.

Letter K

1. Kernel Memory

Memory reserved for core system operations. Kernel memory usage is tracked in megabytes.

2. Key-Value Store

A data storage method that pairs keys with values. Large key-value stores consume many megabytes.

3. Knowledge Base Size

The total amount of stored knowledge in an AI system. Size is measured in megabytes or larger units.

4. K-Means Dataset Size

The amount of data used in clustering algorithms. Dataset size affects memory usage in megabytes.

5. Keras Model Size

The storage required for AI models built with Keras. Model size is measured in megabytes.

6. Keyframe Data

Important frames selected from video data. Keyframe storage contributes to total megabyte usage.

7. Kernel Cache

A cache used by the operating system kernel. Kernel caches store frequently used data in megabytes.

8. Knowledge Graph Storage

Memory used to store relationships between data points. Knowledge graphs require significant megabytes.

9. Kinetic Data Stream

Continuously changing data from sensors or systems. These streams generate growing megabytes over time.

10. K-Nearest Neighbor Memory Usage

The memory required by nearest-neighbor algorithms. Memory use increases as datasets grow in megabytes.

Letter L

1. **Latency**
   The delay between requesting data and receiving it. Latency affects how quickly megabytes move through AI systems.
2. **Layer Output Size**
   The amount of data produced by a neural network layer. Output size is measured in megabytes during processing.
3. **Load Balancing**
   Distributing work across systems so no single device is overloaded. Balancing helps manage megabytes efficiently.
4. **Local Storage**
   Data stored on a device rather than the cloud. Local storage capacity is measured in megabytes.

5. **Log File Size**
   The amount of storage used by system logs. Logs can accumulate many megabytes over time.
6. **Loss History Data**
   Stored values showing how model error changes during training. Loss history consumes megabytes.
7. **Low-Precision Data**
   Data stored using fewer bits per value. Low-precision formats reduce megabyte usage.
8. **Labeled Dataset**
   Data that includes tags or labels for AI training. Labels increase total dataset size in megabytes.
9. **Linear Model Size**
   The storage required for a linear AI model. Size is measured in megabytes.
10. **Load Time**
    The time required to bring data or models into memory. Load time depends on megabytes involved.

Letter M

1. **Memory Allocation**
   Assigning a specific amount of memory for tasks. Allocation is tracked in megabytes.
2. **Memory Footprint**
   The total memory an AI program uses. Footprint is measured in megabytes.
3. **Metadata Size**
   The storage used by descriptive information about data. Metadata adds extra megabytes.
4. **Mini-Batch Size**
   The amount of data processed at once during training. Batch size affects megabyte usage.
5. **Model Checkpoint Size**
   The storage required for saved training states. Checkpoints often consume many megabytes.
6. **Model Compression**
   Reducing model size while preserving performance. Compression lowers megabytes required.
7. **Model Parameters**
   Values learned by an AI model. Parameter storage contributes to total megabytes.
8. **Memory Bandwidth**
   The rate at which memory transfers data. Bandwidth affects how fast megabytes move.
9. **Multimodal Dataset**
   Data combining text, images, audio, or video. Multimodal data uses large megabytes.
10. **Mutable Data**
    Data that changes during processing. Mutable data can increase temporary megabyte usage.

Letter N

1. **Network Bandwidth**
   The capacity of a network connection. Bandwidth controls how many megabytes can be transferred.
2. **Neural Network Size**
   The total storage required for a neural network. Size is measured in megabytes.
3. **Node Memory**
   Memory available on a computing node. Node memory limits megabytes per task.
4. **Normalization Data**
   Values used to scale data consistently. Normalization adds to dataset megabytes.
5. **Non-Volatile Memory**
   Memory that retains data without power. Capacity is measured in megabytes.
6. **Numerical Precision**
   The detail level of stored numbers. Higher precision increases megabytes.
7. **Noise Data**
   Unwanted or random information in datasets. Noise increases data size in megabytes.
8. **Neural Activation Size**
   Memory used to store neuron outputs. Activation size is measured in megabytes.
9. **Network Transfer Size**
   The amount of data sent across a network. Transfer size is tracked in megabytes.
10. **Node Cache**
    Temporary storage on a node for faster access. Cache size uses megabytes.

Letter O

1. **Object Storage**
   A storage method that manages data as objects. Capacity is measured in megabytes.
2. **Offline Dataset**
   Data stored locally rather than streamed. Offline datasets occupy megabytes.
3. **On-Device Storage**
   Storage located on the AI device itself. On-device capacity is measured in megabytes.
4. **Operational Memory**
   Memory used during active AI operations. Usage is tracked in megabytes.
5. **Optimization Data**
   Information used to improve model performance. Optimization data uses megabytes.
6. **Output Buffer**
   Temporary storage for results before delivery. Buffers hold megabytes.
7. **Overhead Data**
   Extra data required for system operation. Overhead increases total megabytes.
8. **Object Detection Output Size**
   The amount of data produced by detection models. Output size is measured in megabytes.
9. **Online Storage**
   Storage accessible via the internet. Online storage limits are measured in megabytes.

10. **Open Dataset Size**
    The storage footprint of publicly available datasets. Size is measured in megabytes.

Letter P

1. **Parameter Count**
   The total number of model values. Count correlates with megabytes required.
2. **Persistent Storage**
   Long-term storage that retains data. Capacity is measured in megabytes.
3. **Pipeline Buffer**
   Temporary storage between processing stages. Buffers manage megabytes in motion.
4. **Preprocessing Data**
   Data created while preparing datasets. Preprocessing adds megabytes.
5. **Precision Reduction**
   Lowering numeric detail to save space. Reduction decreases megabyte usage.
6. **Prediction Output Size**
   The amount of data produced by model predictions. Size is measured in megabytes.
7. **Primary Memory**
   Main system memory used for processing. Capacity is measured in megabytes.
8. **Processing Overhead**
   Extra resources needed during computation. Overhead increases megabyte usage.
9. **Profiling Data**
   Information collected to analyze performance. Profiling data uses megabytes.
10. **Paged Memory**
    Memory divided into fixed-size blocks. Paging manages megabytes efficiently.

Letter Q

1. **Quantization**
   A technique that reduces numerical precision to lower memory usage. Quantization helps AI models use fewer megabytes.
2. **Query Cache**
   Stored results from previous searches or requests. Query caches save megabytes by avoiding repeated computation.
3. **Query Latency**
   The time it takes to retrieve data after a request. Latency depends on how many megabytes must be accessed.
4. **Queue Buffer**
   A temporary holding area for data waiting to be processed. Buffers store megabytes in order.

5. **Quick Access Memory**
   Memory designed for fast retrieval. It handles megabytes needed immediately by AI tasks.
6. **Quantitative Dataset**
   Data made up of numerical values. These datasets are stored and measured in megabytes.
7. **Query Result Size**
   The amount of data returned from a query. Result size is measured in megabytes.
8. **Quorum Storage**
   A distributed storage method requiring agreement across systems. Data is replicated in megabytes.
9. **Quality Metrics Data**
   Information used to measure model performance. Metrics consume storage in megabytes.
10. **Quantized Model Size**
    The reduced size of an AI model after quantization. Size is typically measured in megabytes.

Letter R

1. **RAM Usage**
   The amount of active memory in use. RAM usage is tracked in megabytes.
2. **Read Throughput**
   The speed at which data is read from storage. Throughput affects how fast megabytes are accessed.
3. **Real-Time Processing**
   Processing data immediately as it arrives. Real-time systems manage megabytes continuously.
4. **Recursive Memory Use**
   Memory consumption during repeated function calls. Usage accumulates in megabytes.
5. **Redundant Storage**
   Extra copies of data kept for reliability. Redundancy increases total megabytes stored.
6. **Resource Allocation**
   Assigning system resources like memory and storage. Allocation is measured in megabytes.
7. **Runtime Memory**
   Memory required while a program is running. Runtime memory usage is tracked in megabytes.
8. **Raw Dataset Size**
   The size of unprocessed data. Raw datasets often require many megabytes.
9. **Read-Only Memory Footprint**
   The storage space used by non-modifiable data. Footprint is measured in megabytes.
10. **Retrieval Speed**
    How quickly stored data can be accessed. Speed depends on the number of megabytes involved.

Letter S

1. **Sample Size**
   The number of data examples used in AI training. Larger samples increase megabytes.
2. **Scalable Storage**
   Storage that grows with demand. Scalability supports increasing megabytes.
3. **Serialized Data Size**
   The storage size of data converted into a transferable format. Size is measured in megabytes.
4. **Shared Memory**
   Memory accessible by multiple processes. Shared memory usage is tracked in megabytes.
5. **Snapshot Size**
   The storage required for saved system states. Snapshots consume megabytes.
6. **Sparse Data Representation**
   A storage method that saves space when data contains many empty values. Sparsity reduces megabytes.
7. **Storage Capacity**
   The total amount of data a system can store. Capacity is measured in megabytes or more.
8. **Streaming Data Buffer**
   Temporary storage for incoming data streams. Buffers handle megabytes in motion.
9. **System Cache**
   Memory that stores frequently used data. Caches manage megabytes for faster access.
10. **Synchronization Data**
    Information used to keep systems aligned. Sync data adds to total megabytes.

Letter T

1. **Temporary Storage**
   Short-term storage used during processing. Temporary storage holds megabytes briefly.
2. **Tensor Size**
   The memory required to store multidimensional data structures. Tensor size is measured in megabytes.
3. **Throughput Rate**
   The amount of data processed per unit time. Rate is often described in megabytes per second.
4. **Training Dataset Size**
   The total amount of data used to train AI models. Size is measured in megabytes.
5. **Transfer Buffer**
   Temporary memory used during data movement. Buffers hold megabytes during transfer.
6. **Transactional Storage**
   Storage that ensures data consistency. Transactions add overhead measured in megabytes.

7. **Thread Memory Usage**
   Memory consumed by execution threads. Usage is tracked in megabytes.
8. **Token Storage Size**
   The memory required to store processed tokens. Token data uses megabytes.
9. **Time-Series Data Size**
   The storage footprint of data collected over time. Size increases in megabytes.
10. **Training Checkpoint Size**
    The storage required for saved training states. Checkpoints are measured in megabytes.

Letter U

1. **Unified Memory**
   A memory system shared between CPU and GPU. Unified memory manages data in megabytes efficiently across processors.
2. **Upload Size**
   The amount of data sent to storage or the cloud. Upload size is measured in megabytes.
3. **User Data Storage**
   Storage allocated for user-generated files. Capacity is tracked in megabytes.
4. **Utilization Rate**
   The percentage of memory or storage currently in use. Utilization reflects how many megabytes are occupied.
5. **Uncompressed Data Size**
   The size of data before compression. Uncompressed data often uses more megabytes.
6. **Update Payload**
   Data sent during software or model updates. Payload size is measured in megabytes.
7. **Uptime Storage Logs**
   Logs recorded while systems run continuously. Logs accumulate megabytes over time.
8. **Unified Dataset**
   A dataset combined from multiple sources. Size is measured in megabytes.
9. **User Session Memory**
   Memory allocated for active users. Session memory uses megabytes dynamically.
10. **Usage Quota**
    A storage limit set for users or systems. Quotas are defined in megabytes or larger units.

Letter V

1. **Validation Dataset Size**
   The amount of data used to evaluate AI models. Size is measured in megabytes.
2. **Vector Embedding Size**
   The memory required to store numerical representations of data. Size is measured in megabytes.

3. **Virtual Memory**
   A system that extends RAM using disk storage. Virtual memory is managed in megabytes.
4. **Volatile Memory**
   Memory that loses data when power is off. Capacity is measured in megabytes.
5. **Video Dataset Size**
   The storage required for video data. Video datasets consume many megabytes.
6. **Versioned Storage**
   Storage that keeps multiple file versions. Versioning increases megabyte usage.
7. **Vision Model Size**
   The memory footprint of computer vision models. Size is measured in megabytes.
8. **Vector Database Storage**
   Storage used for similarity search data. Vector databases consume large megabytes.
9. **Virtualized Storage**
   Storage abstracted from physical hardware. Capacity is tracked in megabytes.
10. **Volume Capacity**
    The total size of a storage volume. Capacity is measured in megabytes or more.

Letter W

1. **Weight Parameters**
   Learned values in AI models. Weight storage contributes to megabytes used.
2. **Working Memory**
   Memory actively used during processing. Working memory usage is measured in megabytes.
3. **Write Throughput**
   The speed at which data is written to storage. Throughput affects megabytes per second.
4. **Warm Cache**
   Cached data that is already loaded. Warm caches reduce repeated megabyte transfers.
5. **Workflow Data Size**
   The total data used across an AI workflow. Size is measured in megabytes.
6. **Web Dataset Size**
   The storage required for web-based data. Size is tracked in megabytes.
7. **Weight Compression**
   Reducing model weight size to save memory. Compression lowers megabytes used.
8. **Window Size (AI Context)**
   The amount of data processed at once. Window size affects memory megabytes.
9. **Writable Storage**
   Storage that allows data modification. Capacity is measured in megabytes.
10. **Workload Memory Demand**
    The memory required for tasks. Demand is expressed in megabytes.

Letter X

1. **X-Axis Data Size**
   Data stored along one dimension of a dataset. Size contributes to megabytes used.
2. **XML Data Size**
   The storage footprint of XML-formatted data. XML files often use many megabytes.
3. **XOR Encoding**
   A binary operation used in data processing. Encoded data occupies megabytes.
4. **Execution Context Size**
   Memory required during task execution. Size is measured in megabytes.
5. **External Dataset Size**
   The size of data sourced externally. External datasets add megabytes.
6. **Expanded Memory Use**
   Memory growth during processing. Expansion increases megabytes consumed.
7. **Experimental Dataset**
   Data used for testing AI models. Size is measured in megabytes.
8. **Extraction Buffer**
   Temporary storage during data extraction. Buffers store megabytes briefly.
9. **Extended Storage Capacity**
   Additional storage added to a system. Capacity is measured in megabytes.
10. **Explainability Data Size**
    Data used to explain AI decisions. Explainability outputs consume megabytes.

Letter Y

1. **Yield Data Size**
   The amount of useful output data produced. Yield is measured in megabytes.
2. **Yearly Data Growth**
   Annual increase in stored data. Growth is tracked in megabytes.
3. **YAML File Size**
   The storage footprint of YAML configuration files. Size is measured in megabytes.
4. **Y-Axis Feature Size**
   Feature data along a dataset dimension. Size contributes to megabytes.
5. **Young Generation Memory**
   Memory area for newly created data. Usage is measured in megabytes.
6. **Yield Optimization Data**
   Data used to improve output efficiency. Stored in megabytes.
7. **YourAIStudyBuddy Dataset Size**
   The total data used by AI study tools. Size is measured in megabytes.
8. **Yottabyte Reference Scale**
   A conceptual upper scale of data measurement. Used for comparison beyond megabytes.
9. **Yield Metrics Storage**
   Storage used for performance metrics. Metrics consume megabytes.

10. **Yoked Memory Allocation**
    Linked memory regions used together. Allocation is measured in megabytes.

Letter Z

1. **Zero-Copy Memory**
   A method that avoids duplicating data. Zero-copy reduces megabytes in motion.
2. **Zipped Dataset Size**
   The storage size after compression. Zipped files use fewer megabytes.
3. **Zettabyte Scale (Reference)**
   A large-scale data concept. Used to compare growth beyond megabytes.
4. **Zone-Based Storage**
   Storage divided into regions. Zones manage megabytes efficiently.
5. **Z-Score Normalization Data**
   Statistical values used in preprocessing. Data adds megabytes.
6. **Zero Padding**
   Adding placeholder data to inputs. Padding increases memory megabytes.
7. **Zoomed Feature Maps**
   Scaled representations in vision models. Stored in megabytes.
8. **Zonal Cache**
   Cache divided by region. Cache size is measured in megabytes.
9. **Zero-Day Model Update Size**
   The storage required for emergency updates. Size is measured in megabytes.
10. **Zipped Model Archive**
    Compressed AI model files. Archives reduce megabytes required.

Overview

KNOWLEDGE SYSTEMS

How Intelligent Machines Acquire, Organize, Store, and Apply Knowledge

Book 3 of 20
Module 2: Artificial General Intelligence (AGI)

Knowledge is the foundation of intelligence. Whether human or artificial, every intelligent system depends on its ability to acquire information, organize it into meaningful relationships, store it efficiently, retrieve it when needed, and apply it to solve problems. Without a well-designed knowledge system, even the most advanced artificial intelligence cannot reason effectively, adapt to new situations, or make informed decisions.

Knowledge Systems explores one of the most important technologies driving the evolution from **Artificial Narrow Intelligence (ANI)** to **Artificial General Intelligence (AGI)**. While ANI systems often perform specialized tasks using limited knowledge within a single domain, AGI requires the ability to understand and apply knowledge across many subjects, continually learn from new experiences, and transfer what it has learned from one problem to another.

This book contains **16 carefully structured chapters** that introduce readers to the essential principles of knowledge acquisition, knowledge representation, semantic relationships, memory systems, reasoning, retrieval, learning, knowledge graphs, vector databases, contextual understanding, and intelligent decision-making. Each chapter builds upon previous concepts, allowing students to gradually develop a comprehensive understanding of how intelligent machines organize and use information.

Written in clear, plain English, this book is designed for students, educators, parents, homeschool families, workforce development programs, and anyone interested in understanding how intelligent systems think, learn, and make decisions. No programming experience is required. Instead, readers are guided through complex AI concepts using practical examples, real-world applications, and easy-to-understand explanations.

As part of the **IntelliGloss AI Education Series**, this book helps prepare learners for the rapidly evolving world of Artificial General Intelligence by providing a strong conceptual foundation in one of AI's most essential building blocks.

Teacher's Guide

Purpose of This Book

Artificial intelligence is becoming increasingly capable because it is learning how to manage knowledge more effectively. Before an intelligent system can reason, solve problems, or make decisions, it must first understand how information is acquired, organized, connected, stored, retrieved, and applied.

This book helps students understand that intelligence is more than collecting data. True intelligence comes from recognizing relationships, identifying patterns, drawing conclusions, learning from experience, and applying knowledge to new situations. These abilities are central to the development of Artificial General Intelligence (AGI).

As **Book 3 of 20** in **Module 2: Artificial General Intelligence (AGI)**, this text builds upon concepts introduced in previous books while preparing students for more advanced AGI technologies explored later in the series.

Book Organization

This textbook contains **16 sequential chapters**, with each chapter expanding the learner's understanding of intelligent knowledge systems. Every chapter is designed to build upon previous learning, allowing students to develop their understanding step by step.

Each chapter includes:

- Clearly defined learning objectives
- Plain-English explanations of complex AI concepts
- Real-world examples and applications
- Chapter summary
- Reflection questions
- Student worksheet
- Chapter quiz
- Complete answer key

Additional Learning Resources

To encourage learning beyond the classroom, every book in the IntelliGloss AI Education Series also includes:

- **Family AI Discussion Section** near the front of the book, encouraging conversations between students, parents, and guardians about artificial intelligence and its growing role in everyday life.
- **Comprehensive AI Glossary** located in the back of the book, providing clear definitions of important AI vocabulary introduced throughout the chapters.

These additional resources support independent learning while strengthening communication between school and home.

Learning Objectives

Upon completing this book, students should be able to:

- Explain the purpose of knowledge systems in artificial intelligence.
- Describe how intelligent machines acquire and organize information.
- Understand the differences between data, information, knowledge, and intelligence.
- Explain how AI stores and retrieves knowledge efficiently.
- Describe the role of knowledge representation in intelligent systems.
- Recognize how memory, reasoning, and learning work together.
- Explain how knowledge systems contribute to the transition from ANI to AGI.
- Discuss the importance of accurate, trustworthy, and continuously updated knowledge.
- Evaluate the benefits and limitations of AI knowledge systems.
- Apply critical thinking when discussing how intelligent machines make decisions.

Classroom Implementation

This book may be used as a semester textbook, supplemental reading, independent study resource, or professional development guide.

Educators are encouraged to:

- Introduce one chapter per lesson or instructional unit.
- Encourage classroom discussions using current AI technologies.
- Assign reflection questions to promote critical thinking.
- Use worksheets as formative assessments.
- Administer chapter quizzes to evaluate student understanding.
- Connect lessons to real-world AI applications in education, healthcare, science, engineering, transportation, finance, and business.

Because each chapter builds upon previous learning, students should complete the chapters in order whenever possible.

Skills Developed

This book strengthens many of the future-ready skills emphasized in today's educational standards, including:

- Artificial Intelligence Literacy
- Digital Literacy
- Computational Thinking
- Critical Thinking
- Problem Solving
- Ethical Reasoning
- Communication
- Information Literacy
- Technology Awareness
- Career Readiness

These skills help prepare students for higher education and the rapidly changing workforce shaped by intelligent technologies.

Message to Educators

Artificial General Intelligence will rely on far more than powerful computers. It will depend on how effectively intelligent systems acquire, organize, connect, remember, and apply knowledge. By helping students understand these foundational concepts today, educators are preparing them to become thoughtful users, responsible innovators, ethical leaders, and informed decision-makers in tomorrow's AI-powered world.

Thank you for your commitment to educating the next generation of learners and helping them understand one of the most transformative technologies of our time.

Learn AI. Understand AI. Shape the Future.

Susie Hala
Founder, IntelliGloss Press
Author, IntelliGloss AI Education Series

NOTES:

NOTES:

NOTES:

www.ingramcontent.com/pod-product-compliance
Lightning Source LLC
Chambersburg PA
CBHW041751220926
51847CB00014B/172
* 9 7 8 1 9 7 2 9 2 5 2 4 9 *